"I always thought Bob Lupton was one of the most innovative forces in dealing with city problems. In this book I learn he is simply following principles 2,500 years old. Creative, thoughtful and provocative."

PHILIP YANCEY, AUTHOR OF *RUMORS OF ANOTHER WORLD*

"Bob is a longtime friend of mine, and he's done such an excellent job of improving the quality of life of people in Atlanta. *Renewing the City* is an outgrowth of his many years committed to doing economic and community development from a biblical perspective. I hope this book gets wide acceptance and readership."

JOHN PERKINS, PRESIDENT, JOHN PERKINS FOUNDATION, AND COFOUNDER, CHRISTIAN COMMUNITY DEVELOPMENT ASSOCIATION

"Bob Lupton writes what he knows about. Fortunately for us he knows a great deal. He knows about the concreteness of needy folk in the city; he knows about the city as a system and the powerful who preside over it. He knows about compassion and mercy kept sober by issues of justice. He knows about faith that turns to bold energy and he knows about a biblical script through which to organize all of his learnings into a testimony of faith.

"This book is a modern retelling of the narrative of Ezra-Nehemiah, a narrative in which Lupton himself is cast as a key character. The book lives precisely at the interface between ancient text and current urban transformation. Its powerful testimony will provide guidance and courage for those who read. And we finish the book grateful to Bob and Peggy for their large-hearted urban wisdom."

WALTER BRUEGGEMANN, PROFESSOR OF OLD TESTAMENT, COLUMBIA THEOLOGICAL SEMINARY

"Bob Lupton has captured the essence of Nehemiah's story in the rebuilding of Jerusalem. Bob has taken the biblical truths of Nehemiah and applied them to the terrible deterioration and disgrace facing America's inner cities. This book provides realistic hope through biblical Christian community development. *Renewing the City* is a must-read for anyone doing urban work today."

WAYNE L. GORDON, PRESIDENT, CHRISTIAN COMMUNITY DEVELOPMENT ASSOCIATION

"Bob Lupton *is* Nehemiah. This imaginative, authentic and narrative account of a faith-motivated visionary's calling to rebuild a city devastated by war and abandonment will inspire similar efforts in America's urban neighborhoods."

RANDY WHITE, NATIONAL COORDINATOR FOR URBAN PROJECTS, INTERVARSITY CHRISTIAN FELLOWSHIP, AND AUTHOR OF *JOURNEY TO THE CENTER OF THE CITY*

"In *Renewing the City* Bob Lupton has given us a remarkable glimpse of the confusing realities, the irritating lessons and the crises of leadership that are often a part of urban development work. It's all interwoven with an imaginative, provocative and biblically faithful rendering of the story of Nehemiah. From the realities of regentrification to the competing models of economic planning, Bob's insights are full of uncompromising faith and deep wisdom. This is a must-read for everyone who believes that God loves cities."

STEPHEN A. HAYNER, PEACHTREE PROFESSOR OF EVANGELISM, COLUMBIA THEOLOGICAL SEMINARY

"An engaging book from an author who tops the charts when it comes to credibility. Ageless principles from an ancient story are lifted up for today's reality. Lupton looks for and finds a theology that touches the ground, even when the ground is messy. He writes as well as he thinks, and he thinks as well as he implements. His compelling candor and honesty work well in a world of ambiguities."

ROBERT SEIPLE, FOUNDER, INSTITUTE FOR GLOBAL ENGAGEMENT, AND AUTHOR OF *AMBASSADORS OF HOPE*

REFLECTIONS ON COMMUNITY
DEVELOPMENT AND URBAN RENEWAL

RENEWING THE CITY

Robert D. Lupton

InterVarsity Press

Downers Grove, Illinois

InterVarsity Press
P.O. Box 1400, Downers Grove, IL 60515-1426
World Wide Web: www.ivpress.com
E-mail: mail@ivpress.com

InterVarsity Press® is the book-publishing division of InterVarsity Christian Fellowship/USA®, a student movement active on campus at hundreds of universities, colleges and schools of nursing in the United States of America, and a member movement of the International Fellowship of Evangelical Students. For information about local and regional activities, write Public Relations Dept., InterVarsity Christian Fellowship/USA, 6400 Schroeder Rd., P.O. Box 7895, Madison, WI 53707-7895, or visit the IVCF website at <www.intervarsity.org>.

All Scripture quotations, unless otherwise indicated, are taken from the Holy Bible, New International Version®. NIV®. Copyright ©1973, 1978, 1984 by International Bible Society. Used by permission of Zondervan Publishing House. All rights reserved.

While all the stories in this book are based on real people and situations, some names and identifying details have been altered to protect the privacy of the individuals involved.

The story written by Jonathan Lupton in chapter 24 and the material written by Canadian author Rob Alloway in chapters 16 and 18 have been used by permission of the authors.

Design: Cindy Kiple

Images: kids by brick wall: Zelick Nagel/Getty Images
       bricks and pail: C Squared Studios/Getty Images

ISBN 0-8308-3326-9

Printed in the United States of America ∞

Library of Congress Cataloging-in-Publication Data

Lupton, Robert D.
 Renewing the city: reflections on community development and urban
 renwal / Robert D. Lupton.
   p. cm.
 Includes bibliographical references.
 ISBN 0-8308-3326-9 (pbk.: alk. paper)
 1. Community—Biblical teaching. 2. Bible. O.T.
 Nehemiah—Criticism, interpretation, etc. 3. Urban renewal. I.
 Title.
 BS1365.6.P45L87 2005
 222'.806—dc22

                    2005004493

P	19	18	17	16	15	14	13	12	11	10	9	8	7	6	5	4	3	2	1
Y	19	18	17	16	15	14	13	12	11	10	09	08	07	06	05					

CONTENTS

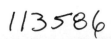

FOREWORD

BOB LUPTON IS THE ONLY PERSON I know who could have written a masterful book on the ancient prophet Nehemiah that is at the same time a book on community development and urban renewal. The worlds of Susa, Jerusalem and Atlanta interact, but with incredible integrity to the unique contexts of each. To write this book, Bob had to plant himself equally in the stacks of theological libraries and in the streets and communities of Atlanta, and that over many years.

Anyone who has ever received Bob's FCS newsletter, as I have for many years, or heard him speak formally or informally, knows that he is a superb teller of stories. He's an artist with words, so I knew this would be a good book. But it's better than that. I've taught Bible and urban ministry at the college and seminary level, but I've never seen anyone get into the mind of Nehemiah, Ezra, their allies and their adversaries as well as Bob does in this book. I also have a pretty good eye for those who curry contemporary audiences by importing our issues into the ancient biblical texts. This book does not do that. The biblical story is treated with wonderful sensitivity and integrity.

The format of the book breaks evenly into two equal parts. Part one explores the thirteen chapters of Nehemiah in story form. The story is artfully told with nuances worthy of the best in Jewish Midrash. Part two merges that story with eleven contemporary urban issues, laced with transparent stories from Atlanta and other cities where transforming leadership gets forged in our day. Bob is equally adept at both nuance and transparency, be it about himself or his friends.

At the same time, several decades on the streets and in the communities of Atlanta have given Bob remarkable insights into the meaning of the text and the drama of Nehemiah's life and career as a leader in the task of renewing a city in ways that empower the local communities and confront the oppressors. What becomes so obvious to any reader is that we are now without excuse in the presence of systemic injustice in an urban world. We have a biblical word and mandate to address these contexts, and they are multiplying in the urban world on all six continents.

Ancient Persia is the same piece of geography as modern Iran. How ironic that this nation, which appears daily in our newscasts, should have produced a "gospel for the city" twenty-five hundred years ago, and that in it, the Iranians get some credit for the rebuilding of Jerusalem and not the destruction of it. Equally ironic perhaps is that in our day there are Iranian exiles living and studying in London in hopes of going back to Iran one day to help reinvigorate God's church, which has suffered but remained present in Iran from Pentecost to the present.

The late Jewish scholar Robert Gordis used to describe the Bible (by which he meant the Jewish scriptures) as the "Divine Library," with its beautiful descriptions of God's concern for the universe, for all life and certainly for the cities. In books like Jonah and Daniel we see God's concern for the two enemy cities of Israel—Nineveh and Babylon. Nineveh had conquered and destroyed the capital Samaria and ten tribes in the north. Later Babylon destroyed Jerusalem and the two southern tribes. Jonah, albeit reluctantly, shared God's gracious forgiveness through his preaching in Nineveh, and Daniel did it by his presence in a government career in Babylon. That is what I like to call the gospel for Iraq, a gospel for cities of violence that may be far away.

Meanwhile, Nehemiah is the other half of the story. Here God gives a faraway government official a call to rebuild and restore the city back home. God is the hero in all these stories, and he is the one who calls people like Ezra and Nehemiah to move back home, or "return flight" as Bob calls it. The God of the Bible is about restoring people and rebuilding communities.

To God be the glory and to the earth be peace.

To Bob Lupton be thanks and to our cities be hope!

Ray Bakke

PREFACE

I COULD NOT REMEMBER THE LAST TIME I had read the book of Nehemiah. It was one of those obscure writings from a confusing period in Israel's history that had never held much interest for me. Because Nehemiah the man never made it into the biblical hall of fame—he wasn't a Moses or Abraham or David with hero status in Sunday school—I knew only that he had something to do with building a wall and that the book came between Ezra and Esther in the books-of-the-Bible memorization contest.

I do clearly remember my wide-eyed astonishment when as an adult I finally did a careful read of the memoirs of this layman who, like myself, left a successful career to pursue a calling in urban revitalization. How had I missed it? I was twenty-five years into urban community development—up to my ears in salvaging deteriorated neighborhoods—before I discovered this biblical blueprint for reclaiming cities. It is the firsthand account of a high-level government official who takes a leave of absence, secures a government grant, organizes the largest volunteer missions project in biblical history, transforms a dangerous ghetto into a secure city, then repopulates it by inducing suburbanites to move in. For a community developer, this book is a treasure trove.

Immediately I drove to the nearest seminary to check out all the books I could find on this remarkable character. To my disbelief, I found not a single book on the man. There were several Ezra-Nehemiah commentaries that translated the Hebrew text and provided historical context, along with a couple of books that used Nehemiah as a springboard for discussions on leadership and character. A wider Web search turned up books on urban housing initiatives and self-help programs that adopted the man's name. But I could not find any writing that focused on Nehemiah as an urban developer.

I discovered in talking with Old Testament professors that little Christian scholarship has been invested in the period of Jewish history between the Babylonian captivity in 586 B.C. and the arrival of Jesus. Finding reliable information on Nehemiah and the context of his mission required sifting through countless obscure journal articles, digging among archeological studies and piecing together ancient Near Eastern history and Jewish scholarship. The effort, though tedious, led me into a world of political intrigue, social conflict, economic crises and moral dilemmas. I tracked Nehemiah into the midst of challenges and quandaries not at all unlike those I encounter daily in the modern city where I serve.

I encountered much disagreement among scholars regarding the chronology, authorship and authenticity of the biblical account. When I finally came to the decision to attempt a book on the subject, I made a choice to sidestep those arguments and accept the text as written. This layman's approach to Scripture may not gain me a seat at the head table in the scholarly community, but it does allow me to dive into the story without distraction. And after all, it is the drama, not an analysis, that speaks most poignantly to our spirits.

I also came across in my research an ancient Jewish tradition known as *midrash*. It was a teaching method first developed by rabbis in Nehemiah's day to illuminate and animate the Scriptures. Through a combination of commentary, parable and poetic imagination, ancient teachers drew their congregations into engaging discussions about the underlying truths of their faith. The text was the portal into history, and midrash brought it to life. Midrash provided images and examples that added color, emotion and texture.

Taking guidance (or perhaps license) from this ancient tradition, yet exercising caution to remain faithful to the biblical account, I have attempted to enter into the world of Nehemiah, to slip into the courtyards and council chambers alluded to in the text and to get close enough to overhear personal conversations. The chroniclers have, of course, preserved many of the interactions among the players in this drama. But many more private discussions, many of the behind-the-text scenarios must be garnered through midrash.

I have braided together three identifiable strands: biblical narrative, midrash color and texture, and contemporary story. My desire is to glean from the life of a remarkable layman those principles that guided his decisions as he reestablished an ancient city, then place those principles alongside the realities of modern-day urban ministry. Some of the ways Nehemiah handled situations will likely spark as much debate among today's readers as they did among his contemporaries. I have not attempted to explain away his harshness or make excuses for his extreme measures. Rather, I have gone with the assumption that Nehemiah, though called by God, was a man like any other man, with remarkable gifts as well as shortcomings and blind spots. I find his candor and spontaneity (or perhaps impulsiveness) refreshing. I can relate to such a man.

I have been diligent in my efforts to retell Nehemiah's story with biblical and historical accuracy. Yet this is hardly a historical textbook. Neither is it a how-to manual on community development. The realities of urban life, both ancient and modern, are far too complex to distill into a one-size-fits-all book—principles, perhaps, but not formulas. My intent is to invite readers to travel back with me to an ancient city, watch and listen as a layman grapples with the challenges of rebuilding, and discover together the striking parallels in the process of restoring vitality to our own cities.

My wish is to provoke candid conversation among those who care about the city and to lay bare some of the dilemmas that elude neat solutions. Should discussion lead to a deeper understanding of the complexities of city life and a greater appreciation for those who, either by choice or by fate, live amid these tensions, my goal will have been half realized. If the struggle becomes a catalyst for personal engagement in redemptive kingdom work, my fulfillment in writing this book will be complete.

PART ONE

THE STORY

The memoirs of Nehemiah as preserved in the scriptural text provide us with a first-hand account of the rebuilding of Jerusalem seven generations after its destruction in 586 B.C. Part one is the retelling of that story, complete with the candor and intrigue of a layman who organizes the largest volunteer community service project in biblical history.

1

CITY IN RUINS

WINDS SWEEPING IN FROM THE WILDERNESS to the east howled and whispered in unpredictable velocity through the dark Jerusalem alleys, adding their grit to the drifts that collected in doorways and on window ledges. Only wild dogs and other predatory creatures of the night (occasionally human ones) would be stirring at this late hour. Nehemiah waited until he was sure the city was asleep—as asleep as an undefended city gets—before he nudged six of his most trusted officers who sat, fully clothed and armed, waiting for his signal. Silently they emerged into the deserted street, waited for their eyes to adjust to the darkness, then moved single-file in the direction of the nearest city exit. Creeping around the city stable, they untied a horse that Nehemiah's horsemen had left saddled and waiting for him, then crept past burnt-out houses, taking care to avoid occupied dwellings that showed yellow lamplight through the cracks of their doors. Reaching a jagged opening in the city wall that was once the Valley Gate, they slipped out of the city, fairly sure they had not been detected.

Earlier that week, the arrival of their royal caravan from the distant capital city of Susa had created no small stir in Jerusalem. The leader of the delegation was none other than Nehemiah, King Artaxerxes' personal cupbearer and brother of Jerusalem's vice mayor Hanani. Regal emblems marked his fine leather saddlebags and a well-armed Persian cavalry detachment trotted proudly at his guard. But what was his business in Jerusalem? For three days the official visitors had been lying low, recuperating from their strenuous journey. And for three days the rumor mill churned out all manner of wild speculation. Were they just stopping over for a rest on their way south to Egypt? What if the Persian government was planning to impose even more taxes on Judah? Or could this be an envoy preparing for the king's armies headed this way? Maybe the king was sending some financial relief, given that the famine, now in its second year, was drying up Judah's crops. From priests to politicians to merchants, the rumors spread, but no one, not even Ezra, the appointed priest-governor of Judah, had any idea why this Nehemiah and his royal entourage had arrived.

The small squad hugged the outside of the wall as they inched their way in a counterclockwise direction around the perimeter of the city, Nehemiah astride his mount, his men on foot before and aft. A silver half moon provided them with ample illumination as they picked their way around boulders and fallen sections of fortification, past Jackal's Well and on toward the Dung Gate—or what was once Dung Gate. A charred post jutting out of a heap of rocks was all that remained. The same depressing sight greeted them at the Fountain Gate—superstructure gone, giant beams and timbers burned away. And between these gaping portals, stretches of wall badly breached and toppled from their once-proud heights. The devastation of the Fountain Gate and the King's Pool was so complete that Nehemiah had to dismount and climb on foot around the debris field. The wall that had provided security for generations of Jerusalem dwellers lay in a huge pile of rubble, exposing the insides of the city like the eviscerated carcass of a dog ripped open by a bear.

Jerusalem was not yet stirring as the men slipped though the Valley Gate opening and made their way back to their quarters. But sleep would not come to Nehemiah this night. His stomach churned with anxiety as the enormity of this undertaking weighed upon him. Hanani, his brother, had indeed painted a bleak picture of the city when he visited Nehemiah at the palace in Susa eight months earlier. But nothing could have prepared him for the immensity of this devastation.

How could this be? Had Ezra focused all his time and energies on temple refurbishment and ignored the securing of the city? Three Persian dynasties had come and gone since the edict of Cyrus freed the Jews to return from exile in Babylon, and still they had no city to anchor their homeland. How long had Ezra been governor here now? Twelve years? Thirteen?

Nehemiah checked the anger that flared up within him. How dare he be critical of such a godly priest! The temple, rebuilt several generations ago, had been upgraded under Ezra's leadership. Many original gold and silver vessels and adornments from Solomon's great temple had been returned from the imperial treasury in Babylon, and he had inspired many Babylonian Jews to give liberally to temple operations. That was certainly important, Nehemiah told himself. But a temple huddling in a burnt-out city laid open to the appetites of predators, a city devoid of the governance of elders at the gates, a city whose economy was little more than a haven for charlatans and loan sharks—what good was a house of God when there was no city of God to implement its beliefs? Indeed it was little more than a broken symbol of some scattered tribal people who once believed themselves to be Yahweh's chosen race.

What about the redevelopment efforts that Ezra was to have begun years ago? These last three days of quiet observation had produced little evidence of city renewal. But then, what could you expect, Nehemiah conceded, of a scribe-turned-governor whose passions were directed more toward compiling ancient writings than toward rebuilding a capital city? Perhaps it was understandable.

2

THE CALLING

BACK AT THE DESK IN HIS JERUSALEM QUARTERS, staring pensively at a flickering candle, Nehemiah was beginning to come to grips with the enormity of his task. The concern that bore down on him was of a different sort from the depression that had consumed him back in Susa eight months earlier. Hanani's report of homeland Jews enduring hardship, of the famine burning dry their land, of Judean villages being looted by Bedouin marauders—it had all been distressing. It was evidence that the society was still in chaos even after all the expectations created by Ezra's royal mandate to return and rebuild.

"Still in ruins! How could this be?" Nehemiah had bellowed at Hanani. His people were free to return to the homeland God had promised them. Judah had godly Jewish leadership once again. And they had money—deported Jews had prospered during their exile. As if that weren't enough, the Persian government had granted them substantial sums to aid in reconstruction efforts. Why was Jerusalem not a viable governing citadel once again? Nothing in his adult life had distressed Nehemiah so deeply.

Hanani's account had taken a toll on Nehemiah's normally optimistic temperament. His life in Susa up to that time had been a satisfying one. What he lacked in physical stature he more than made up for in winsomeness of smile and quickness of wit. He had distinguished himself as a bright and responsible government employee. When Artaxerxes ascended to his father's throne and began the search for a new cabinet and staff, Nehemiah's name was put forward. In time Nehemiah made himself as valuable to the king as he had been to his former bosses, eventually becoming the trusted royal cupbearer with daunting management responsibilities as well as constant access to the king in matters both public and private.

Before Hanani's fateful visit, Nehemiah considered his life to be full and fulfilling. Though connected through both lineage and tradition to the Jews whom Nebuchadnezzar had uprooted from Judah more than a century ago, Nehemiah was Persian born, Persian educated and well assimilated into the ruling class of the Persian culture. More European than Middle Eastern in appearance, with his lighter skin and curly reddish hair, he hardly stood out as a Hebrew. But Jewish he was, through and through. The God of his forebears was his God and the law of Moses was the code of his life. The old prophet Jeremiah, whose words many of the elders in the Jewish community committed to memory, had greatly influenced Nehemiah. "Seek the peace and prosperity of the city to which I have carried you into exile," Jeremiah had heard Yahweh say. "Pray to the LORD for it, because if it prospers, you too will prosper." Indeed Nehemiah and his family had prospered.

But he had been unable to shake off the depression that took hold of his spirit following Hanani's report. So acutely had it affected him that he found it impossible to conceal his gloom behind his naturally congenial appearance. Food lost its appeal. For the first time in his life he had cried out to Yahweh from the depths of his being, pleading for mercy, for hope, for restoration. Worse, in the darkness of his soul came a persistent whisper—not audible but surely unavoidable—telling him that he could, he *must,* do something about Jerusalem. He fasted and prayed mightily for discernment. Was this the voice of Yahweh, he wondered, the same powerful influence that came upon the prophets and patriarchs of old? Or was it merely a function of his Jewishness come of age, a sober sense of duty instilled from his youth to hold tenaciously to the history and traditions of his people? He wished for Jeremiah, who would surely have known what to make of such an impression. But Jeremiah was long asleep in the earth with the ancients.

Never before had Nehemiah been so badly distracted. Or conflicted. His attention to his administrative responsibilities had slipped noticeably over the weeks following his brother's visit. He had even embarrassed himself by missing a meeting with other senior staff. Simply forgot it. This inexcusable behavior only added to the heaviness that pressed down upon him like a millstone. This voice, this obsession, invaded his every waking hour. He would be no good at all to the king if he could not somehow bring this torment to closure. Even in his sleep, his dreams were a series of recurring scenes, all with the same theme—organizing construction activities in Jerusalem.

It was lovely, sensitive Queen Damaspia who first recognized that something was troubling his spirit. A caring and gentle person, she inquired of Nehemiah if he had not been feeling well lately. A powerful urge welled up inside him to spill out everything to her, but instincts restrained him. No, he was fine, he deceived her. But in his mind he had spoken it; he had named the voice a "calling of God." This brief, deceptive interaction had been a defining moment. He knew then that if—rather, *when*—he admitted the truth to his king and queen, he would tell them that this was indeed a divine calling.

A restored Jerusalem, economic and political anchor of the Jewish homeland, center of worship for the followers of Yahweh—this was the vision that grew large in Nehemiah's mind. Once he had accepted that rebuilding the city was his divine assignment, his mind raced ahead to strategy. What materials would be required? What engineers and skilled artisans would be needed? What was the available labor force in Judah? How would he finance the undertaking? His years in government service had exposed him to the complexities of urban development, and he was certainly no stranger to project management. But this mission presented issues he had never before confronted. Palestinian politics had always been thorny, and his decisive manner hardly made him an ideal diplomat. And then there was the matter of transporting a convoy of workers and materials through provinces hostile to Jewish interests. This was a world he had not had to deal with as a member of the Persian elite secure in the king's city of Susa.

All of this strategizing would be useless fantasy, however, unless King Artaxerxes saw the validity of the cause and could be persuaded to grant Nehemiah a leave of absence from his responsibilities. Queen Damaspia would likely look favorably upon such a request. Her genuine affection for Nehemiah, which had grown out of years of his attentiveness to details of the royal household, would make her sympathetic to his cause. But the king was another matter. His trust in Nehemiah was beyond question, but he was a ruler hardened by endless uprisings and political intrigue across a vast empire. He was not one to be moved by sentiment or passion. He would have to be convinced that investing in an urban revitalization project in a small province a thousand miles away would reap tangible benefits for the crown.

Perhaps the case could be made on political grounds, Nehemiah reasoned. Regional stability was a topic of constant concern in the palace. Egypt was forever vying for control of the Mediterranean. A fortified Jerusalem under the rule of a loyal governor might have a containing influence on Egypt's ambitions. Or maybe the economic argument would be better. Jerusalem once controlled a prosperous grain- and olive-producing region. With the infusion of new capital and capable governance, it could once again generate substantial wealth—and tax revenues for the crown. Or perhaps Jerusalem could be a supply depot for the Persian armies that moved along the Mediterranean coast in the unending conflict with Egypt. Jerusalem was a little east of the main corridor, but it was certainly close enough to be a major repository.

The more Nehemiah pondered the strength of these arguments, the more unsure he became of their strategic value to the empire. Of one thing he was sure, however, being a confidant of the royal family: Artaxerxes' most vulnerable spot was the affection he held for his lovely wife. Approach the king when Damaspia was present and her desires would have considerable sway. The queen would clearly be Nehemiah's best chance. He would have to wait for the opportune moment.

By the time the proper alignment of king, queen and opportunity arrived, four months had passed. Four months of gathering intelligence on the provinces through which he would have to travel. Four months of scouting the Persian-Jewish community for engineers and skilled builders who could be recruited for his development team. And many sleepless nights scrawling unending lists of details and contingency plans by the light of his oil lamp.

Strangely, Nehemiah's anxiety over finding the precise moment to take his request to the king consumed less and less of his emotional energy. His prayers now flowed spontaneously from a growing sense of excitement about the mission, requests more for divine wisdom than for relief from the stress of uncertainty. He discovered growing within himself a reassurance that when the right moment arrived he would know it. And though he continued to rehearse in his mind dozens of possible scenarios for his presentation, he somehow felt assured that he would know the most fitting approach and the right wording when the time came.

As it happened, it was neither Nehemiah's timing nor his own initiative that opened the conversation. Perhaps Queen Damaspia, as she reclined with the king in their private dining chamber, casually mentioned her concern that Nehemiah seemed to be feeling troubled about something lately. Artaxerxes, hardly sensitive to such matters so long as the work was getting done, did take notice of Nehemiah's uncharacteristically somber face as the faithful cupbearer ordered silver goblets of wine placed before them.

"Why does your face look so sad when you are not ill? This can be nothing but sadness of heart," the king commented to Nehemiah.

This was it! This was the opening Nehemiah had been awaiting for four months. For a moment he froze in panic, unable to recall a single word he had rehearsed. When he opened his mouth, the only words that came were an unrehearsed stream of feelings.

"Yes," Nehemiah poured out, "there is indeed great sadness in my heart. The city of my ancestors still lies in ruin. Though the great king graciously allowed my Jewish people to return to their homeland and even gave them generous grants to rebuild Jerusalem, they have failed to even secure its gates. This is a disgrace to my people. Yes," he confessed, "I am grieving over this great loss of opportunity."

Who could know if it was the vulnerability of the admission or a subtle nudge of the queen's knee or a sure-enough divine prompting that caused the king to respond as he did? But a how-can-I-help offer from the mouth of the monarch was as close to divine intervention as anything Nehemiah had ever witnessed. The implications of this momentous occasion were as terrifying as they were marvelous. A request that came across as presumptuous could be disastrous for the mission—for one's head!

Nehemiah breathed a silent prayer and implored, "If it pleases the king and if your servant has found favor in his sight, let him send me to the city in Judah where my fathers are buried so that I can rebuild it." Damaspia caught Artaxerxes' eye with a look that would have melted the heart of any man in the empire, and though she said not a word, she left no doubt about what would please her. The king had but one question: "When will you get back?" Damaspia smiled.

With the leave of absence granted and the mission approved, the conversation moved quickly to logistics. Passports would be needed to assure safe passage for a three-month journey across antagonistic jurisdictions, along with a line of credit—no, a grant would be better—to requisition lumber and building materials from the royal forests and storage depots. An official governor's home should be built inside the Jerusalem walls and governing powers conveyed to him in writing. An entourage of trusted assistants, experienced engineers, support personnel and a cavalry detachment would need to be assembled. With the full support of the king, Nehemiah would leave Susa with all the supplies, trappings and authority of a royal envoy.

3

AN IMPROBABLE PLAN

AS THE SKY OVER JERUSALEM BEGAN TO LIGHTEN and the jagged silhouette of the eastern wall became visible through his window, Nehemiah rose from his desk and gathered the loose papyrus pages of his plan into his leather case. He would meet with Ezra first thing this morning to present the documents bearing Artaxerxes' seal that officially established him as the governor of Judah. He anticipated no resistance. The change in leadership would doubtless come as a relief to the aging Ezra, who long ago had admitted to being a better writer than administrator. He would need to rely heavily on Ezra's extensive knowledge of local politics. Ezra would know firsthand the challenges of navigating the crosscurrents between long-time Judaean residents and the more affluent newcomers who had returned from Babylon and other Persian territories with their "civilized" notions of how things should be run. Together, the outgoing and incoming governors would call an assembly of leaders—city officials, influential merchants, ranking priests and nobles who spoke for their clans scattered throughout Judah. Nehemiah would unveil his plan to them, attempt to secure their support, then begin immediately hiring a construction force. The employment opportunities, if nothing else, should be good news for the economically depressed area. This could happen within the week, he figured.

Ezra proved to be as receptive to his new replacement as Nehemiah had hoped. He was a tall, slender man, graceful in manner. *This is a true man of*

God, Nehemiah thought as they sat in the temple quarters that housed the college of priests. The old scribe seemed not at all defensive about the condition of the city's infrastructure. Rather, his demeanor communicated a deep sadness over his inability to galvanize the people into a functioning community.

"The trouble goes back three or more generations," Ezra recounted as he ran his long fingers through a head of thinning gray hair. "It began with the first exiles returning from Babylon." As convoys of Jews began to arrive back in Judah—the children and grandchildren of captives led away by Nebuchadnezzar when he sacked Jerusalem—there was an immediate clash of cultures. Those who had evaded capture and remained in Judah, mostly rural peasants, had assumed squatters' rights over much of the abandoned property. They had developed friendly alliances with leaders of the surrounding provinces and adapted reasonably well to life without a capital city or temple.

Babylonian Jews, on the other hand, were more sophisticated and urbane, a largely professional class that had assimilated into the leadership structures of their homes in exile. Their return to Judah ignited a sort of class war, Ezra related. There were endless disputes over the rightful ownership of land and issues of political control—natives against immigrants, urban elites against the rural "people of the land." And with every new wave of returnees came a new social upheaval.

"That's one reason why we could never get organized enough to rebuild the city," Ezra lamented. "The same conflicts erupted with the crowd that came back with me when I returned."

Originally, the new temple was intended to unify the people, the old priest went on. When King Cyrus of Persia conquered the Babylonian Empire and let the Jews return to their homeland, he put up funds to construct a new temple. A student of human nature, he knew religion could be a strong organizing force within a culture. By supporting the reconstruction of the temples of the ethnic peoples throughout his enormous empire, he would increase loyalty to the crown as well as have an administrative presence in every region. Priests elevated to the level of provincial governors could serve several roles: religious leaders, government spokespeople and administrative overseers. The practice had been so effective that it had been continued by Cyrus's successors. Indeed Artaxerxes had appointed Ezra to these very functions.

But rebuilding the Jerusalem temple, the aging scribe continued, was fraught with problems from the outset. Zerubbabel and Jeshua, Persian-educated leaders who championed the effort, returned from exile along with fifty thousand urbane Jews to resettle Judah and reestablish Jerusalem. The clash of cultures between the indigenous rural dwellers and the more cultured returnees might have been expected, but no one anticipated the volatility of their theological differences. Many of the exiled Jews, the priestly and professional classes, had tenaciously held on to the sacred writings, preserving them against the day the prophecies of Jeremiah would be fulfilled and they would return home to the Promised Land. They determined to cling to their belief in Yahweh as the only true God, to faithfully observe the law of Moses and to keep their culture intact by marrying exclusively within the Jewish community.

Meanwhile, those who were left behind in Judah without a temple or strong priestly leadership assimilated with the surrounding cultures. They were survivors, pragmatists. They adopted many of the customs and practices of the surrounding peoples. Intermarriage was a natural way to secure familial alliances with neighboring tribes and ensure protection and needed trading partnerships. Worship of their in-laws' gods made for harmonious family relationships.

The returning orthodox Yahweh followers detonated a social explosion when they declared that only those who were faithful to the law of Moses could participate in the rebuilding of the temple. The syncretists had defiled themselves by "whoring after other gods," the purists accused, and were thus deemed unworthy to participate in worship at the house of the Lord. The resulting conflict created such deep rifts among the Jews that the temple project was derailed for generations. The edifice was eventually completed—largely through the efforts of the orthodox party, who had the backing of the crown and the prophetic urgings of Haggai and Zechariah—though it was inferior in size and grandeur to Solomon's temple.

This was history that Ezra knew intimately. As an exiled scribe and collector of Jewish literature, he had recorded the entanglements of Jewish repatriation with the same thoroughness that he had given to the copying of ancient sacred manuscripts. Ever since his royal commissioning as minister of state for Jewish affairs, however, he had been far more than a chronicler—he had been a shaper of Judean history. And here the story became highly personal. Nehemiah sat entranced as the old man recounted how he had conducted his four-month journey returning from Babylonian exile, how the Lord had protected from ambush his unguarded convoy laden with priceless temple treasures, how the strife-weary citizens of Jerusalem had welcomed him and his entourage upon their arrival. After years of infighting, Judah was eager for new leadership.

Ezra, though too modest to admit it, had earned a well-deserved reputation as the leading expert in Mosaic law and literature, and he was highly regarded in Jewish circles. The word of his appointment as minister of Judah had come as good news to the conflict-worn Judean Jews. The fact that he was bringing with him many of the sacred treasures from Solomon's temple as well as handsome sums for temple enhancements added to the excitement. It had not been difficult inspiring the Jewish community (to use the term loosely) to rally around the temple refurbishing campaign, Ezra recounted. Not at first. His caravan of several thousand new émigrés, laden with personal effects and treasures from Babylon, ignited celebration in the city.

"But the jubilation was short-lived," Ezra lamented. "The city, of course, was no place to house the newcomers." Before the exile, greater Jerusalem had boasted more than one hundred thousand residents. But after the destruction, only a handful of hardy souls had slipped back in to brave an existence here. Most of the city still lay in ruins. A handful of the returnees—the higher-ranking priests and administrative officials—took up residence in the rebuilt temple facilities and government buildings, but most of the immigrants found housing in the surrounding villages. New neighbors with new money churned much-needed cash into the stagnant Judean economy and just as surely churned up animosity. Capital-rich investors instantly became involved in money lending and real estate speculation—practices welcomed by some but disparaged by others as loan-sharking and land-grabbing. Posturing for economic and political control soon ensued. Similar power struggles erupted in temple life. Persian-schooled priests who returned with Ezra, orthodox in their view of Scripture, were aghast at the syncretism of the Judean priests who embraced the religions of the surrounding cultures. This led to vicious disputes and ugly name-calling quite unbefitting spiritual leadership. Any optimism that Ezra's appointment had sparked was soon doused by bitter ethnic, class and theological rivalries.

It was not as though he had not *tried* to unify the people, Ezra said in his own defense. He certainly possessed not only the legal power but also the moral authority to assemble the Judean Jews and call them back to conformity to the law of Moses. This he had attempted, on several occasions. And there were times when the people wept and repented because of their faithlessness and vowed to do better. These times of recommitment inspired hope in Ezra. But such reforms seemed to have little staying power. Landowners soon slipped back into their back-door trading practices with foreigners in order to circumvent the payment of tithes and offerings to the temple. The elites were back at their power plays and slick deals that always left the innocent holding the short straw. The syncretistic priests were again making concessions for "good people of other faiths" and admitting them into the temple. And of course, there was the unending sabotage of the would-be faithful by their foreign wives and in-laws who were loyal to the interests of other tribes and other deities.

Ezra's face flushed with emotion at the thought of pagan intermarriage. "It's been a thorn in my side since the first day I took office." He wagged his head in frustration. He understood, he admitted, that it made survival sense for those who had been left behind to eke out an existence on the land. A Samaritan dowry could overcome a generation of poverty. But the well-heeled exiles who returned since the Cyrus emancipation had no excuse. Try to build a nationalistic spirit, try to regulate trade, try to implement Mosaic law—it's almost impossible with all those conflicting family loyalties.

"You can never trust a Jew who has married into the family of a Samaritan or a Baal worshiper," Ezra's voice rose in volume. "Pagan marriage is the single greatest barrier to Jewish reunification. You can never build consensus. Some of them don't even speak Hebrew anymore!"

Nehemiah had been listening intently. Much of the history he knew, but the underlying sources of discord and subversion were a revelation. There was far more complexity to reestablishing this city than he could possibly have understood when he sat at his desk in Susa designing what now seemed like romantic and naive reconstruction plans. It was becoming clear the longer they talked that the physical rebuilding of ruined walls—work that could be accomplished with Persian money and hired construction workers—would not be the biggest challenge. A far more difficult task would be drawing a contentious people of varied classes, cultures and dialects into a unified kinship. Unless this fractured group of Abraham's children could be pulled together as one community and rallied around a common vision, there would be little hope for the rebirth of their *Jeru-salem*— City of Peace.

It was the sight of a merchant repairing the stonework on his storefront, visible from the temple room where Nehemiah was sitting, that sparked a bizarre thought in his mind. It was an idea so preposterous that he rejected it as absurd the moment it popped into his head. But it *might* bring the people together, the thought persisted. What if the community—not hired contractors but volunteers—could be inspired to do the building themselves? It was laughable. Possible, perhaps, with many hands and enough skilled supervision. Still, an outlandish idea, a logistical nightmare. It would certainly get a good laugh out of anyone who knew anything about construction, he thought.

As Ezra droned on about the wearisome task of mediating venomous disputes and arbitrating the charges and countercharges that fueled contention among the people, Nehemiah stared beyond the open temple courtyard to

the street where the storekeeper troweled mortar into a crack in the front
wall of his shop. A jewelry store, it looked like. If a delicate-handed jeweler
could patch masonry on his own building, perhaps other ordinary citizens
could be motivated to learn wall-building techniques to repair their city.
How long would it take to train unskilled labor to lay stone with enough engineering precision to construct a secure wall? If he used his Persian-trained
engineers and masons as teachers and supervisors rather than actual builders, the work force could be dramatically expanded. How long would it take
to organize . . .

The silence in the room snapped Nehemiah from his pondering. Ezra had
stopped talking, realizing that Nehemiah was no longer listening to him.
There was no point trying to deny it. Nehemiah hadn't a clue what Ezra had
been saying the last few minutes, couldn't hope to make an intelligent response to cover his rudeness. It was his embarrassment that impelled him to
blurt out to Ezra the ridiculous line of thought that had been distracting him.

But Ezra did not laugh. Nor did he say a word. For a long time, Ezra
stared at the ceiling, twisting his thin gray beard. Finally the old scribe whispered, "That might actually work!"

By that simple affirmation, a bizarre idea became an ingenious strategy.
There could hardly be a more difficult, logistically challenging method of
construction, but there could also be no better way of bringing a fractured
people together. Ezra envisioned the covenant community from the city and
surrounding farms and villages, the priests and Levites, newcomers and indigenous landowners, all working side by side in harmony as one family. Nehemiah's mind was back again on organizing. Local leadership would have
to be convinced. The work force could be rallied if their leaders believed in
the mission. Skilled Persian engineers would be teamed with local workers
and assigned to specific gates and wall sections; volunteers would be assigned to the wall or gate closest to their personal residence. A materials
depot would be set up in the center city near the temple, providing accessible distribution and monitoring. Temple grounds could serve as the command and control center for the operation.

"How long will it take to assemble the leadership of Judah?" Nehemiah asked. It would not take long, Ezra assured him. Perhaps three days. Many of the nobles (as the family patriarchs like to be called) from outlying towns had already collected in the city, the arrival of the royal Persian caravan having signaled that some sort of change was imminent. Couriers could be dispatched immediately to deliver invitations to every village and clan throughout Judah. Everyone must be included.

The sun was directly overhead when Ezra and Nehemiah climbed the wide stone steps of the temple portico and turned to face the assembly. The temple courtyard was filled with clusters of nobles, groups of city officials, priests and temple staff in their dark robes and headwear and, at the periphery of the crowd, the Persian entourage—Jewish, certainly, but distinct in their cultured attire and military garb. Rumors had been rolling like waves of grain in a windstorm from one chattering huddle to the other. But when Ezra and his royal guest turned to face the crowd, no one had to call for silence—a moment with this much intrigue had its own capacity to hush a crowd. In words clear and surprisingly brief, Ezra proclaimed that King Artaxerxes had appointed his own personal cupbearer to be the new governor of Judah. Nehemiah, son of Hachaliah of the tribe of Judah, was now officially taking over the reins of government with the sweeping powers of a satrap. Lifting high the document that bore the king's seal in a gesture designed to validate this transfer of power, Ezra took a step backward, then bowed with deference to the new satrap of Judah.

The first official words out of Nehemiah's mouth were as blunt and spontaneous as his confession to the king and queen months earlier. "You see the trouble we are in: Jerusalem lies in ruins, and its gates have been burned with fire. Come, let us rebuild the wall of Jerusalem, and we will no longer be in disgrace."

There was stunned silence, a hush like the calm before a storm. Every man stared stone faced at this brash new governor, not making a sound, giving away neither head nod nor frown. There had been no warm-up for this startling challenge, no time for pondering or debate. Like a bucket of well water thrown in the face, it took one's breath away.

Before the stunned crowd had time to recover, Nehemiah launched into the story of his calling, saying how Yahweh had prepared the king's heart, how the king had responded graciously to a bold request, how the funds and materials had been allocated and the authority had been granted to rebuild the city. The story, in its retelling, seemed somehow even more miraculous than in its living.

It was obvious that the assembly were deeply moved as they listened. Their silence had become softer, more like awe, even reverence. Could this be the moment destined by Yahweh to reestablish his chosen people in their holy city? With a boldness that surprised even Nehemiah, he bellowed at the top of his voice: "The fullness of time has come to rebuild Jerusalem!"

Again, silence. After a long pause, Ezra stepped forward and with excitement dancing in his eyes proclaimed in a clear tone, "Let us start rebuilding."

The chant was repeated by the priests and then picked up by the Levites, and soon the entire assembly was shouting, "Let's start rebuilding." The moment was electric.

Once again Israel was one, shouting heavenward with one voice. The roar echoed down the city streets, over broken walls and around gaping gate portals and out into the valleys. Ezra and Nehemiah embraced.

4

THE OPPOSITION

THE ENORMOUS UNDERTAKING WAS OFF AND RUNNING. Plans that had been working in Nehemiah's head for months, revised a hundred times and now dramatically altered to accommodate volunteers, were set in motion. Senior project management was appointed and an operations headquarters was set up on the high ground adjoining the temple complex. As groups of volunteers from all over Judah began streaming into the city by the hundreds, each was assigned a specific gate or wall section. Crew chiefs within every work group, selected by skill level and demonstrated leadership capacity, were given an orientation by command center staff. A skilled artisan was assigned to every team of workers to provide instruction and ensure the quality of construction. It would be backbreaking labor, inching huge stones up ramps with levers, raising massive beams into place, forging heavy hinges and bars. But the people were filled with eagerness, their dedication frequently outweighing their skill. They were caught up in a vision of history-shaping magnitude, and everyone, even the women and children, had an important role to play.

In nearby Samaria, at Governor Sanballat's Beth Horon manor, activity of a different sort was brewing. Three cohorts stared at each other across an inlaid wood table, anxiety etched on their faces. A calamity was about to crash down upon the world they had worked so diligently to build, unless they acted quickly and decisively. Sanballat, who had called the emergency meeting, was joined by Tobiah, his subgovernor of Ammonite lands to the east, and Geshem, an Arab collaborator from the south. All politico-religious strongmen and engineers of a provincial governors' alliance, they had positioned themselves to siphon off border tariffs from the trade streams that crisscrossed their jurisdictions. King Artaxerxes, under whose indirect authority they had been appointed, required fixed tax revenues from the increase of their provinces to support the Persian government. But along with their office came the right to levy additional taxes for local government, including their own salaries, homes, staffs and a variety of other perks. Cozy alliances among fellow governors could control the Trans-Euphrates-Mediterranean trade routes. Border-crossing taxes could generate substantial private revenue.

Sanballat, Tobiah and Geshem had been content to see Jerusalem in ruins, incapable of exploiting the network of roads that connected it to the major cities of the region. And it had been child's play to negotiate trade agreements with Judean farmers. Judean clans were happy to avoid paying the Jerusalem temple tax by selling their produce and livestock across province lines rather than through the loosely monitored Judean exchange system. And of course, their net profit was better on the black market. With virtually no enforcement capacity, Jerusalem could do little more than preach sermons at them.

Sanballat and Tobiah had been politically shrewd in their posturing with Judah. Samaria no longer enjoyed the privileges of official governance over Judah as it once had, so Sanballat found other ways to exert control. He had given one of his younger daughters in marriage to the grandson of Eliashib, high priest of the Jerusalem temple. This provided him considerable access to the administrative and religious affairs of the Jews. Ezra had spoken out against such intermarriage from time to time, had even attempted to outlaw it, but the benefits of having a loyal daughter in the chambers of the top religious leader were well worth the risk and aggravation. Tobiah had himself taken a bride from a prominent Jewish family, and his son Jehohanan had done the same. These family ties assured accurate intelligence from inside the Jewish body politic as well as influence in important internal decisions.

Having a new governor in the region, one appointed directly from Susa, was worrisome enough. But when news of the Jerusalem reconstruction project reached Sanballat, Tobiah and Geshem, they were distraught. If the Judean borders were to come under the control of a strong central Jerusalem government and trading practices were legitimized, this could severely affect their lucrative cartel. Further, a fortified Jerusalem with garrisons and gates would soon become a magnet for commerce—quite different from the virtually unregulated and unscrupulous free trade zone that the city for years had been. This would be unwelcome competition indeed. Something had to be done, and quickly.

A servant poured three golden goblets to the brim for the third time. The fine wine imported from the celebrated Aegean vineyards was hardly noticed by the three conspirators as they considered the gravity of the situation. Who was this newcomer Nehemiah, anyway? And how had he been able to rally the people in such a short time? There hadn't been this kind of excitement and unity in Judah since Ezra arrived with Solomon's temple trappings twelve years before. How to sabotage this fellow, undermine his credibility—that was the challenge.

The king appointed Ezra because he was a harmless albeit trustworthy priest, right? Sanballat was going somewhere with this line of reasoning. Ezra never had any messianic fantasies and could always be counted on to submit accurate tribute payments to Susa, right? The other two nodded their agreement, still not sure where Sanballat was headed. What if, he continued, the word got out that this Nehemiah had aspirations to set himself up as king of Judah and declare Israelite independence! It had worked in the past to stalemate other ambitious Jewish leaders. Smiles crept across the faces of the three comrades, and Tobiah lifted his goblet for a toast. They had a plan.

The three dignitaries, adorned in their impressive governors' robes, arrived in Jerusalem the following day at the peak of the preconstruction planning. People of all descriptions were scurrying everywhere, men shoulder-ing heavy timbers, women preparing food, children toting water jugs. The trio wound their way to the temple plaza, where they were told Nehemiah would be. It was a beehive of action, chaotic at first glance but purposeful. And right in the middle of the swirl of activity stood Nehemiah, shuffling through lists, barking out orders and wiping perspiration from his brow. The three approached him, bowing and offering deferential gestures befitting a man of royal appointment. Nehemiah paid little attention to the formality and inquired bluntly as to their business.

It was obvious that this sweaty, ambitious little governor was not about to waste time on diplomatic courtesies, so the delegation got right to the point. "It is not difficult to see what you are up to," Sanballat launched into Nehemiah. "This volunteer building project, absurd as it may be, is an inge-nious method for stirring up Jewish dreams of becoming a sovereign nation with Jerusalem as its capital."

"It is no use trying to resecure the city—for political or any other pur-poses," the others chimed in. "It was tried numerous times before and al-ways failed. And as soon as King Artaxerxes learns of these subversive am-bitions (and he will certainly be informed without delay), this project and its treasonous leader will be dealt with harshly." Sanballat, his eyes now bulging with fury and his finger in Nehemiah's face, had delivered the intim-idating warning.

It was a serious charge, to be sure, and one who did not know the king and his wife so intimately might well have been shaken by it. The critique of his volunteer mobilization strategy might have some validity since it was an untested concept. But the accusation of treason? Had no one told these dolts that he had been Artaxerxes' personal cupbearer and trusted palace ad-ministrator?

Nehemiah stared back coldly into their faces, never blinking an eye. These treacherous men would have no part in the future life of this city or country, connected by marriage or not, regardless of their political status or reputation among the leading citizenry. No longer would they intrude in the affairs of the Jewish community. Nehemiah determined to see to that.

"The God of heaven will give us success," Nehemiah declared to them. "We his servants will start rebuilding. But as for you, you have no share in Jerusalem or any claim or historic right to it."

Not another word was spoken. The trio glowered, wheeled around and stomped back the way they had come, their robes waving behind them. Nehemiah wiped his forehead with the sleeve of his white tunic and continued his work.

5

CONSTRUCTION BEGINS

HUGE MOUNDS OF ROCKS AND BOULDERS, some piles rising higher than the wall itself, began to heap up on both the inside and the outside of the city as eager hands dug through the rubble. Like an army of ants, volunteers swarmed around and over the wall, moving tons of debris into sorted stacks. Men using wooden beams as levers pried loose massive stones and rolled them away from the foundation. Stretches of high wall that had been toppled into valleys required enormous effort as well as engineering prowess to reconstruct. Scaffolds on precipitous inclines rose to dangerous heights to reach the top wall level. Boulders had to be levered and rolled up from the valley floors by teams of workers, then hoisted in canvas slings by block and tackle up the side of the wall to be swung into place. Medium-size stones were carried on strong backs or on stretcher-type carriers between two men, then handed up the scaffolding to waiting masons. Even women and children got in on the act, gathering handfuls of rocks from the debris fields and stacking them in orderly piles.

Fortunately stone, unlike wooden gates, could not be consumed by fire, though much of it still wore the char from the inferno of Nebuchadnezzar's final siege. The wall they were now building would be as strong as the former wall that had secured the city since the time of Solomon and before. It was dirty, backbreaking work, and in many sectors just digging down to solid wall or foundation was taking days, even before the first stone could be fit into place. But the enthusiasm was contagious. Relatives who had not seen each other in years sweated and laughed together. The sound of the Levites singing the hymns of Zion buoyed the spirits of the work force.

For some, such as the college of priests, this was a highly spiritual endeavor, an act of worship full of history and sacred symbolism. They labored as tirelessly as everyone else but with insights and perceptions that gave their efforts special meaning. The rural people who traveled in each day from the surrounding areas were caught up in an exhilarating spirit of civic pride—something Judah had been short on for too many years. A rebuilt Jerusalem could mean the end of exploitation and the return of greatness as Yahweh's favored nation.

For those merchants, temple employees, municipal workers and other brave souls who lived within the broken walls of the city, the thought of twenty-four-hour security for their families and businesses seemed too good to be true. They had been the most skeptical when the reconstruction plan was announced, having been disappointed numerous times before by Ezra's false starts. They had learned to live life on the defensive, relying on street savvy and their own survival devices. Not eager to risk another letdown, they had halfheartedly agreed to help with wall sections near their own homes and businesses. But when it became evident that this Nehemiah was not only serious but also capable, and when they witnessed thousands of volunteers being deployed around the circumference of the city, they joined in with abandon.

It was a sight to behold: Uzziel and Malchijah, leaders in the goldsmith guild, out there with their delicate-handed, slightly built apprentices, grunting and groaning over stones that heartier fellows down the wall tossed with ease. But they had an eye for symmetry. They searched out stones that fit precisely against the next, rough side turned in, sloping up at the precise angle the engineers had instructed. The process was impossibly slow, and for men who had spent their lives shaping and filing meticulously designed goldware, it seemed monumental. But at the end of each day their wall section had moved measurably upward, an emerging work of art.

It seemed everyone had joined in—merchants and shopkeepers, temple servants and musicians, farmers and herdsmen. Shallum, a vice mayor of the city, was out on the line cheering folks on. He and his daughters had committed to a whole section themselves and were getting blisters right along with their well-born friends who volunteered with them. Even Hananiah the perfumer and his employees were out there mopping their brows. There was some good-natured humor going around about the new fragrance Hananiah was wearing. Must be selling well, people grinned, since almost everyone wore the same aroma these days.

Nehemiah's skills in organizing and his understanding of human nature were evident everywhere. Some forty gate and wall segments had been assigned, each with specific beginning and ending points, each to a different construction team, each with engineering oversight. Work crews were formed on the basis of natural affiliations: family ties, village identity, social status or professional membership. Those who lived and worked in the city were given responsibility for sections of the wall that provided immediate protection for their own homes and shops. For one glorious moment, it seemed that everyone—all of Jacob's diverse children—were united in this historic undertaking.

It was a minor thing, perhaps, given the overwhelmingly positive response of the people, but significant enough to be noted in Nehemiah's journal. One delegation that arrived from the small town of Tekoa ten miles to the south attracted attention. The men were enthusiastic workers, but for some reason their elders showed a reluctance to join in. Perhaps these leaders considered this strenuous work beneath the dignity of nobles. Or perhaps, as leaders in their own right, they expected to be elevated to top management roles on the project. Or as some rumored, perhaps they had secret alliances with Geshem. Whatever the reason, they refused to enter into their assigned work on the long portion of wall that stretched southward from the Fish Gate. Like spoiled children who didn't get their way, the Tekoite nobles sulked in the shadows as their men sweat joyfully in the sweltering sun. In contrast to their leaders, the men of Tekoa distinguished themselves as such able and energetic workers that they finished their assigned wall section well ahead of schedule and were reassigned to the demanding task of building the high wall overlooking the Kidron Valley.

The first gate to be completed was the Sheep Gate on the high ground near the temple mount. It was fitting that Eliashib, the high priest, and a large cadre of fellow priests and temple staff had been assigned to this gate. Not only did it protect the temple and their living quarters, but also it was the gate through which the sheep and other sacrificial animals were led to the altar. Damage had been extensive on this part of the wall, since it was the first to be breached by Nebuchadnezzar's troops, and like all the other gates, its doors and superstructure had been burned away. But unlike the rest of the city, which was surrounded by steep valleys, the terrain here was fairly level, allowing the reconstruction work to progress at a faster pace.

It was toward the end of the second week that Eliashib surmised that his crew might be first to complete their gate. This was a motivating realization, and when he shared it with his crew, they redoubled their efforts. Within three weeks they had completed their wall repairs and were laying the final stones in the archway. Meanwhile, those with carpentry skills measured and sawed and chiseled and planed. Other priests shuttled heavy hinges and bolts back and forth from the central forging area, where blacksmiths heated and beat metal bars into hardware. Each timber and board, each piece of iron hardware had to be measured and fit, measured again and refit, until it matched up perfectly. The closer the great doors got to their finished look, the more intense the excitement grew. After measurement for the final time to ensure that the doors would fit perfectly into the jambs, the time had come to hang the first new city gate.

For the first time in four weeks, work all over the city came to a halt. Throngs of sweat-streaked workers climbed the hill toward the Sheep Gate, filling the assembly area, lining the top of the wall and surrounding buildings and spilling out into the open spaces outside the gate. The huge doors, sanded smooth and shining with layers of protective oil, lay prone on blocks before the stone opening, poised for the moment of their erection. Eliashib, surrounded by the dirt-covered lot of clerics, stood proudly beneath the high archway. When he raised his arms to speak, a hush fell across the crowd.

"This is not the work of men," he shouted so all could hear, "but the work of Yahweh. This gate, now consecrated to the purposes of God, will be an eternal symbol of his faithfulness to his people." And with that, the high priest gave the signal and his fellow clerics hoisted the great doors into place.

The crowd exploded with cheers and shouts that could be heard all over the surrounding countryside. Nehemiah and Ezra, who had chosen on this occasion to remain out of the limelight, swapped a knowing glance. It was inspiring to celebrate milestone successes and important, too, to celebrate those who spent themselves in the accomplishment. And it did not hurt to have Eliashib, who had uncomfortably close ties with Sanballat and Tobiah, visibly expressing his support for the project.

6

EXTERNAL THREATS

A MONTH OF STRENUOUS EFFORT HAD PRODUCED remarkable results. The quality of the work was surprisingly high, given that none of the work force had ever tackled a task of this magnitude and complexity before. Severe breaches had been repaired and all the toppled sections had been rebuilt to at least half their original height—an extraordinary accomplishment considering that in some places the wall breadth exceeded twenty feet. The city was being reborn; how could any child of Abraham not be inspired?

Back in Samaria emotions were running high as well, but for different reasons. The provincial governors' alliance had called another urgent meeting to consider next steps to derail the Jerusalem reclamation effort. Sanballat was beside himself with anger.

"What does this bunch of poor, feeble Jews think they are doing?" he fumed. "Do they think they can build the wall in a day if they offer enough sacrifices? Look at those charred stones they are pulling out of the rubbish and using again!" Sanballat waved his arms in exasperation.

"Let the fools build," Tobiah chimed in with a sarcastic sneer. "That stone wall would collapse if even a fox walked along the top of it!" They raged on.

"That insolent Nehemiah seems impervious to verbal threats. Maybe filing an official complaint to Persia would put a stop to this nonsense," Sanballat growled. It had worked before to halt other rebuilding efforts, even the temple reconstruction project. Tobiah and Geshem grew quiet at the thought, and worried expressions darkened their faces. A trumped-up charge could backfire if a royal inquiry found them out.

"Better that we find a way to demoralize these simple-minded Jews," the conspirators schemed. "A smear and fear campaign might just do the trick. Much safer than filing a formal complaint."

An immediate summit was convened—Sanballat's cabinet, administrators and commanding officers of the Samaritan militia, along with key regional leaders from Ammon in the east, Arabia to the south and Philistia on the west. There was no doubt in anyone's mind why the Jerusalem project had to be brought to a halt. The governors explained the gravity of the situation. The Jews *must not* be allowed to dominate this region as they once had done, controlling trade and imposing their bizarre sabbath practices on everyone doing business in Judah. They had to be stopped—now.

"It will take a decisive one-two punch," Sanballat declared, pounding his fist in his open palm. "First, the whole stupid venture must be discredited. Their labor force has to hear from legitimate sources that their ill-conceived wall-building idea will never work." It took years of work by highly skilled engineers and artisans to complete the first wall, Sanballat pointed out. "This volunteer endeavor is pure folly, a joke. A hurriedly thrown-up wall can be tossed apart by any wandering band of brigands. A mixture of reason and ridicule should demoralize a good number of these naive Jews. Threat of bodily harm should take care of the rest."

Sanballat had more. "Second, rumors must be leaked from a variety of reliable sources that military forces from every province in Palestine and from the Trans-Euphrates and Arabian regions are being mobilized for an attack on Jerusalem. That should put the fear in them. Those streams of self-confident volunteers will dry up overnight." Smiles and head nods were exchanged among the conspirators.

On to tactics. The ridicule campaign would be easy enough. Mixed marriages would provide the perfect avenue for undermining the confidence of volunteers. Allied nobles whose sons and daughters had taken Jewish spouses would be enlisted to convince their Jewish in-laws not to participate in the ill-advised project. Also, the ever-present naysayers within the Jewish ranks, though hard to identify at the moment, could be rewarded for their dissent.

Phase two—the military intimidation campaign—could be executed in days, Sanballat assured the others. Militia leaders from each jurisdiction would plan training maneuvers. The siege of Jerusalem would be their target. Neither troops nor populace could know whether these exercises were actual preparations for warfare. Rumors would spread like wildfire as soon as the combatants were ordered to the field and the dust of horses and chariots rose from the plains. The Jews would be shaking in their sandals as soon as they heard that all their surrounding neighbors were preparing to attack Jerusalem.

"Brilliant," the captain of the Samaritan militia grunted, wishing the plan had been his. "Resourceful," another said. "Good use of misinformation." No vote was needed—there was obvious consensus in the room. A timetable was agreed upon, assignments were handed out and a corps of motivated saboteurs headed back to their districts, posts and constituents.

"There is something satisfying," Sanballat commented to his comrades as the gathering broke up, "about having an intimate knowledge of your enemy, designing a well-conceived battle plan and deploying forces in a conquest you are sure to win." Tobiah and Geshem nodded their approval. Had their friend been born in Persia instead of the backwater province of Samaria, he might well be a general leading the king's armies.

The campaign of deception took effect with surprising speed. Unknown to Nehemiah, workers on their daily journeys to and from the city were discussing the feasibility of the project. Some were raising doubts about the stability and permanence of the wall. The management team was first to report a decline in enthusiasm among the volunteers. Even though much work had already been accomplished, enormous heaps of debris still lined the wall—what seemed like mountains of rubble to a labor force wearying of backbreaking toil.

It was to be expected, Nehemiah conceded. It was an awful lot to ask of people to leave their homes and jobs early every morning to work all day in the scorching heat for little or no compensation besides personal satisfaction. But it was more than physical fatigue that registered on the workers' sweat-streaked faces. Up and down the line, a contagion of discouragement sapped energy and depleted vitality. No one had dropped out yet, but production was clearly beginning to slip.

It was an overheard conversation between two young laborers wrestling rocks into their canvas carrying slings that exposed the cause of the work slowdown. Both young men were married to Ammonite brides. Both had been urged by their in-laws to abandon the effort and return to their home responsibilities. The conversation in itself would not have been noteworthy, since the rebuilding project had indeed drawn needed labor away from the farms. What caught the attention of the supervisors was that these two men were reciting the exact same script—almost word for word—that their in-laws had used to dissuade them from participating. This had to be more than coincidence.

The incident was reported to Nehemiah, who immediately dispatched his lieutenants to question every work team and determine the pervasiveness of the assault. The news was not good. Nearly every intermarried couple was experiencing similar conflicts, induced by their non-Jewish in-laws. But it did not stop there. Most of the builders who had business dealings or working relationships with other tribespeople—and that was no small number—reported similar incidents. It was clearly a well-orchestrated attack against the mission. It smelled of Sanballat.

How does one counter psychological warfare like this? Back in Persia, such sedition could be dealt with quickly and harshly. But this wasn't Persia, and Nehemiah had neither the authority nor military strength to launch an attack on Samaria. How does one fight an enemy whose weaponry is innuendo and rumor? *Truth!* That was the only counteroffensive Nehemiah could come up with. That and prayer.

By the end of the day, he had made sure that every worker in the entire city knew the truth about the plot and was armed with a retort to fire back at any who would attempt to sabotage the mission of Yahweh. And it was an equally heated prayer that Nehemiah unleashed before the people: "Oh listen to us, dear God. We're so despised: Boomerang their ridicule on their heads; have their enemies cart them off as war trophies to a land of no return; don't forgive their iniquity, don't wipe away their sin—they've insulted the builders!" And with that, the people returned to their stations, picked up their chisels and trowels, saws and hammers, and resumed building the wall, somehow reinvigorated.

Phase two of Sanballat's cunning strategy did not become evident until the following week. It took several days for the governors to draft orders and marshal their troops for field maneuvers. But as soon as reservists began pouring into the provincial capitals, unconfirmed news flashes of a top-secret mission began to circulate. It was not long before the entire region was abuzz with reports of a major allied offensive being planned. The target: Jerusalem!

The bright flames of vision and optimism that had inspired a people to take on the impossible were doused black in the span of one dreadful day. From no less than ten independent sources the word had come that a massive, coordinated attack was being planned that would destroy all that had been built and more, wiping out all the Jews who were found in or around the city. There could be no effective defense against such a surprise attack. It would come simultaneously from every direction. The high piles of rubble around the city would work to the attackers' advantage, shielding them from view until the moment of assault, then providing them cover for restaging. A cloud of dread settled over the city, and construction activity came to a standstill. Family groups huddled together in whispering discussion. Were all their dreams and lofty ambitions to end in another holocaust?

Project managers, nobles, city officials, ranking priests and security officers assembled in the command center to compare intelligence reports and consider options. The evidence was undeniable. This was a well-coordinated, multiprovincial military action. A rough projection of available arms only added to the severity of the crisis. It was clear that the defensive capabilities of Jerusalem were inadequate to hold off a large-scale attack. In all probability, however, the siege could be averted if the reconstruction effort were to be abandoned. Then Jerusalem would represent no further threat to the region.

But the captain of Nehemiah's guard was puzzled. As a seasoned military leader, schooled in the Persian war college, he could not imagine that appointed governors would be so foolhardy as to declare an unauthorized war on a neighboring Persian-controlled province, particularly one that had just been placed under the leadership of one of the king's most trusted officials. It simply did not make sense. Nehemiah concurred but was at a loss to explain the coordinated regional troop movements on all the Judean borders.

"Saber rattling," responded his captain. "It's an intimidation tactic that the Persian armed forces use all the time when we need to quell an insurrection or, for that matter, take over a country. It can be very effective, especially against weaker or fatigued adversaries. A show of military might is often more effective than an actual invasion."

Of course, Nehemiah surmised, it was another Sanballat scheme. He and his henchmen were probably up to their scare tactics again. And it was certainly working—the entire city was trembling in fear, ready to abandon the whole effort and hunker down behind the half-built walls or retreat to their farms and villages. But to dismiss the military buildup as an empty threat would be irresponsible. The amassing of hostile forces had to be taken seriously.

"Yahweh will come to our defense," one of the priests spoke up. "If rebuilding the city is a vision given to us by God, and we all believe it is, then he will see to it that the mission is not thwarted by heathen." The words were reassuring. Perhaps this was a test of their faith. Would they look to Yahweh to win their battles for them as he had done so many times in their glorious history, or would they run for the hills like scared rabbits? Old Ezra, lifting his arms heavenward and staring upward as though he were gazing at the face of God, began to pray audibly, fervently. The assembly of leaders, with heads bowed in reverence, some dropping to their knees, joined him with animated "amens." Their dependence must be on the Lord of hosts and not on their own strength.

Nehemiah, ever the pragmatist, rose from his knees when the prayer had ended with a plan already formulated in his mind. "From now on, every worker is to be armed," he said. Every available knife, sword, bow and spear would be brought into the city and distributed among family groups and work teams so that no one would go without personal protection.

"In addition to everyone wearing a sword or dagger," Nehemiah continued, "half the workers of each team will be heavily armed and stand guard over the others while they work. Then alternate in shifts—guards and workers trade places." The militia would be deployed to provide security at the lowest, most vulnerable parts of the wall and in areas yet unsecured by gates. Sentries would patrol the circumference of the city day and night and guards would stay on twenty-four-hour high alert. In the event of attack, a trumpet blast would be sounded, at which time all workers would drop what they were doing, collect their weaponry and rush to the location where the trumpet was blaring. Those living outside the city would plan to remain for the duration within the protection of the walls until the city was resecured or until the threat was past, whichever came first.

"Don't be afraid of them," Nehemiah urged. "Remember the Lord, who is great and awesome, and fight for your brothers, your sons and your daughters, your wives and your homes."

And so the plan was implemented. Guards and sentries were posted without delay around the circumference of Jerusalem, and all the arms in the city were distributed to the building teams. By day's end, all those from more distant villages who had set up temporary camps outside the wall had moved their families, servants and belongings inside the city. The following day, to Nehemiah's relief, all the commuters streamed back into the city, carrying additional weapons as well as supplies and provisions to hold them for several weeks. The terror that only hours ago had paralyzed the people dissolved like morning mist as young and old, clergy and laity strapped on swords, slung bows and quivers over their shoulders and reorganized themselves into an alternating work force/fighting force. In the face of over-whelming odds that threatened destruction on every border, the city seemed empowered with a new sense of confidence—false confidence, one might argue, but an assurance nonetheless that came from knowing they were fully prepared to stand and fight if need be.

With renewed energy, they returned to their work on the wall, swords swinging from their sides, half the workers standing guard with spears and shields in hand urging on their stone-toting team members. The work force, now at half strength, extended their hours from the gray of dawn till the evening stars appeared. Remarkably, the construction pace slowed hardly at all.

Though it could not be confirmed for nearly two weeks, the captain of the guard proved to be right in his assessment of the threat. No governor with any sense would risk incurring the wrath of the crown by invading a neighboring subject state of the empire, especially one under the leadership of a personal confidant of the king. The show of force, intimidating though it was, stopped short of crossing Judean borders. Jerusalem remained on high alert until intelligence reports confirmed that all hostile forces had withdrawn and were standing down—an announcement that caused the city to erupt with boisterous celebration. Young men waved their swords and shook their spears over their heads in victory salutes, running up and down the wall and hollering boasts about little Judah backing down the mighty war machines of their foes. The priests joined in the animated cheering, too, though many of them understood that it was likely Yahweh and not sword-waving volunteers who had turned away the enemy.

Nehemiah breathed a deep sigh of relief. The crisis appeared to be past, but he instructed everyone to remain armed, just as a precaution. His captain, a veteran of many conflicts, needed no one to tell him to keep his troops on ready and posted at visible positions. An adversary as crafty and persistent as Sanballat would likely not accept a foiled plan as the last word. High-alert security measures would remain in effect around the clock. All security personnel were ordered to sleep in their uniforms with weapons at their sides.

7

TROUBLE IN THE RANKS

SUMMER DAYS WERE BEGINNING TO SHORTEN by the time Jerusalem could be called a defensible city once again. Not that the final carpentry had been completed on all the gate structures, nor the wall finished to its original height, but the mountains of rubble had disappeared. Stone by stone they had been removed and laid with precision into a strong, defensive barrier that would rival that of any fortress in the land. The engineers were projecting another month of hard work.

Harvest in Judah was a time of feasting and celebration. But the past two growing seasons had been anything but joyous. The drought that had devastated last year's grain and grape yields was nearly as severe this year, forcing prices even higher and necessitating the costly import of food rather than providing the hoped-for profits from exports. It was inflicting direct hardship upon all who lived off the land and had a generally depressing impact upon the entire Judean economy. In a way, the wall-building project had come along at a good time since harvesting meager yields required fewer hands. And volunteering with friends and family on an inspiring project served to keep one's mind off the bleak economic forecasts back home.

The numbers were now coming in, however, and it did not look good. All up and down the wall, families huddled at break times with worried expressions on their faces. There would be barely enough produce to feed farming households through the winter, let alone any margin left for keeping up with their mortgage payments, repaying advances or paying taxes. To make matters worse, the nobles who owned the land or the mortgages on the land were beginning to turn up the pressure to pay up or move out. Several families, it was learned, were losing farms that had been in their clan for generations.

For anyone who had liquid capital, this was prime time for lending. Frantic farmers and herders were eager to borrow much-needed cash and were willing to pay exorbitant interest rates to get it. Many who had already negotiated advances against their crops to cover their tax liabilities to the Persian government were now desperate for additional credit to avert impending foreclosures on their crops, herds and homes. As word of these accounts reached the city, borne by disheartened volunteers journeying each morning from their rural towns and villages, a spirit of dejection spread along the wall. A growing number of households, it was reported, had borrowed against everything they owned as well as years of future harvests—indebtedness from which they could never expect to emerge. Several families had been forced to give up their children as indentured servants to a landlord in order to keep from losing their home.

"It's slavery," one angry young man burst out, "Jews enslaving Jews." Others in his work crew nodded in agreement.

Resentment burned its way from group to group, the kind of bitterness that fuels anger into explosive outrage. Long-harbored prejudices, set aside in the hopes that a new day of justice had dawned for Israel, now flooded back with a vengeance. Nothing had changed, the irate commoners cursed among themselves. Creditors were exploiters; leaders were moneygrubbers; merchants were opportunists. Even those with modest savings were maligned as selfish hoarders. Subterranean fault lines between people of means and people in need began to crack open, deepening the chasms of class that had seemed to be forgotten.

Perhaps it was pride (but more likely fear) that kept the men from openly venting their resentment toward the landed gentry and those whose holdings were enriched at the expense of the common folk. But the women would not be restrained. They found it intolerable to stand quietly by while their children were going hungry and their hard-working husbands were turned into beggars as family inheritances slipped from their grasp.

It was not an organized work stoppage; it was more like hitting an emotional wall. When anger and resentment reached a boiling point, there was no energy left to continue working on the wall. A great vision simply could not go forward in the face of great injustice. Before dawn, hundreds of workers filled the courtyard and streets outside Nehemiah's quarters, waiting for him to emerge. There was no spokesperson to present a cogent case—only sober-faced workingmen with calloused hands backed by emotionally wrought wives and mothers, waiting to voice their complaints to the only one who had the power to correct the injustices that were tearing their families apart.

When Nehemiah emerged, his morning eyes widened with alarm. "Who called this unplanned assembly?" he asked. "Where are the nobles and elders who always speak for the people?"

A woman near the front of the crowd dropped to her knees and cried out, "Our children are going hungry while our men are working on this wall. Our crops have withered up and we can't borrow another penny to buy grain."

Another joined her: "We've mortgaged our fields, our vineyards, our houses just to borrow enough to feed our families and pay our taxes." Confirming shouts from everywhere in the throng assured Nehemiah that these women were not isolated cases.

"We have had to sell our sons and daughters as bondservants to our creditors, and we'll never be able to buy them back," a woman shrieked. Her husband embraced her, but she would not be comforted.

The pleas that spilled from the hearts of these women had a cathartic effect on the crowd. Grave injustices at the hands of their leaders were at last being publicly exposed. Nehemiah's face reddened, partly from embarrassment at being so absorbed in the demands of construction that he had been unaware of the plight of so many of the volunteers. And partly from anger toward leaders who should have been looking out for the interests of their people but instead were using their privilege for personal gain at the expense of the most vulnerable.

"I will get to the bottom of this matter immediately," he assured the crowd.

And then a thought hit him that caused him to break out in a cold sweat. Could any of his Persian entourage be guilty of this oppressive behavior? He knew that many of them had been doing some lending (he himself had made some legitimate business loans), but had his Susa friends crossed the ethical line? As far as he knew, none of them had engaged in any land speculation, but he had to be sure.

This matter would be thoroughly investigated, Nehemiah assured the crowd, and without delay. Calling for his lieutenants, he issued orders to immediately investigate the investment practices of his staff and associates and report back if any unethical practices were uncovered. He then issued a summons to all the nobles and officials for a mandatory meeting at the temple. His ire had cooled only slightly by the following day when he turned to face the leaders who had gathered in the assembly court of the temple complex.

"You are behaving like predators," Nehemiah bellowed at them. "The law of God strictly forbids extracting usury from any of our own people, especially the poor. You are not only entrapping our people with exorbitant interest; you are forcing them into bankruptcy and destitution. You are making slaves out of our own children. This is just wrong."

There was absolute silence. Not a word of denial or explanation. No excuse or justification. Guilt was written all over their faces. This was a matter of community concern, Nehemiah concluded, and would need to be dealt with in an open forum. Motioning for the nobles to follow him, he pushed his way through the well-attired group and headed to the porch that overlooked the courtyard where masses of people waited in the sun for an answer.

Loudly, so that everyone could hear the charges, Nehemiah reiterated the list of offenses that had been brought against the rulers: price gouging, predatory lending, heartless foreclosures, enslavement of children. Many in the crowd nodded their agreement, while others cringed with discomfort at the blatant exposé of men of prestige and high social standing. The leaders stood quietly, eyes cast downward, admitting by their silence their complicity in these deeds.

"What you have done dishonors Yahweh and makes a mockery of our faith," Nehemiah declared. "You are no different from the heathen who despise us and ridicule our God. I implore you, here in the presence of this company, repent from these evil deeds. Put an end to all these practices this day. Cancel the debts that are owed you. Restore the homes, fields, vineyards and orchards you have confiscated. Return to their parents the children you have taken as bondservants. Do what is just. Let us stop charging interest on our loans. Instead, let us share our grain and oil with those in need and require no repayment."

The response of these leaders was unimaginable to families who the day before had despaired of recovering their property. "We will give it back," the leaders answered with one voice. "And we will not demand anything more from them. We will do as you say."

The crowd exploded with cheers and applause. While the family groups jostled and weaved their way through the chaos toward the penitent nobles, eager to express their gratitude, Nehemiah sent word to the high priest to bring his cadre of ranking clerics to the temple courtyard. This promise would be sealed by a sacred oath. Led in formation over to the great altar of Yahweh, all the nobles and elders raised their hands and swore that they would honor the vow they had made to God and to the people.

"And a curse be on you and your families if you break this vow," Nehemiah pronounced as the oath-taking rite ended. Then vigorously shaking out the bottom folds of his robe so that road dust swirled about him, he added, "If you fail to keep your promise, may God shake you from your homes and from your property!" All the people shouted, "Amen!"

8

THE END IN SIGHT

TWO MORE WEEKS. MAXIMUM. That was the consensus of the engineers. The priests, who had completed their gate and wall section, were already discussing plans for a grand celebration. Most of the great doors were completed, oiled, fitted with hardware and waiting to be set on their hinges. The finish carpentry work on the superstructures and gatehouses was also nearing completion. The push was on to complete those high stretches of the wall that had been toppled into the Kidron Valley—the most demanding engineering challenge of the entire project. But the end was in sight and adrenalin quickened aching muscles and joints.

For Nehemiah this was a deeply rewarding time. A spirit of cooperation prevailed. The corrective action he had taken on predatory lending practices seemed to be holding, and sufficient food was being shared and bartered to enable everyone to have an adequate diet. If there was one thing that tempered Nehemiah's satisfaction, it was the continuous stream of communication that flowed between Judean officials and Tobiah.

It was almost impossible to curb this correspondence since Tobiah was himself part Jew, intermarried with the priestly establishment. He was a powerful man in many respects, more than just in terms of wealth. His personal charisma and stately bearing made him a most attractive figure, one whom those striving to move up the social order would boast of knowing on a first-name basis. And he was using his social capital to full advantage these days. He had up-to-date intelligence on every aspect of the construction process and scrutinized every decision Nehemiah made. Tobiah, of course, passed this information on to his fellow governors, who analyzed it carefully for any flaw or weakness that could be exploited to their benefit.

On four separate occasions Sanballat had sent sealed letters to Nehemiah requesting the honor of meeting with him in the Vale of Ono between Jerusalem and Samaria, time and specific place to be Nehemiah's call. Regional concerns, the invitations said. The intent was hardly subtle. At the very least it would draw Nehemiah out of Jerusalem and distract him from his mission. Worst-case scenario could be an ambush. Nehemiah paid little attention to the invitations, dismissing them with a "thanks but no thanks" response, and remained focused on his work.

The fifth letter to arrive was an open letter—a virtual news release—carried by Sanballat's personal servant to report serious accusations against Nehemiah. It charged that reliable sources throughout Palestine and as far away as Arabia had informed him of Nehemiah's intentions to declare himself king of Judah and that prophets had already been appointed to declare this to be divinely ordained. "You can be very sure that this report will get back to the king, so I suggest that you come and talk it over with me," the message concluded.

"Give me strength, Lord." Nehemiah sighed. The tactic had not worked before. What would make Sanballat think it would work this time? His letter didn't deserve the dignity of a response. But just for the record, Nehemiah returned a hasty "open letter" reply that was sure to become fodder for public gossip.

> "Sanballat: There is not a word of truth in your accusations, of that you are fully aware. I have no interest in meeting with you for any reason!"

This accusation of prophets foretelling a new kingship for Israel lingered with Nehemiah for days after his rebuff of Sanballat. Prophets had indeed prophesied the fate and future of much of Israel's history. Their messages, often encrypted in symbolic language and bizarre behavior, did many times represent the voice of Yahweh. But prophets could be dangerous to have around. Sometimes they declared truth that rulers didn't want to hear. And sometimes they were corrupt—false prophets, paid mouthpieces of kings who wanted to portray personal ambitions to be God's will. In truth, the only way to know for sure if a prophet was speaking for God was in retrospect. If his prophecies came to pass, then he was authentic.

These thoughts had been drifting in and out of Nehemiah's mind as the sun was setting on one more long, hectic day of work. He was looking over plans for the next day when a young priest approached and handed him a scrawled letter from, of all people, Shemaiah, a member of a respected priestly family. Shemaiah (whose name literally meant "who Jehovah heard") was holed up in his house, the note said, agonizing over an unwelcome message he had just received from God. The message involved Nehemiah. Immediately Nehemiah's thoughts flashed back to Sanballat's open letter, especially the part about false prophets declaring God's intent to make him king. Hastily he made his way to the prophet's home. He must be cautious in this meeting with Shemaiah. Who was this man anyway? Nehemiah had never met him, knew only that he came from a good family. If this man truly had received a message from Yahweh, it must be received without skepticism and acted upon in faith. On the other hand . . .

Nehemiah knocked on the door of Shemaiah's home and waited for a response. A young girl greeted him, motioned him in and escorted him down a darkened hall to the rear of the house. In a back bedroom, lit only by a candle that cast dim shadows against the walls, a bearded man, hair disheveled, sat cross-legged in a corner on the floor. The man's expression was one of torment. He stared at the floor with horror and intensity in his eyes, like one who had just watched the slaughter of his family and had no power to intervene.

"They are coming," the prophet whispered. Nehemiah crouched down and cocked his ear to catch the muffled words. "Tonight! You will be killed."

He spoke with such awful finality that Nehemiah's breath caught in his throat. Was this the voice of Yahweh speaking to him? Was this some sort of warning to get his life in order before it was snuffed out?

"Tonight!" the prophet repeated, his voice becoming more emphatic.

Was there no "unless" to this message? No contingency? Was this simply a preordained death sentence being announced? Shemaiah slowly lifted his eyes and for the first time looked at Nehemiah. After a long silence during which the prophet seemed to be processing another message, he spoke again.

"There is only one way of escape," Shemaiah said. "You and I must lock ourselves in the inner temple. There the Lord will protect you."

There *was* an alternative after all. Nehemiah breathed a sigh of relief. Yahweh would provide him sanctuary in the inner sanctum of his holy temple. It was as though God was inviting him to come into his very presence for protection. *How gracious is Yahweh,* Nehemiah thought, *and wise.* For even if his hiding place were discovered, no adversary in his right mind, no matter how aggressive, would dare desecrate a people's holy place.

The two of them must leave together immediately, the prophet instructed, and slip secretly into the temple and bolt the doors. As they rose to go, one small concern troubled Nehemiah's spirit, though he was hesitant to mention it to one so familiar with temple protocol.

"Is not the inner temple a hallowed place where only priests are permitted to go?" Nehemiah inquired of the prophet.

"There is an exception in your case," Shemaiah reassured him, "because you are uniquely called by God to accomplish a sacred mission."

Yes, that did make sense, Nehemiah reasoned. Yet something still did not feel right. Certainly Yahweh could ordain whatever means he chose to accomplish his purposes, but would he violate his own law to do so? And who in Jerusalem, save this one prophet, could verify that it was indeed Yahweh who had given these outside-the-law directives? Nehemiah had a special calling from God, but he was still a layman without the priestly rights to enter the sacred place.

"I will feel better if I consult with Ezra and the chief priest before crossing this line," Nehemiah insisted.

"No time for that," the prophet urged. "We must act immediately!"

It was the nervous, impatient body language and an angry flash in She-maiah's eyes that raised a red flag in Nehemiah's mind. Nehemiah was not going to be pressured by an untested, self-proclaimed oracle into a hasty de-cision that even a layman knew was in violation of God's command. Besides, what kind of a message would sneaking off and hiding in the temple send to those who looked to him for leadership?

Sensing the growing resistance, Shemaiah became openly agitated. In a menacing tone he pronounced, "Our people's blood will be upon your head, should you refuse to accept God's means of salvation for yourself and the city."

"Should a man like me run away?" Nehemiah retorted. "Or should one like me go into the temple to save his life? I will not go!"

A true prophet of God does not curse and swear the way Shemaiah did when Nehemiah rejected his "prophecy." There were soldiers enough to pro-vide protection should there be an attack tonight, Nehemiah reassured him-self as he headed back to his quarters. The greater danger, he concluded, was having a false prophet in the city, obviously paid by Sanballat and Tobiah to publicly discredit him. This imposter would be dealt with another day.

9

THE WALL IS COMPLETED

ON THE MORNING OF DAY FIFTY-THREE, Jerusalem awakened early as usual. But there was nothing usual about this day. The familiar sounds—the clinking of hammers on chisels and the cracking of rock against rock—were noticeably absent. The forges were cold and the scaffolding was gone from the walls. This was the first morning workers filed into the city not in dusty work clothes but in garments normally reserved for sabbaths. With them came their families and servants, carrying picnic food and blankets. This was not a scheduled feast day in the temple calendar, but it was a day for feasting nonetheless. In an astounding fifty-two days, and in the oppressive heat of the Middle Eastern summer, the walls of Jerusalem had been completely rebuilt and new gates at every entrance were securely hung in place.

Every open space filled with family groups and village friends, spreading their blankets on the ground and building cooking fires for a grand picnic. Merchants set out tables arrayed with cheeses and imported wines and fresh fruit of every sort. Children chased up and down the crowded streets and menfolk proudly assisted their wives and daughters up the stone stairways to the top of the wall for a panoramic view. The city had not felt this kind of vitality since the glory days of the monarchy.

Suddenly, from the hill beyond the temple came a sound that stopped everybody dead in their tracks. Trumpets! The piercing blast arrested the at-

tention of militiamen and sent picnickers scurrying for their swords. It was
the dreaded alarm that signaled an attack, and all the men remembered their
instructions to race toward the sound with weapons drawn. And then a second blast, this time joined by other brass horns blaring what resembled a
royal announcement. Strange. Not the clear, shrill call of battle bugles. Then
a third, with crashing cymbals and a swell of stringed instruments. Emerging
from the northernmost part of the temple courtyard came a long column of
robed clergy, strumming harps and lyres, beating drums and cymbals, blaring rams' horns and trumpets—a cacophony of music parading out into the
city. And following the raucous orchestra, a choir of priests lifting their
voices in song. Roars of laughter exploded all over the city as men sheathed
their swords and mothers released protective grips on their children.

It was not clear who had organized this musical extravaganza. Certainly
no one from the civil defense corps! Likely it was the talented Jezahiah, mu-
sician extraordinaire and conductor of the temple choir, who was known to
have a flair for the theatrical. Whoever it was had certainly selected the right
music for the occasion. The crowd immediately picked up the rhythm. Into
the wake of the priestly procession flowed women and children, burly farmers and gaily attired merchants, even sophisticated city officials—all dancing
and singing and clapping to the beat. The parade snaked its way along wide
streets that followed the new wall, gathering members as it went. By the time
it completed its route around the wall and came back to the temple plaza,
nearly everyone had joined the march.

It could hardly be considered a ceremony; there was too much cheering
and hollering to dignify the occasion by such a description. A senior priest,
trying his best to be heard above the clamor, yelled to the crowd that there
were some people present who deserved special recognition. "The hard-
working men of Tekoa . . ." The crowd erupted in yowls and whoops and
wild applause before the priest could get words of congratulations out of
his mouth. The same bellowing hoorahs exploded as soon as the priest
mentioned the names of Uzziel and Malchijah of the goldsmith guild. More
than forty times the crowd responded in thunderous applause as the iden-

tity of each of the working groups was called out. Finally the priest, now nearly hoarse, motioned for Ezra to come forward. As the saintly old leader made his way to the front, the crowd shushed one another in order to hear his words.

"There is one person," Ezra declared in his loudest voice, "without whose vision this day would never have come." Every eye turned toward Nehemiah. "Yahweh has used this man to restore Israel's dignity and respect among the nations. It is fitting that we express our great appreciation to our leader, Nehemiah!" It was a full five minutes before the applause died down enough for their new governor to speak.

It was the most challenging and rewarding experience of his life, Nehemiah told them. And the incredible dedication and self-sacrifice demonstrated by everyone to accomplish such an achievement was deeply moving to him. He was not much for flowery speeches, he admitted, but those who had placed their trust in him as their leader could count on him to govern them justly and uphold the law of Moses.

Then, moving on to some important governance matters, Nehemiah announced the appointment of a number of new public servants who would provide leadership for the city. It came as no surprise that Hanani, his brother, would be the new mayor of Jerusalem. Hananiah, a trusted friend and veteran soldier, would be in charge of all military and civil defense forces. Levites would be called back to the city to serve as overseers of all ceremonial regulations as well as temple security and management, roles required by Mosaic law but abandoned with the decline of temple resources. Additionally, they would be charged with the responsibility of keeping the city gates, monitoring traffic flow in and out of the city and enforcing sabbath observance as prescribed by Scripture.

"From this day forth," Nehemiah declared, "the gates of the city will be locked before sundown and not opened again until well past sunrise." Anyone was welcome to spend the night within the city—welcome to move in permanently, for that matter—but no one would be permitted to enter or exit once the doors had been shut. Guards would remain on duty in the guardhouses from predawn until nightfall, and round-the-clock sentries would be visibly posted. A volunteer civilian security corps would provide backup for the militia, supplying additional coverage on stretches of wall nearest their homes. It was the first time in anyone's memory that Jerusalem felt truly safe.

10

REPENTANCE AND RECOMMITMENT

THE NIP OF AUTUMN WAS IN THE PREDAWN AIR. Harvest was in. Sparse though it was, it did not dampen the spirits of families who made their way along a network of dusty trails and roads that led up to Jerusalem. From farms and villages throughout Judah they streamed, thousands of them, many leading pack animals laden with tents and firewood and fresh produce from the yields of their fields. Families had been eagerly anticipating this trip for many weeks, weaving colorful cloth from wool they had spun and dyed, sewing new garments, preparing spicy delicacies, saving their best wine. They were on the road long before dawn, allowing them to arrive in time to witness the opening of the gates and hear the first trumpet blast that announced the beginning of the festive month of celebrations. A good number of the travelers had already seen the secured Jerusalem—volunteer workers who had traversed these roads daily during the construction project. Many of the women and children, however, and men who had stayed home to tend herds and flocks and village affairs, had only heard the stories of the historic undertaking. Today they would see it for themselves.

A new day was about to dawn. The travelers could sense it in their souls. More than the brightening that illuminated the silhouette of a strong fortress city against the eastern horizon, something was new in the spirit of the people. During the past few weeks, a noticeable feeling of optimism and cooperation had appeared in the air, even between the poorer people of the land

and their moneyed, newcomer neighbors. Today they would all listen to readings from the holy book of Yahweh, the words that defined them as a chosen race, words nearly forgotten during too many turbulent years of political infighting and social wrangling, words they were somehow now ready to hear. The elders had appealed to Ezra to personally read from the sacred scrolls—a duty typically handled by the college of priests. And Ezra, whose reputation as scribe laureate was legendary in Jewish communities throughout the empire, had readily agreed.

By the time the sun was peeking over the high hills to the east, immense throngs had assembled outside the gates of the city. Inside, host families and shopkeepers and clerics of every rank were scurrying about in last-minute preparations for the first of the three traditional fall celebrations—the Feast of Trumpets. At the appointed time (the precise moment when the sun broke into clear, unshielded view) a trio of trumpeters atop the wall released a long, clear call that reverberated off the hills and sent echoes down the valleys. With military precision, the heavy iron bolts on the gates dropped and the great wooden doors swung wide. A cheer erupted from the crowd.

By the thousands they poured through the magnificent gates, curious eyes darting from gleaming doors to great archways to towering walls. How strong the city looked! How proud were the workers who had cut and joined the massive beams and chiseled and wrestled boulders into tight, smooth surfaces! Wives and children gazed admiringly at the quality work their men pointed out to them. Engineers, arms gesturing and waving in the air, described to appreciative listeners the geometric calculations required for the job and the machines they had improvised to lift and slide huge stones into precise sockets. Team leaders joked and laughed with volunteers they had spent the summer sweating alongside, remembering saw cuts made on the wrong end of boards and wheelbarrow loads of rock tipped over by overconfident youth. There was much good-natured banter about whose wall section was strongest or straightest or highest, along with teasing of those who worked on sections beside their homes—humorous accusations about their wall being twice as thick.

In the large plaza near the temple, just inside the Water Gate, a tall wooden platform had been erected. The elders who had prevailed upon Ezra to keynote the day with Scripture reading wanted to make sure that everyone would be able to see their venerated spiritual leader. Word spread quickly that this was the place where Ezra would be addressing the congregation, and soon every square inch of ground was spread with blankets and expectant listeners. A strange mix of jubilation and gravity stirred through the assembly, like the joy of a wedding celebration interwoven with the solemnity of taking lifetime vows. Excited chatter dropped to a whisper as the crowd spied Ezra emerging from the temple followed by an entourage of clergy and Levites.

When Ezra reached the wooden structure and climbed the stairs to the platform, a hush fell over the crowd. One of his assistants handed him a scroll, and with great reverence he gently unrolled it and held it high for all to see. The entire assembly spontaneously rose to their feet, some with eyes turned heavenward, others with heads bowed. The sight was more than the old scribe was prepared for, and all that would come forth from his mouth was an emotion-choked "Praise God!" Like sparks from a campfire, words of praise broke out across the assembly, and soon the whole plaza was caught up in a spirit of worship. "Amen, amen," the people responded. Women began waving their hands with shouts of hosanna. Others bowed low to the ground, some even prostrating themselves before the Lord. It was the kind of Spirit-ignited worship that no priest could plan or control, a rekindling of the soul of a people grown cold with worldly cares.

When the crowd quieted and Ezra regained his composure, he began to read aloud from the law. Stationed throughout the audience were Levites with copies of the sections from which Ezra would read. After each passage was read from the platform, Levites circulated among the people to explain the meaning. For many this was the first time they had heard directly and understood clearly the commands of Yahweh, and frankly they found it to be disturbing. A sobering realization began to dawn on the people: the distance between the law of God and their lifestyles was immense. Most had not committed murder, but in many other aspects of the law they were serious offenders.

Ezra's voice touched something deep within their spirits, and with every verse the weight of the convicting reality grew more intense. Downcast eyes and slumping shoulders. Then an occasional sniffle and dabbing of moist eyes. From a group that sat near the temple courtyard wall, there could be heard a man's uncontrollable sobbing. Another passage of Scripture was read and explained. The sobs could then be heard all over the plaza, grown men weeping unashamedly before their wives and children and servants. A contagion of guilt and grief gripped the people. How far they had strayed from the commands of Yahweh! How deeply He must be displeased with them! Some in the congregation began to wail aloud as they would at a wake.

This was not what the day was supposed to look like, Ezra finally commented to one of his assistants during a break from reading. This was not to be a day of mourning; this was the kickoff day for the harvest feast. Making his way up to the stand once again, Ezra held the scroll above his head, and rolling it closed declared, "Today our God has told us to celebrate, and celebrate we will! Enough tears. It's time to feast." Furthermore, Ezra instructed the Levites, as they fanned out into the crowd, "Tell them not to cry."

To reinforce the old scribe's admonition with the stamp of governmental authority, Nehemiah mounted the platform and called out to the people: "Go and enjoy choice food and sweet drinks, and send some to those who have nothing prepared. This day is sacred to our Lord. Do not grieve, for the joy of the LORD is your strength." And with that the weeping ceased and the feasting began.

For the next seven days the Jewish community, both in the city and throughout the countryside, camped out in makeshift lean-tos, observing the ancient and long-abandoned practices of the Feast of Booths. The daily public reading and interpretation of Scripture restored meaning to the festivities far deeper than the gratitude everyone felt for another harvest and for their restored capital. On rooftops, in open courtyards and out in the fields, they ate and drank their fill of the yields of the harvest. Those with abundance shared with those who had little. Around campfires they all cooked and sang and danced. And at night they slept under the stars, sheltered only by branches of fresh-cut olive, myrtle, palm and fig trees. And Israel remembered and celebrated the goodness of Yahweh, who had led their people out of captivity in Egypt and who once again had freed them from enslavement and given them back their promised homeland.

Three weeks later the community was again pouring into Jerusalem. The last day of October was set aside in their calendar for the great Day of Atonement—the final event of the month of harvest celebration. This time they came not in gay apparel, nor weighed down with rich food and wine, but in drab sackcloth and with only enough nourishment to keep the children from crying. They led animals selected from their flocks and herds to be sacrificed on the altar. In the plaza before the Water Gate the congregation assembled, reverently and silently. Once again the book of the law of the Lord was opened, and from the platform Levite leaders took turns reading aloud. There was no need for interpretation this time. The people understood what the commands of Yahweh required of them. Their hearts and minds had been prepared, and they were ready to publicly confess their sins and receive the promised forgiveness.

It had been planned as the traditional service of repentance—Scripture reading, a prepared antiphonal confession read by the Levites with "amen" responses from the people. And indeed, this was how it began. But at some indistinguishable point during the corporate confession of the unfaithfulness of their forebears, the "we, your people" became a personal prayer. The neglect of sabbaths and the withholding of tithes were *their* sins, not just their ancestors'. And the worship of other gods and giving of their sons and daughters in marriage to foreign infidels was *their* transgression. In the silences that interspersed the reading of prayers, the meaning sank into their souls.

It was during one of these silences that a leading Levite invited the congregation to confess any personal sins they had committed against one another. It was the prompting many seemed to be waiting for. A mother quietly apologized to her child for cutting words she had spoken in anger. Brothers separated over jealous competition moved toward each other. Scattered throughout the crowd were businesspeople who had undercut and deceived others through shady dealing. There were families embroiled in land disputes who had not spoken a civil word to each other in years. There were priests who had harbored deep resentment against other priests and had made false and damaging accusations. One by one, individuals made their way through the crowd to face those they had wronged or offended. The sorrow and weeping that had erupted spontaneously in this same place earlier in the month now expressed itself in personal acts of reconciliation and healing.

The confessing and forgiving and hugging and restoring went on for nearly three hours. Joyful smiles, like rays of sunlight breaking through an overcast sky, shone through the dirt-covered faces and disheveled hair of the drably attired crowd. A deep cleansing was taking place. The Levites felt it among themselves, for they, too, had experienced the releasing power of forgiveness. "Stand up and praise the LORD your God, for he lives from everlasting to everlasting!" one of them shouted out to the congregation. "Praise his glorious name! It is far greater than we can think or say," some of the others responded. And the people did just that, with great joy and passion.

The confession and praise ended with a prayer offered by Jeshua, ranking Levite. And then, in an unusual move that puzzled everyone except the handful of senior priests and Levites who knew about the plan, Nehemiah mounted the platform and took his place among the Levite leaders. He carried with him a leather folder from which he removed a document of some sort that he handed to Jeshua. The crowd quieted as the Levite raised the page over his head for all to see.

"It is an official pledge," Jeshua informed the congregation, a written oath to which the people were being asked to bind themselves. "Listen to its words," he called out.

The document, which focused on three specific areas, had been drafted by senior priests and Levites at Nehemiah's request. Pagan intermarriage, the most troubling and contentious of issues, topped the list. "From this day forward," it read, "we promise not to give our daughters in marriage to the peoples around us or take their daughters for our sons." Next was a commitment to keep the sabbath holy: "When the neighboring peoples bring merchandise or grain to sell on the Sabbath, we will not buy from them on the Sabbath or on any holy day." The long-abandoned practice of sabbatical year observance was also reinstituted: "Every seventh year we will forgo working the land and will cancel all debts."

Tithing was the third area, one that was felt by the drafters (who were hardly disinterested parties) to require specificity: (1) an annual assessment of an eighth of an ounce of silver to cover the cost of temple operations, including feasts and festivals and a schedule of prescribed rituals and special offerings; (2) a lottery for supplying wood to fuel the altar; (3) a firstfruits offering of all agricultural products and the firstborn of all flocks and herds; (4) firstborn sons dedicated to the Lord for spiritual leadership; and (5) one-tenth of everything produced, including the best-quality flour, grain, fruit, wine and olive oil. The document outlined exactly how these resources were to be used, where they were to be stored and who was accountable for their collection, management and distribution. The temple storehouse system was to be reestablished with a priest-Levite check-and-balance system to ensure its integrity. The text concluded, "We will not neglect the house of our God."

The crowd responded with an enthusiastic "amen." Farmers and singers, clergy and militia, patriarchs and peasants, everyone from aged grandmothers to children old enough to understand raised their right hand and with one voice repeated their solemn pledge "to obey carefully all the commands, regulations and decrees of the LORD our Lord."

Nehemiah then stepped to the front of the platform and, in businesslike fashion, declared that an oath, in order to be properly ratified, required signatures of all those holding positions of leadership. The official sealing of this covenant would take place immediately at the temple portico.

Nehemiah led the signing procession, writing his name boldly at the top of the signature space. Senior priests and heads of the Levitical families followed suit. (Curiously, high priest Eliashib somehow missed out on the signing ceremony.) Then all the nobles, princes and clan patriarchs lined up and one by one sealed their solemn promise in their own hand.

11

RENEIGHBORING THE CITY

THE CITY SEEMED COLD AND STRANGELY SILENT. A scant population of permanent residents—hardly enough to fill a village—had settled into their routines now that the autumn festivities were over, and for the first time since the vision to rebuild the wall had been unveiled, a sobering stillness descended upon the city. It was safe, true. The temple stirred with priestly activity (though most of the clergy and Levites lived outside the city), and government staff went quietly about their business. Nobles occasionally occupied their city residences, and a modicum of commercial traffic trickled in and out of the gates.

But Jerusalem was far from being a vibrant capital city. Many streets were still lined with vacant lots and abandoned shells. What rebuilding had taken place was in clusters around the temple and on less damaged blocks, leaving whole sections of the city uninhabited. The spaciousness that was welcome during wall reconstruction and the fall festival season now seemed bleak and cavernous. Commuting clergy, merchants and weekend worshipers could hardly restore the city to social and economic viability. Nehemiah was painfully aware that a vital urban center had to be filled with permanent, vested residents engaged with self-interest in every facet of city life. Abandoned real estate shouts out disinvestment and devaluation. Depopulation has the smell of death. The city, in order to be a desirable place to live, had to be rich with educational and cultural interest and alive with vigorous commerce.

Such vitality begins with an educated and resourced population.

How could Jerusalem be reneighbored? Nehemiah was making lists again. He was familiar with a variety of urban revitalization strategies that had been implemented throughout the Persian Empire: large-scale civic improvement projects, inducements of cheap or free land, highway and waterway construction that attracted residential development, the importation of conquered peoples . . . (Nehemiah shuddered as he remembered the devastating impact the latter had upon his own people.) None of these options seemed to fit the unique situation in which Jerusalem found itself. First of all, there was no more urban development money forthcoming from the king's treasury. That ruled out public works projects to create jobs and jumpstart residential and commercial development. At the moment, the city was generating only a fraction of the wealth that the suburbs and the rural land were producing. Employment, apart from tax-supported government and temple jobs, was largely outside the city limits. And then there was the endless morass of title disputes over city property that stretched back a century and a half—expensive legal work that put a damper on development.

Good demographic data was needed, Nehemiah concluded. He wanted to know just how many employed or employable workers now lived in Judah, what kind of population growth rates could be measured and anticipated, what was the current and projected wealth-generating capacity of the region that would require the banking-lawyering-marketing-soldiering support services of the capital. Such documentation, if it contained reliable genealogical data, could also serve to unravel many of the property title entanglements. And so he commissioned a national census.

As the information flowed in, an encouraging picture began to emerge. Judah was much stronger than official Persian statistics revealed. In spite of the depressed market, blamed largely on drought conditions, the people were hard workers and inventive entrepreneurs. Their families were growing, as were their flocks and herds. The influx of returnees from cities throughout the empire was replenishing the culture with capital as well as professional expertise. It was obvious to Nehemiah that Jerusalem was poised to become the economic and political powerhouse of Palestine. He could make that case to the people, he was sure.

A wall dedication and grand opening celebration. Yes! That would be a perfect event for marketing the city to the populace. The dedication of the first gate and the somewhat impromptu wall-completion celebration had been inspiring affirmations for the builders, and the harvest feasts and atonement fast had been incredibly important to the spiritual life of the community, but no consecration of the wall itself had yet been scheduled. This could be another occasion for a corporate praise service and an opportunity to showcase the benefits of city living, Nehemiah reasoned. Ezra concurred when Nehemiah shared the idea with him. The old scribe was no urban strategist, but one thing he knew—something needed to be done about all those burned-out buildings and deserted streets.

The plan would have to be intelligently and artfully conceived. The priests and Levites could do a good job of creating liturgy, music and choreography for the occasion. Their capacity for pageantry always produced inspiring results. But it was the marketing of the city as a desirable place of residence that presented the greatest challenge. The streets would have to be cleaned of trash and debris, and existing homes and buildings would need to be renovated and whitewashed. Palms and greenery should be planted and the ancient fountains and pools cleaned and repaired. And this would be the perfect time to use the remaining funds in Nehemiah's government grant reserved for the construction of a governor's home.

The idea soon took on a life of its own. The college of priests dug into historical archives to unearth prayers and speeches offered by earlier leaders at special dedications. Psalms and other poetic writings were selected for the occasion. Levites with musical talents were recruited from all over the province to compose orchestral and choral pieces. On the streets, home and business owners jumped into the renovation process, and volunteer days were scheduled to clean up public areas. The most ambitious construction project was the governor's new home—hardly a mansion but elegant in its simplicity and style. To have it completed by early spring, in time for the dedication date, was optimistic, but certainly the exterior and landscape could be ready to put on display.

By the time spring breezes began to melt the chill of winter, the city had put on a much brighter face—some streets might even be called charming with their new shutters and fresh coats of plaster and whitewash. But there was one issue that kept troubling Nehemiah's mind. What if comfortable rural and village folk were simply not interested in urban living? Those most likely to buy in, he suspected, would be the recent immigrants from cities throughout the empire who had not yet set roots in the Judean countryside. That would be a good start but hardly a representative body. Jerusalem needed a citizenry from every township and region to link it directly to the commerce and local politics of Judah.

A review of historic documents filed in temple archives, together with recent census data, revealed that a surprising number of families once held title to Jerusalem property. After the destruction of the city nearly 150 years earlier, most of those claims were either abandoned or forgotten. Jerusalem had become a city of squatters, and with the exception of the temple properties, most claims had never been disputed. Now was certainly no time to contest the chain of title on property occupied by current residents; these folk had surely earned the right of possession. But hundreds of other plots—most vacant, many with ruins—were unclaimed but traceable to family ancestry. Suppose, Nehemiah pondered, these families could be motivated to reclaim family land and reestablish their rightful place as citizens of Jerusalem. Suppose they could come to see it as a privilege to have a stake in the affairs of the governing city. Some of the forward-thinking folk would doubtless seize upon the opportunity. Others would have to be convinced. Some, he knew, would simply be uninterested.

He would approach it from two angles. There was time enough for Nehemiah to pay visits to the leading nobles and clan leaders to introduce the reneighboring strategy prior to the wall dedication. Those families who volunteered to relocate to the city would be celebrated publicly during the program and honored for their commitment. Their example should encourage others to sign up. Then, after the dedication, he would institute a draft—no, he would call it a "sacred tithe" of the people. He would ask every family, every village, to select by lottery 10 percent of their people to move into Jerusalem. If the right attitude prevailed, this could be an exciting adventure, not to speak of an attractive investment opportunity.

Months of rigorous planning and organizing, endless orchestral and choir rehearsals, and strenuous construction, renovation and beautification efforts culminated on the morning of the great dedication day. Again the city was packed with Jews from all over Judah. Those who would play assigned roles in the event numbered in the hundreds. Hundreds more would receive public recognition of one sort or another. And for thousands of others in the audience, this would be an opportunity to participate in a historic moment to be retold for generations. The city looked beautiful! Streets were swept clean and adorned with greenery; houses wore brightly colored coats of fresh stucco; shops and markets displayed their wares in tantalizing array; the temple shone like a gem in the morning sun. And in prominent display, on prime real estate across from the temple courtyard property, stood the new governor's mansion. No one alive had ever seen Jerusalem as stunning as it looked this morning.

Despite the congestion of the crowds, there was an orderliness in the city. Levites and other temple personnel wearing brightly colored armbands that distinguished them as official hosts moved about the throngs, answering questions, giving directions and informing guests about the various activities of the day. In the plaza just inside the Valley Gate, a large gathering of priests, nobles, city officials, choir members and musicians with their instruments were forming up in two long lines. Jezahiah, headmaster of the Levitical musicians guild, hurried about, arranging orchestra and choral groups in proper position. At his signal the procession began filing silently up the steps that led to the top of the wall and spread out along the broad stone surface of the fortification. Into two directions they split, Nehemiah leading one group northward in a clockwise direction and Ezra proceeding south and east with his assemblage. When the two great parades reached the midpoint in the wall, they halted and turned to face inward.

A silence fell across the city. An octet of trumpeters raised their horns and sent out in unison a clear, perfect blast that echoed down the city streets and off the opposite wall. Eight trumpeters from the opposite wall answered back across the city. Chills ran up and down the spines of the crowd who stood below. Again the trumpets called out, this time in three-part harmony. The response came back in kind. The boom of large drums next broke the silence, and again a deep reverberating answer from across the city. Then an explosion of harmonious sound erupted from the northern wall as the full orchestra called the city below to worship, and from the south and east came an antiphonal response. By the time the full power of choral voices joined in the concert, lifting songs of praise, there was scarcely a dry eye in the crowd. The magnificence of the production was more than awe inspiring; it was celestial! And when Jezahiah invited the whole assembly to join in the singing, the volume of triumphant praise that rose up was heard even from far off.

The processionals converged near the temple and filed down from the wall into the open plaza where the priests had prepared an inspiring dedication service. "This day the prophecy of Zechariah has been fulfilled in our midst," shouted a priest who had been selected for his deep, booming voice. "This is what the Lord Almighty says: 'My love for Mount Zion is passionate and strong. I am returning to Mount Zion, and I will live in Jerusalem. It will be called the Faithful City, the Holy Mountain. Once again old men and women will walk Jerusalem's streets with a cane and sit together in the city squares. And the streets of the city will be filled with boys and girls at play.' "

The day far exceeded Nehemiah's expectations. Ezra's too. The assemblage before the temple proved to be an almost perfect setting for corporately thanking God for their new, safe, beautiful city—and (not that Nehemiah would have admitted being so crass) a superb marketing opportunity as well. It was certainly the perfect backdrop for publicly celebrating those who had volunteered to relocate into the city. The crowd's enthusiastic response to these urban pioneers was contagious. What once would have felt like a risky venture now seemed normalized by the example of respected friends and neighbors—suburban and rural folk excited about urban living. Good security and improved conditions made it not at all difficult to envision how city life could afford a comfortable and stimulating lifestyle, not to mention the investment opportunity. To Nehemiah's satisfaction, no one had to be pressured to move into Jerusalem. The inducements, along with a nudge of encouragement, was all that it took to produce long lines of applicants ready to reclaim historic family properties. Real estate values in Jerusalem began to improve.

The great dedication day yielded another, quite unexpected result. So many people—from elders to women and children—raved about the magnificent music the Levites had performed that several nobles approached Nehemiah about the possibility of hiring a full-time temple orchestra and choir. It was a splendid idea, one that would enhance worship and add richness to the cultural fabric of the city. Though a professional company of musicians would require additional funding, the consensus was strong enough to convince Nehemiah that the people would support it with generous offerings. Besides, it would bring that many more talented neighbors—musicians and their families—into the city as permanent residents.

The idea was floated to the congregation and the response was overwhelmingly positive. Their eagerness to provide a heaping share of tithes and offerings to cover not only the basic costs of temple operations but also the additional Levitical functions of gatekeeping, storehouse management and now a ministry of music signaled an important shift in public attitude. Tithes and offerings, often sarcastically referred to as "temple taxes," were being viewed as acts of worship and community building. This was the spirit of the law that Ezra had long preached but seldom witnessed.

12

THE GOOD YEARS

AN ABUNDANT SUPPLY OF DRINKING WATER flowed from Gihon
Spring through Hezekiah's Tunnel—an engineering marvel carved through
more than a quarter mile of solid rock—filling restored city pools and fountains and topping up the great subterranean cisterns beneath the temple hill.
Another life-giving stream flowed through Jerusalem as well—a vigorous
trade stream producing revenues that swelled the city budget. Land values
in the citadel had experienced steady appreciation during the years following the dedication. The construction industry was booming. Vacant buildings had been demolished and in their place fine homes had been erected.
The charred shells of abandoned storefronts had been snapped up by investors and razed to make way for new commercial development. With a hearty
tax base, the temple complex had been renovated and enlarged, and a new
government administration building had been constructed. Modernized
sanitation, paved streets and beautifully terraced public plazas reflected the
influence of architects from world-class Persian cities.

Another marvel had been introduced into the regional economy—
money! Once political stability had returned to Judah, Nehemiah initiated a
system of coinage that had proven effective in the more urbanized areas of
the empire. Barter only worked well in an agrarian society. Gold and silver
were risky since it was difficult to verify their purity and since scales could
be easily manipulated. But a coin, minted by the king and bearing his in-

scription, offered the assurance of accurate weight and purity. Once introduced into the Judean economy, money accelerated the process of local exchange and positioned Jerusalem to capitalize on international commerce. Traders from as far away as Egypt and Greece flooded into the new market, bringing fine wines, exotic tapestries and delicately woven fabrics, expensive oils and perfumes, and most any other commodity that could be sold for a profit. Fish from the Mediterranean, thoroughbred horses from Arabia, fresh produce from all over Palestine, crafts from local artisans—every available shop, vending table and stall displayed the wares of eager merchants. Prosperity flooded back into Judah.

Stable, ethical government was the major factor. A progressive, well-managed city, positioned at a crossroads of travel routes, was naturally a nexus of exchange so long as convoys could journey in safety and merchants could make their deals free from the threat of robbers. Jerusalem now afforded both. A secure mountaintop fortress looking down on its region with a protective eye was a welcome invitation to the trading world—the very opportunity Sanballat and Tobiah most feared. Jerusalem was rapidly becoming once again the powerhouse of regional commerce.

Speaking of Sanballat and Tobiah, they and their comrades were now safely out of the picture. Their threats and schemes had been exposed as the hoaxes they were and the two had been stripped of their holdings and status in Jerusalem. This afforded Nehemiah no small sense of satisfaction. The pagan marriage issue that had given Ezra so much trouble had also been appropriately dealt with. The heads of Judah's clans were holding to their oath of ethnic purity, and the strength of the economy was serving to diminish any lingering temptation.

Tithes and special offerings were also coming in as promised, and the system of checks and balances for managing religious affairs was working well. Yahweh was Israel's God, their *only* God, and his law was their law. Syncretist priests had yielded their pluralistic positions in favor of purist theology. Levites, counterbalancing the long-standing priestly domination of all things religious, were now in charge of many of the temple management functions and most of the ceremonial law enforcement.

The vision that long ago in distant Susa had taken over Nehemiah's life had blossomed into reality before his eyes. Indeed it had become a reborn Jerusalem, city of God, strong economic and political anchor of the Jewish homeland, center of worship for the faithful followers of Yahweh. And it was deeply satisfying.

Nehemiah was tired. Fulfilled but tired. And frankly, it was starting to show. It was time, he concluded after consulting with his brother and several other trusted leaders, for him to return to Susa for some much-needed rest. Israel was in capable hands. It would be good to carry back to the king a personal progress report and hopefully secure a royal blessing to extend his duties as governor of Judah. Besides, it had been a long time since he had seen his family. And so, after twelve intense years of rebuilding, reorganizing and redeveloping, Nehemiah left his Jerusalem home and returned to Persia.

13

ENFORCING THE RULES

HOW LONG NEHEMIAH STAYED IN SUSA he did not record in his journal. What he did write, however, is that his governorship was extended for a second term. When he returned to Jerusalem he discovered that several distressing situations had developed in his absence.

The first hint of a problem came as he and his entourage, laden with baggage from their long return trip, passed by the temple on their way up the hill to the governor's residence. He could have been mistaken, but he thought he saw someone who looked like Tobiah ducking into the temple compound. Anger flared up inside him like an erupting volcano. The thought of this despised enemy of the faith being allowed to enter the city, let alone the *temple*, released a surge of bile into his viscera. He hoped mightily that the strikingly dressed fellow he had seen was only someone who resembled the conniving foe. *God help those responsible if Tobiah has been permitted back in*, Nehemiah seethed as he broke from his escorts and marched toward the temple entrance.

It was worse than he feared. It was indeed Tobiah he had seen entering the temple grounds, a junior priest innocently confirmed. Tobiah's quarters were in the old storehouse area. *His quarters!*

"Where's Eliashib?" Nehemiah roared. Eliashib—no longer the high priest but still wielding influence over temple affairs—had to be the culprit. He had always had a cozy relationship with Tobiah, endorsing him as basically a good person. Hearing his name used in less than endearing tones, Eliashib poked his head around a doorway and inquired who might be asking for him. The priest's face immediately reddened as his eyes met Nehemiah's. There was no denying his complicity and little point in defending what was clearly a serious infraction of the law. "Take me to him," Nehemiah ordered Eliashib.

A large storage area intended for grain and oil offerings for local welfare needs, and two smaller adjacent rooms for consecrated incense and worship trappings, had been converted into an apartment for Tobiah. Woven carpets imported from the East covered the floors and gold-laced draperies adorned the plastered walls. The furnishings were equally opulent, obviously selected and arranged by a talented interior designer, creating an atmosphere befitting a dignitary on his visits to the city.

"Outrageous! The desecration of this sacred place is bad enough," Nehemiah raved, "but inviting a pagan and enemy of Yahweh to move into the holy temple—this is utter blasphemy!" Snatching a tapestry from the wall, he threw it to the floor and stamped on it. Eliashib, along with several other priests who had come to see what the commotion was about, backed out of the doorway and into the courtyard. An expensive vase crashed against the wall and shattered into a thousand pieces. Out came Nehemiah dragging a velvet lounge cushion and flung it onto the dirt in front of them.

"Clear everything out," he shrieked at the wide-eyed priests. "Throw it all into the street! I want this place scrubbed and fumigated! Then put everything back the way it is supposed to be."

This was hardly the homecoming celebration Nehemiah had envisioned. He should have seen to the retirement of Eliashib before he left for Persia. *Amazing, when vigilance is relaxed even slightly, how quickly ambitious people can infiltrate places of influence, even the house of God,* he thought. Tobiah had slipped out the rear of the compound and made a rapid retreat from the city, but his instincts for power and greed would in no way be diminished. He would have to be watched, Nehemiah knew. And by the way, where were the tons of grain that should be filling the temple storehouse? The stockpiles of new wine and olive oil were gone as well. And where were the Levites who should have been tending to these affairs? This would be Nehemiah's second disappointment of the day.

"No money to pay them," the senior priests reported. Most all the Levites had to go back to work on the farms. All the musicians and worship leaders and guards and temple administrators—all the staff commissioned to manage religious life among the people—had been dismissed and sent home due to lack of funds. What had become of the signed commitments all the leaders of Judah had made under oath? Withholding of tithes and offerings could not be blamed on a famine, not this time. The land was yielding in abundance and the economy was booming. An assembly would have to be called immediately to determine what had gone wrong.

An official communiqué was hastily dispatched from the governor's office to all the elders and clan chiefs as well as city and religious officials. "Why is the house of God neglected?" Nehemiah confronted the leaders who gathered as per his instruction in the temple courtyard. Though he already knew the answer, he waited, arms crossed, for a response.

After an awkward, shuffling silence, a noble from the rich growing region northwest of Jerusalem offered a candid explanation. "Greed, I'm afraid," he admitted. A few of the larger landholders had delayed payment of tithes and then others followed suit. This resulted in some staff layoffs among the Levites, including some of the tithe collectors. It was a downward spiral from there. With diminished accountability, the temptation to withhold tithes became irresistible. This was an honest and embarrassing admission, but the downcast expressions and head nods in the crowd confirmed that the practice had become widespread, like a contagion of greed that had swept the country.

"Well, the Levites are going to be reinstated," Nehemiah declared. "All of them, with back pay. And you are going to fulfill the solemn oaths you swore before Yahweh and the people." He stared into every eye that would look up. "All back tithes *will* be caught up, with interest, and from this moment forward they *will* be kept current. That includes the rotation of firewood offerings for the altar. I want these storehouses filled to capacity and the temple fully staffed. We have made a covenant with Yahweh, and we *will* keep it! Any questions?" There were none. This would no longer be an honor system, he continued. And motioning forward four men who had been standing beside the temple porch, he introduced his compliance team: one priest, one scribe, one layman and one Levite. All of them were men of sterling reputation and unquestionable ethics, men whom he was appointing to monitor the collection and management of the storehouse distribution system.

Prosperity had proven to be a wonderful blessing but a highly seductive one, Nehemiah reflected. Famine tempted the rich to opportunism, but abundance seemed to spawn greediness in all sectors of the population. Withholding of tithes and offerings was but the first sign of greed he would encounter upon his return to Judah. The following sabbath, on an early morning stroll, he was alarmed to discover that all the Jerusalem shops were open for business and commercial traffic pressed in and out of the gates like on any other business day. The winepresses were turning; donkeys pulled wagonloads of grain through the gates; the farmer's market was jammed with tables of fresh-picked produce; international merchants displayed their imported delights; a livestock auction was just beginning.

These signs of Israel's new prosperity would have brought a smile of satisfaction to Nehemiah's face normally. But this was the sabbath, the day that Abraham's children everywhere held apart as a sacred day of worship and rest. Jews in exile had paid a high price for their refusal to work on this day. And now, here in Jerusalem, everyone was disregarding it, treating it as a normal business day. What was exceedingly distressing to Nehemiah was that when he reprimanded several of the farmers and merchants, they looked surprised, as if they didn't understand what he was so upset about. The summons went out the following day for another elders meeting.

"What is this wicked thing you are doing—desecrating the Sabbath day?" Nehemiah confronted the assembly of leaders. "Didn't your forefathers do the same things, so that our God brought all this calamity upon us and upon this city? Now you are stirring up more wrath against Israel by desecrating the sabbath. It's bad enough that you withhold your tithes and force our

Levite brothers to abandon their posts. But then you take advantage of their absence and violate Yahweh's holy day. Well, the Levites are coming back to their stations, and I've instructed them from now on to close down the city every Friday at sunset and not open the gates until Sunday morning. No passage in or out except for worship or residential traffic. All businesses will be closed during that time. That goes for trading both inside and outside the wall. No working the farms either. We made a promise to our God to keep his day holy, and we *are* going to keep it! I am going to see to that personally," Nehemiah pledged—or threatened, as some read it.

It was later the following week, as he was headed for the temple administration building to see to the arrangements for Eliashib's retirement, that the sound of playing children caught Nehemiah's attention. The laughter of children was not an unusual sound in this area, since many of the priests' families lived in the residences surrounding the temple. What did arrest his attention, however, was the unfamiliar language two of the little ones were bantering in. It certainly wasn't Hebrew or colloquial Aramaic. He paused to listen more closely to see if he could identify the dialect. *Sounds like Horonite,* he thought.

"Whose children are these?" he asked a robed member of the clergy who was passing by.

"Joiada's son," was the reply. "Eliashib's grandson."

"What language are they speaking?" he inquired.

"Horonite. Their mother is one of Sanballat's younger daughters." Nehemiah's face turned grim. Would there be no end to Eliashib's sacrilege?

"It's not all that uncommon these days, especially among the young people," the priest explained.

It was beyond Nehemiah's comprehension. This matter had been clearly dealt with in the covenant signing years ago. Pagan marriages were banned. Period. How could this practice, which had been so destructive to the integrity of the community and so corrupting to the faith, have crept back into acceptability in such a short time? Into the heart of the temple community! Nehemiah managed to restrain his outrage. If indeed this practice was slipping back into the culture, he would have to deal with it at its source. He whirled around, walked back to his office and ordered his staff to begin a quiet investigation of all families in Judah who had intermarried with foreign infidels.

With accurate data in hand, Nehemiah issued an official invitation to Eliashib, and all other priests and elders found with pagan marriages in their households, to meet with him at the governor's complex to discuss "an important matter." After welcoming his guests and extending courtesies befitting men of leadership, Nehemiah motioned to a priest to bring the box containing the original documents that every noble and family patriarch had signed years earlier promising to abide by the law of Yahweh. Drawing specific attention to the section on refraining from giving their children in marriage to pagans, he asked if anyone could offer a reasonable explanation for their compromise on this point.

"Young people these days," one of the elders whined, "they just don't value our traditions. They think we're out of touch with the modern world."

"They think multiculturalism is a good thing," another chimed in. "And raising their children to speak multiple languages is preparing them to be world-class citizens." Eliashib's grandson, who had accompanied the old priest to the gathering, smiled smugly.

"Wasn't this exactly what led King Solomon into sin?" Nehemiah threw out. Anger was starting to flash in his eyes. "He was our wisest leader ever, but even he was led into sin by his foreign wives." It was the condescending smirk on the face of Eliashib's grandson that finally pushed the governor over the edge.

"Out of here," Nehemiah shouted, "you and your whole family! I want you out of the city today. You are officially banished from Jerusalem!" Eliashib immediately jumped to his grandson's defense, as did several other men who objected to the severity of the governor's order. Snatching the closest objector by his beard and hair, he shook him and roared, "Any covenant breaker who thinks he is wiser than Solomon and believes himself to be above the law will be given the same treatment. You will be condemned as infidels and excommunicated." And with that he pushed the man back into the arms of his stunned friends. There would be no further discussion of this matter. The final decision on pagan marriages had just been made.

Out of another captivity the children of Jacob had been delivered and restored to a land flowing with milk and honey, a land promised by Yahweh himself centuries earlier as an inheritance to them and their children forever. Exiles scattered over a vast empire were returning to their homeland, secured once again by the crown jewel of Judah: Jerusalem. The sacred writings of Moses and the prophets had endured the flames of destruction and the brutal dismantling of the culture and were now, thanks to Ezra and other faithful scribes, rewritten and safeguarded once again in the temple. Judah was in full bloom, like a rose in the desert. And a people at peace were building homes and planting vineyards and bearing children, secure in their own land. As in the days of old, Yahweh had once again shown himself to be a faithful and gracious God.

To Nehemiah there could have been no greater privilege than to receive a divine call in a crucial moment in Israel's history, a call to rebuild Jerusalem and reorder the homeland society according to the instructions of Yahweh's Word. Some would find him abrasive and abrupt, lacking in diplomatic skills. Others might accuse him of being overzealous, of being too harsh with those who opposed him. But none could fault the superior quality of his leadership or his unswerving commitment to accomplishing the task to which he had been called. He left little doubt among the citizens of Judah that the law of God would be the law of the land so long as he was governor. Whether out of grateful hearts or because of the threat of expulsion, the people of Israel would, under his administration, live by the sacred writings that had been preserved down through centuries of turbulent history. Israel would from this time onward be known as the people of the Book.

"Remember me, O my God, for good." This was the final entry in Nehemiah's journal. A layman's simple prayer.

PART TWO

THE
ISSUES

In part one, the account of Nehemiah's experience is retold largely as it has been preserved for us in scriptural text (with the texture and license of midrash). Part two zeros in on issues that Nehemiah encountered—issues that are remarkably relevant to our present-day urban context. The challenges he faced are lifted out of the part one story, examined in greater depth, given touches of midrash, and then placed alongside related situations taken from actual experiences in contemporary urban life. While the flow of part two moves back and forth across more than two millennia of history, the similarities become obvious. Nehemiah gives us a vantage point from which to view our age.

14

WHAT MAKES A LEADER?

TO THE AVERAGE CHURCHGOING READER, Ezra and Nehemiah are the titles of two obscure books of the Bible. Few would recognize them as the names of the two men who rescued and preserved for the Judeo-Christian world both the Old Testament canon of Scripture and the city of Jerusalem. These two godly leaders, similar in education and background, called to a similar mission, could not have been more dissimilar. Twinned in an overlapping moment in time, their separate impacts on Jewish history were complementary but as distinct as day and night.

They were both children of the diaspora. Their families, generations before either of them was born, had been force-marched from Judah following the siege of Jerusalem in 586 B.C. and pressed into servitude in Nebuchadnezzar's Babylonian Empire. Ezra's family—clerics descended from the line of Aaron—retained their priestly identity and, even in exile, clung to the sacred traditions of the faith. The religious pluralism of Babylon accommodated the practice of Judaism, a liberty the priestly families exploited into a network of synagogues in cities throughout the empire. Nehemiah, on the other hand, came from a lineage of landowners and Jewish nobility. Though his family was stripped of all holdings when uprooted from Judah, their leadership in the exilic community remained intact, and in time, they emerged into positions of responsibility in Babylonian society.

By the time Ezra and Nehemiah were born, their families enjoyed the full rights and benefits of Persian citizenship. Nebuchadnezzar's tyrannical rule was long gone, vanquished by Cyrus of Persia (539 B.C.), who introduced a reign of benevolence that was to endure for nearly two centuries. In this hospitable climate the Jewish community flourished, enjoying the opportunities of commerce and the freedom of religious worship. Though permitted by royal decree to emigrate to Palestine, many of the Jews chose to remain in the thriving cities of the empire. Such was the case with both Ezra's and Nehemiah's families.

But thoughts of the homeland were never far from the minds of exiled Jews. Any shred of news from Judah was devoured and dissected, then faithfully passed along like nutrients in the bloodstream throughout the Jewish network strung across the civilized world. These reports became the grist for endless theological debates about Israel's unfaithfulness, Yahweh's judgment, the predictions of prophets Jeremiah, Haggai and Zechariah, and the timing of Jewish repatriation. These were household discussions young Ezra and Nehemiah grew up with.

Both boys were the beneficiaries of the sophistication of Persian society— its renowned system of laws, its art and music. And in the synagogue schools they studied the language, history and law of their own Hebrew culture. Early on, the young men mastered the balancing act of assimilating into the dominant culture while at the same time holding to the traditions and beliefs of their heritage.

From childhood, Ezra was a reader. He had a special fascination with the sacred writings. The stories of how the priests in his family had heroically smuggled copies of the Torah out of the burning temple as Nebuchadnezzar's troops sacked Jerusalem had captivated his imagination. It was the sacred duty of the priests, he was often reminded, to protect and preserve the words of Yahweh. To everyone's delight, when he reached the age of decision, he elected to pursue the profession of scribe.

Nehemiah, on the other hand, was intrigued with the ways of government. Growing up in the capital city of Susa, he was exposed to an endless stream of visiting dignitaries with their regal caravans and frequent military parades that displayed the might of the empire. Though thoroughly Jewish in his faith, he was nonetheless captivated by the inner workings of secular government and the remarkable governance structures that controlled a vast and diverse empire. It came as no surprise to Nehemiah's family when he pursued and landed a job in the imperial service corps, a position that gave him access to the political process. Trustworthiness, he soon saw, was a quality highly valued in the service of the king.

Though contemporaries, whether Ezra and Nehemiah ever met as young men is unknown. Ezra, the older of the two, grew up in the suburbs of Babylon, while Nehemiah was raised in the royal city of Susa two hundred miles to the east. Certainly, however, as they emerged into positions of influence in their own spheres, they learned of each other. By the time Nehemiah moved up through the ranks of the Persian government to the powerful position of cupbearer to King Artaxerxes, Ezra had already distinguished himself as the leading authority on Mosaic law. Scribe laureate of the Jewish people, he had assembled the most complete texts of the Pentateuch, the Wisdom Literature and the Prophets that had ever been compiled. Copies of the sacred canon, under his leadership, had been distributed to synagogues throughout the Persian Empire and as far south as Egypt.

Jerusalem was never far from the minds of exiled Jews. A number of floundering attempts had been made by returnees to rebuild the ruined city, and a scaled-back temple had finally been constructed after several false starts. But Judah remained a quagmire of political infighting and social chaos. One of the major factors in this was the constant conflict over religious purity. Returning Jews were for the most part devout Yahwists, schooled in the Mosaic law, thanks in no small part to Ezra's efforts. Homeland Jews, on the other hand, had assimilated with the cultures and religions of surrounding tribes and saw no harm in intermarrying and embracing others' gods. To rebuild a unified covenant community, given this serious theological chasm, was a nearly impossible task. Many said it would take someone like Ezra, revered by homeland and exiled Jews alike, to pull it off.

EZRA WAS NOT VOLUNTEERING FOR THE TASK. Not that he hadn't thought about it a thousand times. But he was a scribe, not an administrator. Yet when King Artaxerxes, troubled by an alliance between the Greeks and Egyptians that was threatening his control of the western front, inquired who might be most capable of consolidating the Judean population, Ezra's name was put forward.

Ezra appeared before the king and his council wholly unprepared for the barrage of questions that were fired at him. Yes, he would need other capable leaders from the Jewish community to accompany him, and yes, he would like to collect an offering to take back with him. Yes, the king's gracious offer to release the remaining gold chalices and artifacts confiscated from Solomon's temple would elicit enormous gratitude from Jews everywhere. When asked about Persian troops to ensure safe passage for himself and such treasures, Ezra replied with preacherlike confidence: "The gracious hand of our God is on everyone who looks to him, but his great anger is against all who forsake him." In other words, no, he would not be needing military escort.

Why the king would entrust such confidence and sweeping judicial power to a scribe with no experience in governance would be the subject of much conversation over the following busy months of preparation. Some said it was Yahweh, pure and simple. Others said it was Ezra's reputation. Still others wondered if a young Jew named Nehemiah on the king's personal staff had something to do with the decision. Regardless, when Ezra assembled his convoy of five thousand eager émigrés for the four-month journey back to Judah, he had amassed far more Persian assets than he would ever have dared ask of the king—twenty-four tons of silver bullion, more than seven tons of gold, priceless temple treasures and three thousand devout volunteers and their families with all their livestock, savings and household goods. And in a leather pouch bearing the royal emblem was a letter from the king that read in part:

Artaxerxes, king of kings,
To Ezra the priest, a teacher of the Law of the God of heaven:
Greetings.

Now I decree that any of the Israelites in my kingdom, including priests and Levites, who wish to go to Jerusalem with you, may go. You are sent by the king and his seven advisers to inquire about Judah and Jerusalem with regard to the Law of your God, which is in your hand. Moreover, you are to take with you the silver and gold that the king and his advisers have freely given to the God of Israel, whose dwelling is in Jerusalem, together with all the silver and gold you may obtain from the province of Babylon, as well as the freewill offerings of the people and priests for the temple of their God in Jerusalem. With this money be sure to buy bulls, rams and male lambs, together with their grain offerings and drink offerings, and sacrifice them on the altar of the temple of your God in Jerusalem.

You and your brother Jews may then do whatever seems best with the rest of the silver and gold, in accordance with the will of your God. Deliver to the God of Jerusalem all the articles entrusted to you for worship in the temple of your God. And anything else needed for the temple of your God that you may have occasion to supply, you may provide from the royal treasury.

Now I, King Artaxerxes, order all the treasurers of Trans-Euphrates to provide with diligence whatever Ezra the priest, a teacher of the Law of the God of heaven, may ask of you—up to a hundred talents of silver, a hundred cors of wheat, a hundred baths of wine, a hundred baths of olive oil, and salt without limit. Whatever the God of heaven has prescribed, let it be done with diligence for the temple of the God of heaven. Why should there be wrath against the realm of the king and of his sons? You are also to know that you have no authority to impose taxes, tribute or duty on any of the priests, Levites, singers, gatekeepers, temple servants or other workers at this house of God.

And you, Ezra, in accordance with the wisdom of your God, which you possess, appoint magistrates and judges to administer justice to all the people of Trans-Euphrates—all who know the laws of your God. And you are to teach any who do not know them. Whoever does not obey the law of your God and the law of the king must surely be punished by death, banishment, confiscation of property, or imprisonment.

Ezra's life as a scribe was over. He was now minister of state for Jewish affairs. On the banks of the Ahava Canal, at the western outskirts of Babylon where his caravan was assembling, he would give his first official order: *pray!* For the first time it hit him just how vulnerable they actually were. Once they crossed the river, they would be moving westward along unpatroled roads while carrying tons of treasures, wagons laden with personal possessions and domestic animals ripe for the picking, not to speak of the women and children. And not a single soldier or armed cavalryman to protect them! We must fast and pray earnestly, Ezra told everyone. Too late now to ask the king for a military escort, especially after he had spoken so confidently about God's protection.

During the next three days of fasting and praying, another overlooked detail was brought to Ezra's attention. As the priests whom he had commissioned to organize and manage the trip were getting an accurate head count, they discovered that no Levites had volunteered for the journey. Everyone from the priestly establishment knew that Mosaic law was clear about Levites performing a range of religious functions. This was a gross oversight, one that he must correct before proceeding if he had any intention of reinstituting faithful temple worship in Jerusalem. So, calling together a group of his most respected leaders, he exposed the problem and implored them to find, if they could at this late hour, any Levite volunteers. To Ezra's great relief, his scouts returned two days later with more than 250 Levites, along with their hastily gathered belongings and harried families.

From April until August they traveled, a strenuous, dusty journey in the sweltering Middle Eastern summer. But God was gracious. They encountered not a single threat or mishap along the way, not even so much as a wolf attack on a lamb. When they came within sight of Jerusalem, the word of their arrival had long preceded them and hundreds of waving well-wishers lined the road with shouts of welcome. The city was overjoyed about their new leadership, especially because it was Ezra. And the temple treasures he brought, along with new capital for refurbishments and other investments, were welcome arrivals indeed.

Ezra's first act upon entering the city was as much personal as it was official. So moved was he with gratitude to Yahweh for the near-miraculous protection on their journey that he made immediate arrangements to offer sacrifices at the temple. From the best of their flocks and herds, he and his company pulled out twelve head of oxen, ninety-six rams, seventy-seven lambs and twelve goats—a magnanimous offering to the Lord and a sign before an onlooking populous that the worship of Yahweh would receive the highest priority in this administration.

There was no apparent resistance to Ezra's appointment. Regional governors welcomed him and pledged their financial support of the temple renovation. The Jewish community was more than enthusiastic about the project and began immediately to organize a local capital campaign. Talk of rebuilding Jerusalem stirred once again among the people. All seemed positive until several of the newly arrived priests overheard a discussion between two local clergy about a dispute one was having with his Canaanite in-laws. The new priests could hardly believe what they were hearing. Intermarriage with pagan women was a flagrant violation of the Mosaic law, especially for a priest. "A lot of priests have foreign wives," the two offered without hesitation. "It's a fairly common practice here in Judah."

Ezra, like most of the Jewish community back in Persia, had assumed that the orthodox priests who had returned to Judah years earlier were trustworthy guardians of the faith. They had been commissioned to go back to the homeland to reactivate Yahweh worship and reestablish Mosaic law. It was a surprise to no one that morality and religious life in the land had been badly corrupted after Nebuchadnezzar led the clergy and educated classes away in chains. But the exiled community took comfort in the knowledge that the priests they sent back to Judah—devout, well grounded in the Torah, seasoned by the disciplines of exile—were more than capable of restoring faithful temple worship and right living in the homeland. This shocking report of infidelity hit Ezra like a falling boulder.

Community elders confirmed the report as they met with Ezra in the temple courtyard the following day. The practice of marrying women from pagan tribes was extensive in Jewish society. The clergy who were supposed to set the standard were some of the worst offenders. As a matter of fact, there was not a guiltless household in the entire priestly establishment. This was staggering. A profound grief came over Ezra and he sank to the ground. As the gravity and extent of this great disobedience penetrated his spirit, he began to sob uncontrollably. In agony of soul he cried out and tore at his clothes and pulled hair from his head and beard.

There the governor sat, rocking and groaning in the dirt of the temple courtyard all day long, too sick at heart to utter a word to anyone. Quietly, others who were sobered by the situation joined him on the ground in what could only be described as a silent wake. By late afternoon, as time approached for the evening sacrifices, cold winds were whipping the garments of onlookers and rain was beginning to spit. The temple plaza was jammed with people wondering what this strange behavior of their new governor could mean.

Finally Ezra began to straighten his cramped legs, rose slowly to his feet and lifted his eyes toward the heavens. It was hardly the image the people of Judah had expected of a royally appointed governor—garments torn and covered with dust, hair and beard disheveled, face stained with tears. A prophet's behavior, perhaps, but not a governor's. Yet who, save the stoniest of heart, would not be moved by the sight of this grief-stricken leader. Ezra lifted his arms upward and cried out, "O my God

. . ." and then fell to his knees, collapsing under what seemed to be a
crushing weight.

He began again:

O my God, I am too ashamed and disgraced to lift up my face to
you, my God, because our sins are higher than our heads and our
guilt has reached to the heavens. From the days of our forefathers
until now, our guilt has been great. Because of our sins, we and our
kings and our priests have been subjected to the sword and captivity,
to pillage and humiliation at the hand of foreign kings, as it is today.

But now, for a brief moment, the LORD our God has been gracious
in leaving us a remnant and giving us a firm place in his sanctuary,
and so our God gives light to our eyes and a little relief in our bondage. Though we are slaves, our God has not deserted us in our
bondage. He has shown us kindness in the sight of the kings of Persia: He has granted us new life to rebuild the house of our God and
repair its ruins, and he has given us a wall of protection in Judah
and Jerusalem.

But now, O our God, what can we say after this? For we have dis-
regarded the commands you gave through your servants the prophets
when you said: "The land you are entering to possess is a land pol-
luted by the corruption of its peoples. By their detestable practices they
have filled it with their impurity from one end to the other. Therefore,
do not give your daughters in marriage to their sons or take their
daughters for your sons. Do not seek a treaty of friendship with them
at any time, that you may be strong and eat the good things of the
land and leave it to your children as an everlasting inheritance."

What has happened to us is a result of our evil deeds and our
great guilt, and yet, our God, you have punished us less than our
sins have deserved and have given us a remnant like this. Shall we
again break your commands and intermarry with the peoples who
commit such detestable practices? Would you not be angry enough

with us to destroy us, leaving us no remnant or survivor? O LORD, God of Israel, you are righteous! We are left this day as a remnant. Here we are before you in our guilt, though because of it not one of us can stand in your presence.

And with that Ezra slumped back to the ground. Those close around him were sobbing quietly. The watching crowd, sobered by the intensity of Ezra's grief, was now sniffling too—some out of genuine sorrow for their sins and some from fear of impending judgment. For an unbearably long time, Ezra lay with his face buried in his hands, groaning.

Finally, Shecaniah, a leader from one of Jerusalem's prominent families, assumed the role of spokesperson for the people and called out so the entire congregation could hear: "Ezra is right. We have been unfaithful to our God and deserve his wrath. But there is still hope for us. Let's make a covenant to divorce our foreign wives and from now on obey all the commands of Yahweh." The crowd registered their agreement with amens and head nods. Ezra did not move.

"Will we obey all the counsel and instruction of our spiritual leaders?" Shecaniah called out. The congregation voiced their response: "We promise to obey!" Ezra still did not move.

At the risk of appearing presumptuous, Shecaniah moved hesitantly to where Ezra lay prone and, stooping down, spoke softly into the governor's ear. "It's time to get up and deal with this," he said. "We're with you, but we need you to take the lead." It was the nudge Ezra needed. Immediately he picked himself up off the ground, brushed the damp dirt from his robe, smoothed his hair and beard and scanned the audience for the priests and Levites.

With sadness in his reddened eyes, yet firmness in his voice, he addressed the clergy leaders: "Let it be as Shecaniah has said. I want everyone here, everyone in all of Judah, to take a solemn oath that you will cease this forbidden practice. And we will start with the priests and the Levites!" The crowd, relieved at seeing their governor on his feet and behaving gubernatorially once again, responded with a resounding "We pledge to do as you say!"

Without another word, Ezra gathered up the folds of his robe and, pushing his way through the assembly, disappeared into the temple complex. The following morning Shecaniah found him sitting alone in the apartment of one of the priests, the same tormented expression on his face, refusing any food or drink. His official decree needed to be dispatched to all the towns and clans of Judah, Shecaniah reminded him. A proclamation should be issued requiring the mandatory attendance of every intermarried Jewish household at a meeting in Jerusalem three days hence. And it needed to have teeth. Those who refused to come would forfeit all their property and be excommunicated from the temple. "Yes," Ezra agreed. "Let me sign the order right away."

Three days later a winter storm was in full fury. Under the threat of expulsion, racially mixed families from all over Judah had braved the driving rain and sleet and now huddled in the muddy temple plaza. Steam emanated from their noses and mouths. Frightened mothers attempted to quiet whimpering children as they pulled tent cloth and blankets about them to shield them from the elements. It was a terrifying moment that none could have anticipated. Leading priests, farming families, merchants and herdsmen—the weight of Yahweh's wrath bore down on these wayward families and, because of them, the whole society. At some level they all knew that they had strayed beyond the limits of the Mosaic code, but it was the clergy who bore the greatest guilt. Those who knew the law best had by their example invited their fellow countrymen to indulge in this forbidden practice. Now, together, they trembled in the cold.

"You have sinned grievously, for you have married pagan women," Ezra declared to the frightened assembly, "and have brought condemnation upon Israel. Now confess your sin to the Lord, the God of your ancestors, and do what he demands. Separate yourselves from foreign entanglements and from these pagan women."

There was not a dissenting voice in the crowd. In spite of the traumatic breakup of families that this decree would require, there was a collective sigh of relief that the fierce anger of God might be averted. "We will do as you say!" voices called out from all over the crowd.

"But must we separate right now, this minute?" one hesitant fellow ventured. The question was on everyone's mind. Splitting up families would be wrenching enough, but turning their wives and children out onto the roads in these chilling torrents with no means of survival would be depraved. Confusion and turmoil erupted as terrified women clutched at their husbands' arms and children began scream.

It was the levelheaded Shecaniah who intervened once again, pulling together some of the more respected leaders in the crowd. "This isn't something that can be done in a day or two," they suggested to Ezra with all humility. "This involves a great number of people and there are too many issues to deal with at this time, certainly not here and in this miserable rain. Let our leaders act on our behalf and schedule times for each family to have their case reviewed by a judge."

Ezra agreed with Shecaniah's plan. He dismissed the crowd with instructions that every affected family should meet with the clan chief or community leader who would be appointed to represent them. A panel of judges would be named to investigate each situation, he reiterated to them. As it worked out, it would take several months for the process to be completed and for every family to be dealt with appropriately.

This should have been the end of it. Ezra's personal memoirs end with this crescendo of repentance and revival that highlighted the beginning of his governorship of Judah. But Nehemiah, who followed him as governor a dozen years later, would tell quite a different story. The issue of intermarriage was far from over, as was the problem of pluralism that accompanied it. By the time Nehemiah arrived on the scene, Judah had been through several such reforms. And each time the people would slip back into the former practices. Ezra, a passionate preacher beloved by his Jewish people, seemed to lack the gifts required to sustain the reforms he inspired.

This is what Nehemiah had found so depressing when his brother Hanani paid him a visit in Susa with the news of the deplorable conditions in

Jerusalem. Nehemiah, like other faithful Jews in synagogues across the empire, had pinned hope on the rebirth of the homeland under Ezra's governorship. But twelve years of Ezra's leadership had produced only sporadic and unsustained spiritual awakenings and negligible urban renewal. Though Ezra's sermons were powerful and his knowledge of Scripture was unsurpassed, his mind did not go to issues of administration. Even with the support of the crown, and with a royal decree to establish the Mosaic law as the law of the land, and even with the full authority to impose "death, banishment, confiscation of goods, or imprisonment," Ezra could neither organize nor expedite an orderly plan. Spiritual leadership without accountability, the people soon figured out, could be quite inspiring, even convicting, but in reality allowed them to live their lives pretty much as they chose. Thus the practice of tithing dried to a trickle, sabbath observance became largely ignored and intermarrying continued.

Nehemiah, on the other hand, was most comfortable when he held the reins of control tightly in his own hands. Because administrative skills flowed so effortlessly into his daily work, he quite naturally, quite incorrectly, assumed that any leader of the stature of Ezra would have similar capabilities. He should have seen the red flags. The government paperwork coming out of Jerusalem from Ezra's administration was perfunctory and vague. Perhaps it was denial on Nehemiah's part or his deep sense of reverence for the scribe that allowed him to ignore what would otherwise have given him concern had it been any other Persian province. It took his own brother's firsthand, uncensored report to finally bring him to his senses.

Jerusalem needed to be managed. Biblical teaching was essential but not sufficient. If the city would ever be rebuilt and restored to its prominence as the Jewish capital, it would have to be governed by a no-nonsense, hands-on leader. It was this realization that triggered Nehemiah's call.

A passionate leader inspires; a pragmatic leader executes. King Artaxerxes was moved by Ezra's confident words and absolute trust in Yahweh's personal protection on the journey back to Judah. But the frightful reality of launching into hostile territory loaded with tons of treasure and not a single armed guard sent Ezra to his knees. Embarrassed then to ask the king for military escort, he implored his party of random volunteers to earnestly pray and fast for three days before they embarked. "Trust God, expect a miracle, have faith! And oh, by the way, can we round up any Levites to go with us?"

Nehemiah, on the other hand, carefully thought through all that he would need to assure safe passage and a successful mission. With no less faith than Ezra, but with substantially more forethought, he requested from the king a leave of absence, a government grant, passports and visas, a team of professional engineers and project managers, documents authorizing the requisition of materials from royal supply depots, and a detachment of cavalry and foot soldiers. Both Ezra's and Nehemiah's caravans arrived safely in Jerusalem, one rejoicing in the miraculous protection of Yahweh along the treacherous roads and the other grateful for their uneventful, well-planned journey. Ezra headed immediately to the temple to offer sacrifices of thanksgiving; Nehemiah formed a scouting party to assess the magnitude of the rebuilding challenge.

A passionate leader weeps over sin; a pragmatic leader secures public confessions and signed oaths. Ezra collapsed in the dirt, overcome by sorrow over the unfaithfulness of the people. He realized, as perhaps no other could, the serious consequences of yet another blatant offense thrown in the face of Yahweh. He grieved; he cried out to the Lord; he tore at his clothes; he prostrated himself before God and the people. He would not be comforted. Only at the insistence of his counselors did he pick up the scepter of governorship and authorize corrective action. Nehemiah's reaction to sin was quite different, not that he viewed it any less seriously. He saw transgression through the lens of societal impact. Marrying into pagan families leads to the acceptance of other gods, which leads to the corruption and erosion of Yahweh worship, which depletes temple revenues and staff, which diminishes the monitoring and enforcement of the laws of God. Intermarriage is sinful not only because it is forbidden by Mosaic law but also because it is bad for the covenant community. Thus, when Nehemiah confronted sin, he exposed it publicly, required offenders to take a public oath and sealed their promise with a signed contract that he then kept on file. If necessary, he would not hesitate to use these documents as evidence for excommunication.

The people loved to hear the passionate Ezra preach. No one had a command of history or a knowledge of Scripture to equal this scribe. And there was something about his deep voice, the way he expressed truth—even the way he read from the Torah—that resonated deeply within the soul of the Jewish people. By popular demand, Ezra was pressed into service as the plenary speaker for the first weeklong harvest feast held in Jerusalem after the walls were rebuilt. A special platform was erected for him so that everyone in the great crowd could both see and hear this astounding speaker. On the opening day of the festivities, Ezra mounted the podium and rolled open the sacred scroll, yet before he could read a sentence, the congregation erupted in emotional praise. When he did declare to them the Word, they were so moved with conviction that he had difficulty calming them down. Nehemiah had to come to the platform and order them to stop weeping and get on with the feasting. Hearing Ezra was like hearing from God.

Hearing Nehemiah was like being called to attention by a drill sergeant. His abruptness and matter-of-fact manner were hardly endearing. He barked out orders with little sensitivity to the feelings of others. One thing could be said of him, though: you always knew where he stood. He was candid, direct and totally at ease with giving directions. His ability to create orderly systems and appoint capable people to places of authority inspired confidence in the citizenry. If Ezra's words came from his soul, Nehemiah's came from his gut. Even his prayers were emotional outbursts that erupted from the joys or frustrations of the moment. Though some accused him of being impulsive and harsh, no one ever doubted his commitment to obeying and implementing the law of God. Where Ezra inspired, Nehemiah brought order.

A vision without a plan is as impotent as a plan without a vision. In Ezra's mind was a picture—a somewhat romantic picture perhaps—of a faithful covenant community living peacefully in the land Yahweh promised to Abraham and his descendants as an inheritance forever. After years of immersion in the study of Israel's rich past, and after endless hours of writing and memorizing the words of Moses, the songs of David and Solomon and the visions of the prophets, a tapestry of Israel's future destiny was woven into his consciousness.

No doubt all Jews held a fantasy of Jerusalem as their shining homeland city, but none was informed by the depth of spiritual insight that Ezra possessed. In his vision the temple was the central focus of all community life. Here the soul of the people embraced and was embraced by the spirit of Yahweh. In this holy place, offerings of thanksgiving, sacrifices for repentance and gifts of charity were like a sweet-smelling aroma of praise rising to a faithful God from a grateful people. Priests and Levites, sanctified for divine purpose, taught from the Scriptures, preserved the purity of worship and sacred rituals and interceded on behalf of the nation. From this spiritual center all communal life flowed.

When King Artaxerxes agreed to return the remaining gold bowls and other artifacts of Solomon's temple that had been stored in the royal treasury in Babylon, Ezra saw it as a sign from God that the fullness of time had come for the reestablishment of Jerusalem. His vision inspired Jews all over the empire to give liberally to the cause of completing the restoration of the temple. Thousands of eager men sold their homes and businesses in Babylon to journey with him to Jerusalem and support this mission. Little wonder why he was so shattered when he discovered that the temple had been badly corrupted by foreign influences and the law of God was sorely neglected. It was understandable that he would invest all of his energies in restoring the purity of temple worship and obedience to the commands of Scripture. If there were no vital spiritual center, nothing else would matter.

Nehemiah's vision was somewhat different. The synagogue in Susa that had nurtured his faith was a spiritual and social haven in a sea of powerful economic and political forces. The synagogue thrived, in part, due to the vigorous business climate supported by a stable government. He had always envisioned a restored Jerusalem as a prosperous capital city, not as large as Susa but just as vital, with the temple, rather than king's palace, as the centerpiece around which other development would emanate. The law of the Lord would be the law of the land, and the people would flourish because they lived by the principles and ethics that assured their prosperity. Nehemiah visualized a well-designed, well-staffed temple complex supported by abundant tithes and offerings and managed by devout and capable clergy. It would be the guiding spiritual force in Judah and a light to the trading nations that flowed in and out of Jerusalem's gates. But the temple could thrive only when it was supported by a thriving city. Little wonder why Nehemiah was so distressed when word reached him in Susa that after twelve years of Ezra's administration the walls of Jerusalem still lay in ruin. And not surprising that he would devote his first energies to rebuilding the city.

Same vision, different perspectives. Same calling, different roles. It is not likely that Jerusalem would have been rebuilt had it not been for Nehemiah's pragmatic leadership. Nor is it likely that there would have been a spiritual awakening without the passionate preaching of Ezra. Two effective leaders, equipped with different gifts and abilities, chosen to serve in tandem by their Creator to alter the course of history.

Leadership has many facets, far too many to adequately examine in this book. However, the examples of Ezra and Nehemiah and the interplay of their unique personalities and styles can stimulate interesting discussion on ways leadership plays out in our context. The following episodes depict common if not predictable dilemmas faced by urban leaders and the people they attempt to lead.

LEADERSHIP LEADING US WHERE?

I first met Dean when he was contemplating a move into our inner-city neighborhood. Pastor to a small fellowship of committed believers, Dean had compassion for those who were wounded and broken. That was his primary motivation for wanting to relocate—to be a neighbor to people who struggled with life-controlling issues. After much prayer and discussion, he and several members of his house church decided to move to our neighborhood and become part of a community church we were attempting to start.

From his first encounter with the poor who attended our midweek lunch and worship, it was clear that Dean had a unique ability to relate to them. His ease of manner, his patient attentiveness to the tangled details of their lives, the seriousness with which he addressed their every concern—these were special characteristics that drew bruised people to him like metal shavings to a magnet. Perhaps he was naive to accept at face value every story of woe, but like all of us who were called to urban ministry, he wanted to believe the best in others. The people of the community immediately embraced him as their "preacher."

These were exciting days in the life of our young church. A diverse blend of races and cultures and ages was attracted by its energy and vitality—senior homeowners, Latinos and African Americans, Appalachian whites, young professionals of varied ethnic backgrounds, homeless and addicted people of every stripe. "Unity in diversity" became our motto. Several young ministers, impelled by a calling to the city, joined the church and began employing their gifts in teaching, music and youth work. A ministry-team approach was adopted, though Dean, because of his spiritual maturity and people skills, emerged as the lead pastor. Preaching was rotated among the ministers and gifted laypersons, offering variety, but it was obvious that most of the congregation preferred to hear Dean's gentle candor.

While Dean remained the constant pastoral influence, other ministers and lay leaders came and went—and that eventually became a concern. With all the talent the church attracted, for some reason it did not retain its members over time. The church seemed to be doing all the right things. Frequent congregational meetings were held where mission statements, core values and membership commitments were explored together in detail. Small support groups were created to provide spiritual nurture and accountability. A calendar of church outings, Bible studies and retreats brought members together for fellowship and teaching. There were times of great excitement and enthusiasm, moments when unity seemed to be working. But it was hard work keeping a congregation as diverse as this one pulling in the same direction.

Dean was most energized by his ministry among the poorest of the congregation, most of whom attended the Wednesday noon service and meal but seldom came on Sunday. And though he continued to occupy the senior pastor position, many of the responsibilities of church leadership wore on him. He was excellent at group process—too good, perhaps. He preferred consensus to majority rule, and this resulted in decisions being stretched out for weeks, sometimes months, of wearisome discussion, decisions that could have been made in a single meeting. It was nearly impossible to act decisively. While the consensus process strove for inclusion and unanimity, younger members grew frustrated by the church's seeming inability to set a course and move ahead. And they came and went.

For more than two decades this cycle repeated itself. And all the while Dean faithfully ministered to those who remained and to the needy of the community. He was pleased when new leaders joined, pleased to let them exercise their creative talents. In fact, too pleased. He was pleased to allow them to preach and lead worship, for his sermons had grown somewhat stale and unimaginative. He was pleased for them to pick up responsibility for the management of church affairs and for visioning the church's future, since his energy for these things was largely depleted. But try as they would, the newest generation of leadership could not get a new vision off the ground.

Finally, in desperation, the dedicated core called a closed meeting to get to the bottom of this dilemma. Dean was relieved that he did not have to attend. The mission of the church was as viable as ever, they concluded. It could use some updating, but fundamentally it was sound. Nor was the problem a lack of talent—the church had had more than its share of gifted people over the years. At the risk of appearing disloyal, the group tiptoed into the issue of Dean's leadership. In many ways he was a model of the

Christian walk, living simply, even sacrificially, quick to prefer others ahead of himself, devoted to family, not given to ego trips. But there was something about his leadership (or was it the lack of it?) that landed the church again and again right back in the same place—stuck in a quagmire of endless process. To Dean it was unthinkable for the church to move on and leave a dissenting member behind. To do so would be insensitive, devaluing, fragmenting. "Trust the process," he would say. When others were ready to cut their losses and move ahead, Dean held firmly to the conviction that the body must be unified and no one was dispensable. And how could anyone argue with that?

Dean was a fine counselor, the group unanimously agreed. But a counselor and a leader may not be the same thing. The kind of leader the church needed to move it forward was a visionary risk taker, one who was willing to innovate and take chances, one who elicited the confidence of others and mobilized them to action. Come to think of it, there were a couple of sharp young ministry types currently in the church who had these very qualities. The congregation loved their lively preaching and their creative ways of drawing the audience into worship. And then a sobering reality descended like a pall upon the group. It was doubtful, they realized, that anyone would ever be able to assert enterprising leadership so long as Dean's influence played such a dominant role in the culture of the community.

How could this committee of leaders, respected though they may be, ever say in public what they were all thinking in private? Dean had to go! It would crush him. It would devastate his family. It could split the church. But to allow things to continue as they had been would mean surrendering to a slow, painful death. The church had a fatal flaw that would have to be removed surgically if it were ever to flourish. It would have to be done thoughtfully, carefully, as sensitively as humanly possible, but it would have to be done decisively.

Once the excruciating decision was made, the group put a plan into motion. Dean was nudged gently to tender his resignation. He was hesitant, a bit resistant, but he was offered no alternative. His pleas for more time and a more thorough process were kindly but firmly rejected. His wife was furious. The congregational meeting to announce his resignation was somber but well ordered and without contention. The end—or the new beginning—was bittersweet. But the church had learned a painful yet vitally important lesson about leadership.

Change by its nature is difficult, they learned, and human nature instinctively resists it. Growth, which always requires change, will inevitably upset and alienate some. A leader committed to consensus decision making, while highly sensitive and inclusive, gives veto power to the one most resistant to change. Sometimes growth necessitates cutting one's losses, as hurtful to some people as it may seem.

They also found that norms established by a founding leader are highly resistant to change, especially when that leader remains on the scene. It takes a strong new leader with persuasiveness and persistence to effect and sustain significant changes in an established church culture.

In retrospect it became clear that the church had been at its healthiest when it had true team leadership. Dean's counseling gifts, when balanced with the creative, entrepreneurial talents of a copastor, invigorated the church both as a community and as an organization.

ON REPLENISHING ENERGY

A few years ago, I suffered from a severe case of burnout. I loved my work, perhaps too much, and had taken too little time away from it. My energy reserves finally ran dangerously low and my board, recognizing the telltale signs, recommended that I take a three-month sabbatical. A beach house on the North Carolina coast offered to us by some caring friends was exactly what I needed. In this picturesque setting I was able to rest, read and reflect over the past two decades of ministry. The following are some reflections I jotted down on what had depleted my energy and what was needed to restore it.

This world seems far away from the city, far from the life in which I have been immersed for the past eighteen years. I am in the third month of a three-month sabbatical from urban ministry. Some gracious friends offered their home in this North Carolina coastal village as a place of rest and relaxation for our family this summer. Long uninterrupted hours of reading books, taking walks, fishing and playing have done much to deepen our relationships and to begin reparations to my soul.

In the quietness there is time to reflect. I have wondered why my life has become so stressful in recent years. Urban living brings its own pressures, to be sure. And there are increasing leadership responsibilities as the ministry expands. But the type of stress that precipitated this sabbatical comes from a deeper source.

The internal tensions that have been building in me distance me from people. I have become increasingly irritable, impatient, detached. With many exciting projects demanding my attention (developing new urban communities, converting an old prison, planning an urban institute, to name a few), I have had less and less time for people who are not directly related to these priorities. Friends, neighbors and even staff whose interests are not project related have begun to feel like intrusions. Accomplishing the important tasks of ministry has become my guiding value. Anything—anyone—that interferes with the timely achievement of these objectives is an irritant to me. Eventually I have found it difficult to distinguish whether I am mobilizing God's talented people for kingdom work or merely using them to achieve my own goals. But I have had little time for pondering these concerns.

The urgent and challenging projects to which I have been committed propelled me ever onward. Finally my body shouted, "Enough!" I had barely enough energy left to jump-start my day. I tried to keep gutting it out, but Peggy knew something was wrong. It was clearly time for a sabbatical.

A remarkable thing has happened during these past few weeks away from the pressures of projects. I have begun to enjoy people again. I realized the other day that I was actually enjoying chatting with John, the next-door neighbor, and helping him fix his old lawn mower. I am surprised to rediscover that I have a genuine interest in the details of people's lives—their children, their work, their life experiences. I even feel an eagerness to get back to the city to spend time with staff who I scarcely know and with friends and neighbors I have held at a distance. How strange that one trained in a helping profession and called to serve the people of the city should have to rediscover after eighteen years that he actually does like people!

When I think about returning to work, however, my stomach begins to tighten and my shoulder and neck muscles tense up. The activities of ministry have obviously become something more than the joyful use of my talents in God's service. Too many red flags are waving—too many concerns over success and failure, too much self-worth tied to performance. Before I can rightly reengage, I must learn once again how to serve without controlling, how to be responsible without picking up responsibility never intended for my shoulders. Like an amusement park carousel, this horse has come around before. I know that I am not called to be successful, only faithful in those things God defines as important—like caring about people. I know this. But living it is quite another thing.

The distance of this peaceful place has brought clarity to another unexamined area of my life: my job description. The broad list of duties that await me back in the city churn up a mix of emotions within me. Some things energize me, such as vision casting and plotting new community development strategies. I would rush back to them tomorrow. But the day-to-day management of the organization depletes my energy (I feel acid pouring into my stomach even thinking about it). If I am to survive for the long haul in this work, I must find a way to major in the areas of my giftedness and entrust the rest of the ministry to others suited to fulfill those leadership roles.

A formation of pelicans just sailed by. Mullet are jumping everywhere. The tide is ebbing now and a steady breeze is blowing across the barrier islands. It will be a good evening for walking. No mosquitoes. I still have most of a month left to enjoy the important things—and a lifetime to learn to keep them in proper priority.

THE FIGHT

It was the worst fight I have ever had, as an adult anyway. And Jon was my good friend. That's what made the conflict so startling.

Jon had been the executive director of our ministry for five years. He took over the CEO position following my sabbatical when I had come to the painful realization that I was not well suited for that role. I was the founder of the organization and its primary vision caster, but management was not one of my better talents. Jon had done a masterful job bringing structure and order to the freewheeling array of programs that had evolved under the umbrella of FCS Urban Ministries. He had standardized employee pay grades, centralized administration and fundraising, and restructured our board of directors to better reflect the diversity of the communities we served. He had even received an award from Atlanta's leading community foundation for our becoming the "most improved nonprofit of the year."

But after five years of hard work, Jon was running out of steam and he knew it. I could see it, too, from the sidelines where I sat as the hands-off president. He was multitalented and thrived on a challenge, but he was not a manager by temperament. The day-to-day was wearing him down and the slippage was beginning to show. We both knew it was time for him to step aside. We had sharply differing opinions, however, on how the transition should take place. Our board chairman offered to host us for a weekend retreat at his Florida beach house to help us sort out our disagreements and come to a mutually acceptable plan of action. It was while walking along the beach that the fight took place.

Jon had done a lot of reading about organizations, and his research had led him to the conclusion that the founders of organizations were seldom best suited to manage their companies in the long term. Entrepreneurs are great at initiating but not so great at maintaining. I concurred. His research further indicated that as long as the founder retained a controlling influence in the organization, its new growth would be stunted by his hovering shadow. Jon's conclusion was that, for the best interests of the ministry, both he and I should leave. I disagreed.

It was clear to me that Jon's decision to resign as CEO was the correct one, but I was not ready to give up my role as president. After all, I had invested nearly twenty of my best years building this organization and had no intention of relinquishing leadership. Besides, I still had a good bit of visionary energy left in me. It was right that I stay out of management, but to leave the organization altogether? Not unless the board felt that I had become counterproductive. I looked over at our board chairman to see if I could get a reading, but he was preoccupied with lathering a fresh coat of sunscreen on his shoulders and arms.

It would be disastrous for the ministry if I took back the reins, Jon was emphasizing with the conviction of one who knew what all the experts said but had never himself started a company. He was doubtless envisioning all his hard work going down the tubes under my mismanagement. My role as president for the past five years had been hands off. It worked best that way with Jon and me. Now, with the systems all working efficiently, his final act to position the organization for its next generation of leadership was to sweep the deck clean. It was the only right thing to do, he insisted. It was good theory, but I wasn't buying. And the decibel level rose.

It was not clear to me whether my attitude came from founder blindness on my part or from the realization that I had not yet felt released from a calling. What was clear at that moment was that I was not about to walk away from the ministry I had spent my life creating. And I told Jon so. At this he exploded with a ferocity that I think surprised even him. It would spell certain death to the ministry, he bellowed. This set off a volley of incendiary accusations and indictments between the two of us that could be heard above the crashing surf. Our wide-eyed board chair made no move to intervene.

And then it was over. The sound of seagulls could be heard once again. For better or worse, the die had been cast. Jon would resign as executive director. I would remain president and take back the CEO reins until a replacement could be found. With my heart still pounding from battle, a strange sense of excitement stirred within me. Though I promised my board chair that during the interim I would do as little damage to the or-

ganization as possible, I felt the beginnings of an adrenalin rush reminis-
cent of the sort that once surged in my viscera when a new vision was taking over my life. And visions create chaos, I reminded myself and did my
best to conceal a smile.

POSTSCRIPT

Fast-forward a decade. Contrary to conventional wisdom, the ministry continues to grow and thrive with both Jon and me still actively involved.
Strong, young leaders have assumed responsibility for running things, while
Jon and I—the old bulls—have carved out roles that suit our gifts but keep
us away from operational functions. The ministry benefits from our experience, our connections, our credibility. Jon is free to consult with community
organizations in Atlanta and elsewhere, which he enjoys immensely. I have
time to write, help staff with their fundraising and launch a new vision now
and then, which keeps me happy. I suppose my stature in the organization
does cast a bit of a shadow, but the young leaders seem to treat me more as
a company asset to be exploited than an obstacle to be overcome. I still retain enough influence as board president to get my opinions considered, but
the reins of the organization are firmly in the hands of a new generation of
visionaries who need to test out their talents and ideas on a rapidly changing
urban landscape.

A maturing ministry must eventually give thought to succession planning. Can aging Ezras and Nehemiahs, essential in the earlier days, remain
assets to their organizations, or does their hovering presence reach a point
of diminishing returns? It all depends on their control needs. In my case, I
guess the jury is still out.

15

GENTRIFICATION WITH JUSTICE

gen•tri•fi•ca•tion (jĕn´-trə-fĭ-kā'-shən) n.
*The restoration and upgrading of deteriorated urban
property by the middle classes, often resulting in displacement of lower-income people.*

CLOUDS OF DUST LIFTED FROM the plains of Ono, stirred by
thousands of hooves and sandals. For months this river of humanity and
livestock had snaked its way southward along the trade routes from Babylon, traveling under the protection of King Cyrus, benevolent ruler of the
Persian Empire, who had decreed that exiled Jews could return home. Tons
of household goods and personal belongings were stacked and roped
aboard ox-drawn wagons, and pack animals, laden with bulky bundles of
food and water jugs accessible for roadside consumption, were tethered
in a single file. A detachment of armed cavalrymen flanked a delegation
of priests and Levites, carefully guarding treasures that generations earlier
had been looted from Solomon's temple. Though dust covered and road
weary, these children of Jacob were high in spirits, for their destination at
long last lay within sight: Jerusalem!

These returning exiles brought with them far more than household
goods. They brought expertise. They knew how cities ran. In their years of
captivity many had emerged into positions of responsibility and leadership
in the urban centers to which their forebearers had been disbursed. They
understood commerce, not simply the bartering of a goat for so many

bushels of wheat, but money that could be flexibly and safely exchanged for any commodity in any amount. They understood banking and legal contracts and titles—the tools of a civilized society. And they certainly had well-discussed opinions about how Jerusalem should be run once the Jewish leadership returned from exile and the law of God was reestablished in the land.

They were also, surprisingly, people of the Word. The destruction of Solomon's temple, the sacking of sacred artifacts and the enslavement in foreign lands were designed by Nebuchadnezzar to sever the Jews from their heritage and their God. How could the tyrant have known that it would do the opposite? In their bondage they clung tenaciously to their religious practices and reconstructed from memory, as well as from smuggled copies of Scripture passages, a remarkably complete version of the Torah. A network of undercover synagogues sprang up across the Babylonian Empire—places where the law of God was taught and the sacred rituals observed. Someday, every exiled Jew believed, they would return and rebuild the temple in Jerusalem.

And now they were arriving, just as the prophets had foretold. This would be the first and largest of many organized migrations—fifty thousand strong, they were, and under the leadership of Prince Sheshbazzar, whom King Cyrus had appointed as governor of Judah. Other caravans would accompany the entourages of later governors appointed by subsequent kings. Still others would come on their own initiative. And with each infusion of residents, Judah became richer, the beneficiary of the wealth and education and culture that prosperous Jews from the empire brought home.

Every returning Jew understood himself or herself to be the living fulfillment of Jeremiah's prophecy:

This is what the LORD says: "You say about this place, 'It is a desolate waste, without men or animals.' Yet in the towns of Judah and the streets of Jerusalem that are deserted, inhabited by neither men nor animals, there will be heard once more the sounds of joy and gladness, the voices of bride and bridegroom, and the voices of those who bring thank offerings to the house of the LORD, saying,

'Give thanks to the LORD Almighty,
for the LORD is good;
his love endures forever.'

For I will restore the fortunes of the land as they were before," says the LORD.

And when they assembled at the temple site with their best lambs, eager for the first time to offer sacrifices at the spot where their ancestors had worshiped, their hearts nearly burst with joy.

Unfortunately the euphoria was always short-lived. Locals—"the people of the land" as they were referred to by returnees—were not quite so enthusiastic. These whom Nebuchadnezzar left behind in Judah following his bloody siege of Jerusalem were peasant shepherds and poor farmers, discarded like so much worthless baggage when Babylonian troops led the citizenry into captivity. They had survived off the land, moving their meager flocks and herds from one poor grazing patch to the next, hiding in remote canyons from bands of thieves, making lopsided alliances with the stronger tribes around them. Over time, however, these ragged remnants grew in numbers and strength, spread out over much of the Judean countryside and reoccupied many of the sacked towns, including Jerusalem. By the time Cyrus defeated Babylon some fifty years later, a Jewish homeland society had re-formed—nothing to parallel the former glory days when the proud fortress city of Jerusalem ruled supreme in the region, but a functioning society nonetheless.

Now exiles were returning with their splendid clothes and educated children and priestly orthodoxy. They came in triumph, not humility. Heirs of Jewish aristocracy, they marched into Judah to assume their place as leaders of the homeland society. Little wonder that the "people of the land" did not share their excitement. By the time Ezra and Nehemiah returned from exile to assume their respective governorships, the feuding had been going on for generations. Bitter disputes still raged over historic land rights. The temple, which had taken more than twenty years to rebuild due to vicious infighting, was still a deeply fractured institution. Indigenous priests had accommodated the gods of Israel's historic enemies, which was viewed by the returning "purist" clerics, disciplined by their exile, as religious whoring.

It would ultimately be a losing battle for the "people of the land." They would lose much of their land at the hands of skillful title lawyers armed with ancient documents and to speculators poised with ready cash to "help" at a moment of financial hardship. They would also lose most of their power. Their tribal leadership style and agrarian bartering system were no match for the sophisticated leadership methods and economic muscle of the returnees. Besides, the exiles arrived with the blessing of the king and with authority to take charge of Judah. What chance did the locals really have to compete with such overwhelming might?

"But why must this be cast as a win-lose conflict?" the newcomers argued. Was not the infusion of wealth and education, the capable leadership and well-schooled priesthood, in the best interests of all Israel? Indeed, was this not the fulfillment of the divine promise? The temple could now be rebuilt, the city walls and gates could rise again from their rubble and prosperity could return to bless all the people. If the locals could only see the larger picture, then they might be able to understand why change was necessary.

But the change that the exiles brought—*imposed,* as the locals viewed it—was hardly a minor or temporary "discomfort." It was cataclysmic! Their grazing and farmlands were confiscated, their priests were discredited and their families were broken apart—all in the name of Yahweh. The pain inflicted by these "necessary" changes and the venom that poisoned the Jewish community would endure long after the smoke of sacrifices rose from a new temple, long after Jerusalem sat proudly once again as the citadel of Judah. 🔥

GENTRIFICATION REDEFINED

Gentrification is a disparaging description of the process by which middle-income professionals buy and restore homes in depressed neighborhoods. I have seen firsthand (yes, inadvertently participated in) the devastating impact that gentrification can have on the poor of an urban community. I have faced panicking families at my front door who had just been evicted from their homes, their meager belongings set out on the curb. I have helped them in their frantic search to find affordable apartments and have collected donations to assist with rent and utility deposits. It is heart-rending to see families being pulled apart as survival forces them into separate night shelters, to see their children, uprooted and confused, slip behind educationally, losing precious ground they will never regain.

But I have also seen what happens to the poor when the "gentry" *do not* return to the city. The effects of isolation are equally severe. A pathology creeps into a community when achieving neighbors depart—a disease born of isolation that depletes a work ethic, lowers aspirations and saps human initiative. I have seen courageous welfare mothers struggle in vain to save their children from the powerful undertow of the streets. I have witnessed the sinister forces of a drug culture as it ravages the lives of those who have few options for escape. Without the presence of strong, connected neighbor-leaders, a neighborhood becomes a dead-end place.

The romantic notion that the culture of a poor community must somehow be protected from the imposition of outside values is as naive as it is destructive. Neighborhoods that have hemorrhaged for decades from the out-migration of their best and brightest need far more than grants, technical assistance and well-meaning partners to restore their health. More than anything else, they need the return of homeowning, goal-driven neighbors who once gave their community vitality. In a word, they need the gentry.

This leaves us in a quandary. The poor need the gentry in order to revive their deteriorated neighborhoods, but the gentry will inevitably displace the poor from these neighborhoods. The poor seem to get the short end of the stick either way.

But must gentrification always spell displacement for the poor? Probably so. Yet displacement is not always bad. There are drug dealers and other rogues who *need* to be dislodged from a community if it is going to become a healthy place to raise children. Overcrowded tenements and flophouses *should* be thinned out or cleaned up, and this inevitably means displacement of some of the vulnerable along with their predators. Bringing responsible property management back into a neglected community does spell disruption for those who have chosen or been forced by necessity to endure slumlord economics. But what may be disruptive for the moment can become a blessing for those who yearn for a better way of life *if*—and this is a big "if"— the poor are included in the reclamation process by the returning gentry.

Gentrification with justice—that's what is needed to restore health to our urban neighborhoods. Needed are gentry with vision who have compassionate hearts as well as real estate acumen. We need gentry who will use their competencies and connections to ensure that their lower-income neighbors have a stake in their revitalizing neighborhood. The city needs landowning residents who are also faith motivated, who yield to the tenets of their faith in the inevitable tension between value of neighbor and value of property.

Gentrification. It's time to redefine it as a word of hope for the city.

GENTRIFICATION WITH JUSTICE

New life is discernible in our urban centers. Of particular interest to one who has invested his life in the city is a refreshing breeze of change beginning to stir in the urban economy. Flight from the city has finally ceased. The current census reveals an uptick in Atlanta's population, the first time in thirty years. It is the same in most other U.S. cities. Young professionals, full of adventure and ambition, and no longer willing to spend hours in maddening daily commutes, are returning to the city. Abandoned warehouses are being transformed into loft apartments, avant-garde studios and gourmet eateries. Long-neglected neighborhoods are being rediscovered and their charm is being restored. Developers small and large are recognizing the opportunity. Development inside the beltway has become more than merely interesting; it is hot!

Business, too, is returning. The Publix grocery chain is building a new store in the once infamous, now rebounding East Lake—the first substantial business investment in the community in fifty years. And this is not an isolated example. Banks are now willing—even eager—to lend money in formerly red-lined areas. The corporate world, always sensitive to the winds of change, is venturing back into the city.

There are signs of institutional change as well. The HUD bureaucracy, which once blighted our urban neighborhoods with its pathological poverty compounds, is now at the forefront of mixed-income housing development that actually helps reignite market forces. The welfare system is returning to its original mission of offering a hand to those needing temporary assistance to get on their feet. Even the intractable public education system is showing signs of change. Vouchers, home schooling, charter schools and other reform initiatives are forcing open a system long closed to innovation.

And—who would believe it?—crime is on the decline in every major city in the country, including Atlanta. A recent *Los Angeles Times* article documented a five-year decline of 13 percent in the national crime rate, while during the same period network news coverage of crime increased 336 percent. Though it may not seem like it, violent crime is at its lowest level since 1973, according to Department of Justice figures.

These are encouraging signs for the city. For the first time in decades, the recent Atlanta mayoral race concerned itself with managing growth—a welcome change from years of fretting over an eroding tax base and crumbling infrastructure. A spirit just short of euphoria is building. Fiery debates among neighborhood groups, developers and city planners over limiting versus increasing density are the necessary and welcome pains of rebirth.

Less noticeable and to date unresearched is another change that is gaining momentum. The poor, whose meager earnings have historically provided them habitation in deteriorating rental property, now discover themselves in the path of gentrification. Rental prices soar as apartments are renovated and a resurgence of home ownership displaces renters. Densely populated housing projects are being replaced by mixed-income apartment communities, and with each conversion, affordable units are lost. And where are the poor going? To the suburbs, says Alex von Hoffman of Harvard's Joint Center for Housing Studies, who is studying this question. Poverty is suburbanizing.

American cities are different from most of the cities of the world. Most large cities in other countries have their wealth concentrated at the center and poverty spreads outward toward the less developed periphery. In developing nations people migrate from the rural areas, settle in poorer edge cities and try to work their way toward the prosperous center. U.S cities, on the other hand, are like doughnuts with a hole in the middle and the dough around the outside. Our center cities are where our poverty is concentrated.

But all this is about to change! A massive demographic shift has begun. The twenty-first century signals a great reversal for U.S. cities as wealth returns to the core and poverty is pushed to the periphery. U.S. cities will begin to follow the pattern of most other cities in the world. In Atlanta the early signs are obvious. Public discourse has only just begun to acknowledge what will certainly become a diaspora of the poor.

The people of faith have a unique mandate to care for the needs of the vulnerable and the voiceless. We cannot rightly take joy in the rebirth of the city if no provision is being made to include the poor. It will not be enough to offer food baskets at Christmas to migrating masses of needy people who are being driven by market forces away from the vital services of the city. Nor will our well-intentioned programs and ministries suffice for those being scattered to unwelcoming edge cities. We must be more intelligent than this, more strategic.

We can create innovative housing policies that will induce developers to include lower-income residents in their plans. We can pass ordinances that that will give tax relief to seniors on fixed incomes so they can remain in their homes. We can establish loan funds to give down-payment assistance to lower-income home buyers. If we are both caring and *thinking* people, we can use our influence to develop the means by which our waiters, janitors, bus drivers and mechanics can share in the benefits of a reviving city—and foster growth at the same time.

The new century has broken upon us with realities unimaginable a decade or two ago. My prayer is that the winds of change that stir afresh in our cities will bring with them a goodly measure of justice as well as prosperity.

THEY'RE SHOWING UP IN MY COMMUNITY!

Mile High Ministries in inner-city Denver was the victim of its own success. The poor were rapidly disappearing from the neighborhood and it no longer made any sense to keep busing them back to the ministry center from the suburbs. When Jeff Johnsen started the program two and a half decades earlier, its location in the heart of Denver's roughest neighborhood was strategically on the mark. He acquired dilapidated houses and commercial buildings for a song, rehabbed them using volunteers and donations, and created an array of life-reclaiming services. But much had changed in twenty-five years. Starbucks had arrived. Boarded-up storefronts now housed popular eateries. Flophouse hotels had become lofts. The destitute, the addicted, the people of the street—they had disappeared.

Denver's mayor, of course, was delighted. Mile High Ministries had done a remarkable job of cleaning up the area. Its school for street kids had intervened where the public school system could not. Its drug treatment home had turned addicts into job-holding citizens. Its neighborhood crime watch helped make the streets safe again. Mile High was precisely the kind of frontline ministry needed to reclaim a devastated community.

The mayor of nearby Aurora was not so elated. Jeff had assumed that he would be pleased to have the support of Mile High Ministries. After all, Aurora was the edge city where many of the poor from Denver were migrating to. And besides, the mayor was an active Christian.

"The poor are not coming here," the mayor declared to Jeff as they drove together toward Aurora's poorer side of town. Jeff knew differently, of course. His staff had been spending excessive amounts of time and gas money shuttling folks back and forth from Aurora to their Denver center. Attempting to tactfully correct the mayor's misperception, Jeff proceeded to point out some of the apartment complexes and cheap motels the urban migrants were moving into. "You misunderstood me," the mayor interrupted. "The poor are *not* coming here!"

It was his duty as mayor, he said as he looked Jeff straight in the eye, to keep his city safe and prosperous. "As a Christian, I love what you are doing. But as a public official, there's just no way I can support your bringing this kind of thing to my city." The influx of the struggling masses with their vice, their pathologies, their propensity toward lawlessness was not welcome in his town. He would do everything within his power to keep these influences out. And no, he wanted no services, Christian or otherwise, that would make the troublesome feel more welcome in Aurora.

The incident is not unique to Denver and Aurora. The same scenario is being played out all over the country. After a half century of disinvestment and decline, our cities are springing back to life. The idyllic promises of picket-fenced suburbia have lost their attraction for a younger generation. In-town living is in. Cheap urban land and decaying buildings are attracting developers like moths to a porch light. And with condos, lofts and gated communities selling like hotcakes to a moneyed gentry, eateries, boutiques and branch banks are rushing in for their market share.

It takes little imagination to understand why big-city mayors are thrilled by gentrification. For decades, smoggy, congested urban life could not compete with the lure of half-acre wooded lots in pleasant suburban communities. And money followed the market out of the city—en masse. The resulting decline in urban property values became an immediate attraction for the less advantaged who were drawn in by cheap housing, public transportation and accessible human services. Meanwhile the prosperous edge cities were enjoying the security and abundance that a vibrant economy affords, largely immune to the woes that were plaguing the city. By the latter years of the twentieth century, the situation had grown so dire that many cities despaired of recovery ever coming. The urban plank had disappeared from the political platforms of state and national politicians, social programs were bankrupt and a postindustrial economy seemed to be doing just fine without city centers.

And then, almost magically, the giants began to stir. The cities were alive after all! There are doubtless a dozen valid explanations for the awakening. But the short answer is this: the market woke up to an opportunity. Devalued real estate, coupled with the appetites of a younger generation for the stimulants of urban life, became an irresistible combination. Gays, artists and gutsy urban pioneers were first to venture back, followed by waves of educated singles, professional couples and empty nesters. By the dawn of the new millennium, it was a full-fledged movement.

What is good news for the Denvers of the nation, however, means bad news for the Auroras. Or so it would seem at first glance. As urban real estate values escalate, rising rents and condo conversions push low-income residents out to the periphery of the city, out to thirty-year-old class-B apartment complexes now owned by real estate investments trusts (REITs). Because many of these properties have impersonal owners (you and I may own minute pieces of them in our retirement portfolios), they are valued for their bottom line rather than the quality of life they provide. As persistently as water finds its way to lower ground, rivulets of the displaced trickle into suburban communities, taking advantage of the reduced rates. These uninvited neighbors show up in the classrooms of affluent schoolchildren. They appear at the rapid-rail stations where once only commuters in business attire and their incoming maids passed. The presence of these unwelcome intruders triggers fears that the problems of the big city are invading the suburbs.

Suburban paranoia is understandable. But the arrival of these new neighbors need not signal trouble. Rightly planned for, these newcomers could mean the arrival of a much-needed labor force. A host of important, difficult-to-fill jobs (food service, construction, landscaping and so on) beckon eager workers. And for the people of faith who have spent millions on mission trips, there is now an opportunity to serve the culturally different right in their own back yards.

This diaspora of the dispossessed signals the need for new paradigms in ministry. Inner-city ministries are at a crossroads—either switch to active community development work that creates opportunities for the poor to remain and share in the benefits of reviving communities or become passive migrant ministries with vans and mobile satellite centers that follow the streams of displaced poor out of the city. The suburban church, which has led the way in constructing volunteer-built homes in the inner city, now faces the need for affordable housing in its own communities. And it will take more than youth groups and paint-bucket brigades to get the job done. The kind of mixed-income housing strategies that will adequately accommodate the need requires the talents of the church's real estate developers and its bankers and property managers. The church, above all institutions, can lead the way in creating healthy, affordable, well-managed apartment communities where its members extend hospitality and enter into neighborly relationships.

Significant changes are upon us. Exciting changes for the new urban gentry. Fearful changes for the displaced. And much ambivalence for those whose protected lifestyles are about to be changed. It is a moment that presents us with the opportunity to get it right. I hope we are up to the challenge.

16

THE PROBLEM OF PURITY

EZRA HAD SPENT MOST OF A LIFETIME gathering and compiling the historic documents that recorded both the bloodline and the sacred teachings of his people. Himself a Persian exile, he saw it as his divine calling to preserve the genealogy of his family—a family through which the entire world would be blessed. Yahweh had declared this. Ezra, like generations of priests before him, was possessed with the unshakable belief that his were a people of destiny. Perhaps his people saluted a Persian king as a temporary monarch, but this king's rule would not ultimately prevail. Someday the free children of Jacob would again worship Yahweh in their own land under their own divinely anointed king. So said the sacred texts.

Their survival was contingent upon their purity, Ezra had preached and written to the exiled synagogue communities that stretched the length and breadth of the empire. The same kind of purity that Moses had commanded when they first took possession of their homeland must be adhered to in this time of exile—purity of worship, purity of behavior and purity of race. Though other gods abounded in the pagan Persian world, Hebrews were to worship Yahweh alone. Though they were engulfed by a lascivious culture, they were to adhere to his moral law. And their ethnic identity would survive only if they took wives exclusively from among their own people.

Only one who had spent a lifetime in exile promoting racial and theological purity could know the euphoria of leading thousands of the faithful back to reclaim their homeland. Ezra had been appointed by Artaxerxes, benevolent king of Persia, as the new governor of Judah precisely because of his reputation as an expert in Mosaic law. He returned to Jerusalem under royal mandate to reestablish Judaism in its pure form, just as the sacred law dictated. His people had escaped yet another annihilation attempt and were returning home triumphantly. Ezra could imagine no more glorious moment to be alive.

How distressing to discover upon his arrival in Jerusalem that the orthodox priests who had returned years earlier along with convoys of other émigrés had abandoned some of the essential tenets of the faith! Allowing other gods to infiltrate their worship was serious enough to corrupt their souls, but intermarriage with foreign tribes could threaten their very survival. Ezra was anguished. His people, after enduring a devastating diaspora that scattered them to the four winds, were now—whether out of lust or greed or political advantage—choosing a path toward their own extinction. This was flagrant disregard for Yahweh's commands. Ezra shuddered to think of the anger of the Lord.

"What's so wrong with building good relations with our Palestinian friends?" the local priests and leaders argued. "As long as we put no other gods before Yahweh, have we not obeyed the first commandment? And the Torah never actually forbids intermarriage with other cultures, except in its most ancient proscriptions. And those were for a different time. Besides, some of our most respected patriarchs had foreign wives."

The priests' challenge, though deeply troubling to Ezra, was hardly an unfamiliar one. He had heard all the arguments before in unending debates back in Persia when parents struggled with teenage sons who had fallen in love with beautiful Persian girls and vice versa. Wouldn't it be all right if she converted to Judaism? Wouldn't it be all right if he got circumcised? Emotions run strong in matters of love, strong enough to cause young people to leave their families and abandon the faith. These were delicate matters. But sooner or later the Word of the Lord had to be applied to daily life, and sometimes you had to just cut your losses. On the side of the law is where Ezra always came down.

The seed of Jacob, he had preached from synagogue to synagogue, were a chosen people, a holy nation. Through their bloodline all the nations of the world would be blessed. Though Yahweh had allowed (caused, according to some of the prophets) their vine to be severely pruned, a shoot from the stump of Jesse would surely blossom in time and the fruit thereof would be the spiritual food of the nations. To preserve their roots was their sacred and solemn duty.

But, like gravity, the pull of the environment is relentless. It pushes persistently for adaptations to cultural realities. Judah was no longer a land of military occupation. Its people were not exiles. Judah was homeland. The threat of extinction was now a thing of the past. It may have been fresh in the minds of newly returned exiles like Ezra and Nehemiah, but for those who had acclimated to the homeland culture, the fear had dissolved like a bad dream in the bustle of a new day. The law, especially this intermarriage command, needed new interpretations to make sense in a free and modernizing Jewish society, so said those who had adjusted to the new realities. Certainly marrying within the family tree was a wonderful tradition—one to be honored and preserved—but to make it a rigid legal matter could cause more pain and dissension than it was worth. The cure could prove worse than the ailment.

Must theology and culture remain perpetually in tension? Must purity of doctrine and purity of love forever pull against each other? By what measure is one to discern when passion for rightness is to supersede compassion for people? And when, if ever, is it appropriate to move the boundaries of the law to accommodate the new realities of society? Such perplexing matters are left to frail humans to decide. And for better or worse, Ezra and Nehemiah came down squarely on the side of the law. 📖

"Good theology often wears garments of pain," says author Rob Alloway as he peeks behind the veil of suffering imposed by the returning purists. Listen to the story he tells of one family's heartache.

ELIASHIB'S WIFE

Some of us welcomed those Jews who first came back from Babylon. They were the children and grandchildren of the exiles, deported under Nebuchadnezzar during his campaigns against Jerusalem. They'd come back to rebuild the temple, and though it took most of twenty-five torturous years, they succeeded. Of course, we married their men. These returning exiles weren't bad people—quite the opposite. There was a purity to their zeal, a freshness to their careful attention to Yahweh worship that made them attractive. And for them, our families were established in the land. Mixed marriages weren't unheard of. Some of their prophets and patriarchs had even endorsed the practice while these same people lived in Babylon.

I married a man named Eliashib. In time I learned to love him. He was a cantor, as his father and his grandfather had been before him. Music was not part of my own worship, but I tell you, when he sang, even I could glimpse the majesty of the God whom he served. At times I would steal close to the temple just to listen to his bright, clear voice raising up the ancient songs of praise. It was not for me to love his God, but that did not stop me from loving what my husband did in his service. Years passed and we had children. Eliashib was as faithful to me as I was to him. We respected our differences.

And then Ezra arrived from Babylon. He was a scholar-priest, come to teach the ways of Yahweh. It helped his cause that he also carried a commission from our Persian overlords authorizing his mission. More Jews had come with him, energized in their mission to reestablish their faith after so many years of subjugation in Babylon. That was when the trouble began. Little by little I watched as my husband fell under the spell of Ezra. Little by little the call for a return to the old laws of Moses grew—a call for purity and single-minded devotion to Yahweh. Eliashib's voice joined in, and while the music was grand and majestic, my ear detected a descant of toughness. Not until the problem of "foreign wives" surfaced did I realize how harsh and unrelenting the ways of Yahweh could be. His race of chosen people could not marry any but their own. In the exiles' march toward purity, I, and hundreds like me, had suddenly become a liability.

I remember a summons came for all the exiles and their families to appear at the temple. There was no escaping the edict. It was a day of heavy rain, which prompted Ezra to keep his words short and terse.

"You have committed treason against our God by marrying foreign women," Ezra was shouting from the temple steps. I stood, soaked through from the rain and numb from his words. Eliashib stood beside me, his face raised and radiant, heedless of the rain that pelted him. I wondered afterward if he felt they were holy scourges, sent to extirpate the sin from his life. *Who was this man who holds such power over my husband?* I thought. *Who is this God?* Ezra continued, "There is only one thing to do. Confess your sins, ask mercy of God and put away your foreign wives."

"We will do it!" The eagerness with which the men roared back their assent left no room for us wives or the children we had brought. And looking at my husband, I knew that I had lost him. The details were not decided there in the mud of the temple square. The Jews were not barbarians. They made me and a hundred other problem women return for a personal inquisition. The whole sordid separation took three months before everyone was processed. Perhaps they thought this court of inquiry would soften the blow or make it easier to explain to our children why their father was sending us away. I do not know. I know only that if you look you will see my husband's name preserved among those who loved Yahweh with such purity that they put away their wives and children.

The preservation of bloodline has little relevance in our age, but the preservation of the family is certainly one of our major concerns. Nowhere is the breakdown of the family more severe than among the poor of the city. Listen in on the following conversations and get a glimpse of how perplexing is the challenge of restoring wholeness.

A Matter of Survival

"You need to either get married or put him out," her pastor said. The alternatives were that clear. Living with a man who was not her husband, living that example before her children, was both immoral and destructive. Regardless of the benefits of such an arrangement, it was fundamentally wrong. Even if she weren't a Christian and had no understanding of scriptural truth, common sense would tell her that living together without the commitment of marriage kept a relationship insecure at best. But Shirley *was* a Christian and had made a commitment to live by God's Word. Even if it meant sacrifice, her pastor told her, she must be obedient and turn away from sinful practices. God could be relied upon to sustain her even if she had to raise the children alone.

"You *can't* marry him, Shirley!" her incredulous social worker exclaimed. No matter that he was the father of her children. It would be a disaster to marry a man who hadn't held a steady job in his whole life. She would lose her welfare benefits, her health coverage for the children. It would be foolish to threaten the fragile support system that had taken her so long to work out, just for the sake of being able to say she was married. If he were disabled, that might be different. Then he'd at least have an excuse and some sort of predictable income. But getting married now would serve no constructive purpose. And why put him out? He might be lazy and irresponsible, but he was good to the children, right? A leech, perhaps, but he didn't run around on her. And there was something to be said for the children's daddy being in their lives.

"Broken families will never be changed unless we have faith enough to trust God and do what's right in his eyes," the pastor urged. He understood the social worker's pragmatic reasoning, he said, but it was devoid of moral grounding. It's the way society thinks: make whatever compromises you have to in order to get by. How would we ever make a redemptive impact on our world unless we chose the higher ground, difficult though that may be?

Honorable work, keeping the law, striving to be a people of the highest integrity—this is what God requires of his children. Do this and we can count on him to supply all our needs.

"And who's going to watch the children while you're at work?" her social worker challenged. Child-care would be far too costly, even for one child, let alone three, especially on a minimum-wage job. Their grandmother was not able to do the job. It might work if their daddy were at home. Yes, that would probably be the best solution. And staying under thirty hours per week would not threaten their government health coverage. A full-time job with a family health-care plan would not be a reasonable expectation for an entry-level worker like Shirley. Work was important, her counselor affirmed, but first priority was taking care of those babies.

"So you're not going to get married?" her pastor inquired. "And continue living in sin?" Disappointment registered in his eyes. If she put it off until the children were through school, as she was hinting, much of the damage would already have occurred. The broken model of family that would be imprinted in the children's values would inevitably be replicated in their lives. When would it end? When would children of the city see living examples of godly courage, of women who demanded to be treated with respect, of intact families with two parents committed to each other and sharing equally in the joys and responsibilities of home? Perhaps she was just too weak, too beat down to muster the strength to do what was right.

"I'm amazed at your strength," her social worker affirmed. To work a nearly full-time job, keep a household running, juggle the schedules of three children, endure the frustrations of an unproductive live-in boyfriend, keep the government agencies at bay, and still find time to have the kids clean, dressed and ready for church every Sunday—this was a monumental accomplishment. What love! What an example to her children!

ANOTHER ISSUE OF PURITY

"How can we let Gloria lead the service when we know she is living in sin?" The issue was finally coming to a head. The church elders who gathered in the pastor's study for their regular officers' meeting had known for some time that Gloria had allowed a man to move in with her—she had made no secret of it. Michael was a Christian, she said, and was a real help to her financially and with the kids too. It was obvious that she was in love. She hadn't been this giddy and animated since she was a teenager. And spiritually she seemed more alive than ever. She said that they read the Bible together and would sit and talk for hours about God. But they couldn't discuss marriage seriously, at least at present, since he was still married to a woman back in Mexico. He didn't love the woman, Gloria said, hadn't seen her in years. But for him to return to Mexico to divorce her would be risky—immigration problems.

"It's certainly no issue for the Wednesday lunch crowd," the pastor commented, leaning in Gloria's favor. Everyone who came to the midweek service and community lunch knew Gloria well. She had grown up with most of them on the streets. They knew what she had been, had seen her in her wild days, knew the change Christ had made in her life. Everyone knew where her house was—the one that the churches had built for her—and many had knocked at her door in times of personal crisis. Gloria was their homegrown missionary, always ready with a hug and a prayer and some extra food or clothes, never too tired to get out of bed to take a mother with a sick child to the hospital or sit for hours sipping coffee with a despondent drunk. No, her credibility with the poor and broken folk who attended the Wednesday service was solid. To them this matter of living with Michael was a nonissue.

"They may not care, but we certainly should," one of the elders responded. "We have a responsibility to see that the leadership of the church is striving to live according to biblical standards." He was right, of course. And everyone knew that for a woman to live with a man to whom she was not married, especially one who was married to another woman, was a significant moral compromise. A small compromise, perhaps, in the eyes of broken people whose lives had been devastated by abuse, who had lost their children to the system, who clung to survival by a thread. A much larger compromise to a ruling body charged with the responsibility of overseeing the ministries of the church. Was not God's Word clear about this matter?

"For all her strengths, Gloria certainly does have her share of problems, doesn't she?" another elder commented. On many occasions the church had bailed her out of financial straits—gas being cut off, no car insurance money, unpaid medical bills. The stipend the church paid her was not enough for her to support herself, let alone three kids, and the child support from the children's father was sporadic. It was a dilemma, really. The church valued her ministry but had scarcely enough money to pay the pastor and basic overhead. Small grants from the denomination and suburban friends kept the community outreach going, including Gloria's stipend, but it was a long way from providing her a living wage. And so for years she lived by faith, depending on God and miracles and the goodwill of others to get by. In a way, this kind of life kept her sensitive to the plight of others who struggled daily with survival needs. In another way, her financial problems could be blamed on a church that encouraged her ministry but was content to allow her to struggle for years at a subsistence level. This uncomfortable awareness moved the elders' discussion off her finances and back to the issue at hand.

"Are we saying that someone who is wounded cannot be a wounded healer?" the pastor challenged. It was a powerful point. Indeed Gloria was a wounded person, crippled by poverty and neglect, abandoned by her husband. She knew pain. She also knew the transforming work of Christ that penetrated her despair with hope and brought healing to her broken life. Those who observed her life could not deny the dramatic change. And though the ghosts of her past were never far away, her spirit had been freed to love—both herself and others. The grace she extended to struggling addicts whose cycles of recovery and relapse were as predictable as nightfall was far beyond that of their families and treatment counselors. She would sit for hours beside the hospital bed of woman who had been beaten bloody by a drunken boyfriend. She would invite into her home frightened children who had run away from violent domestic conflict. To the disheartened and ill-treated and injured, she was the very embodiment of Christ.

"Caring though she may be, should we have someone representing the church who isn't strong enough to resist immoral behavior?" It was tantamount to endorsing it, the discussion continued. Wouldn't Jesus forgive the offense but say, "Go and sin no more"? Or was this one of those nonabsolutes that allowed for some cultural wiggling room? And didn't we all have areas of imperfection, some blind spots, in our lives? On and on the debate meandered. In the end there was little question about Gloria's desire to serve God nor about the effectiveness of her ministry. And there was general agreement about her lack of strength to resist certain temptations. They could, perhaps should, remove her from her position until she had this matter resolved. This would force her to choose between Michael and the ministry. It would also create an enormous outcry among the community folk who would see her termination as a great injustice. If the elders gave her an ultimatum and she asked Michael to leave, did they have an obligation to come up with additional funding to adequately provide for her needs?

Finally one of the officers reminded the group that there were other pressing items on the day's agenda—the pastor's request for a sabbatical and what to do about the roof leak in the sanctuary, to mention two. They decided to table Gloria's issue, make it a matter of prayer and discuss it at a later date.

17

DISCERNING A VISION

IT WOULD HAVE BEEN MUCH EASIER if a high priest like Samuel had anointed him or if a prophet like Elijah had laid the mantle of responsibility upon his shoulders. Nehemiah would even have settled for a special dispensation from a presiding priest. But Yahweh was choosing to remain silent, unless you could somehow attribute to Yahweh the tumult that raged within Nehemiah's spirit. He scratched into his journal a churning of overpowering emotions and one-way outcries to his God. But no divine voice. The decision that would finally emerge out of this layman's private grappling was the closest thing to a divine calling he would get.

The need for capable, steady-handed leadership in Jerusalem was apparent. Yet just because Nehemiah could conceivably mobilize the resources and manpower for a large-scale rebuilding project was hardly reason enough for him to consider taking on the challenge himself. The need, after all, does not constitute the call. There were always more needs pulling at him than he could begin to address, every one important, every one urgent. God had placed him in this strategic position from which he could accomplish much good for his people and for the people of the empire. To request a leave of absence so that he could focus all his energies in faraway Judah was hardly good stewardship. Unless God were actually calling him to this specific task. He would have to be convinced beyond any reasonable doubt.

Some of the prophets of old received visions from Yahweh—specific assignments or detailed instructions to convey to the people. What Nehemiah was experiencing was surely not like that. But it was a vision of *some* kind that played over and over in his mind in the days following Hanani's visit. Like a recurring dream of tangled, surreal scenes, his mind was drawn again and again to images of Jerusalem still lying in waste. And always visions of a new, rebuilt holy city. It was tormenting, an obsession that dominated both his waking and his sleeping hours. Try as he would to fill his mind with the responsibilities of the day, he could not hold these invading thoughts at bay.

At some point, weeks after Hanani's report, Nehemiah conceded within himself that Yahweh was indeed calling him—*imposing* upon him the task of rebuilding Jerusalem. How else could he explain this irrational fixation that plagued him, interfering with his ability to concentrate on his professional duties? It was the loneliest decision he had ever faced. Obviously, he could not breathe a word of this to any of his associates, nor give a hint of it to the king. Jewish family members who enjoyed the benefits of his privilege would probably panic at the thought of his leaving Susa. And the elders of the synagogue, wise and learned though they were, would be as conflicted as he. He wondered if the prophets and patriarchs felt such vacillations in their spirits, if they too had to figure out for themselves the mysterious voice of Yahweh and the dreadful consequences of reading his voice wrong. In the end, it was his decision and his alone.

Once he was decided, however, there was no turning back. He knew that as soon as he revealed to his king that a higher calling had been placed upon his life, higher than his single-minded attention to the affairs of the palace, the search for his replacement would begin, for what monarch could abide a chief of staff whose heart was not fully in his work? But this calling—Nehemiah would now claim it as such—strangely emboldened him. He *would* pursue this course, he determined. With all the terrifying unknowns, with no assurance that the king would grant him a leave of absence, he would nevertheless lay his future on the line. *This must be*

what faith is about, Nehemiah contemplated in quiet hours alone, surrounded by the luxury and security that were the envy of an empire—*risk-
ing it all on a gut feeling that you are accurate in deciphering the mysterious will of God.*

If this sense of calling gave him courage, it was the vision that ignited
his imagination. Familiar renderings of ancient Jerusalem painted by
Jewish artists now became more than nostalgic artwork on synagogue
walls; they were the blueprints for a vision. Dimensions of walls, number
and position of gates, location of the temple and other key structures, water supply and sanitation system—these and a thousand other matters
whirled endlessly through Nehemiah's mind. The logistics would be
daunting. Architectural design, materials lists and accurate cost estimates
would be difficult enough to project from a distance, but transporting
lumber and iron for a new city and the army of skilled engineers and artisans needed to rebuild it would be as complex as it was costly. The challenge was exhilarating.

In his most honest moments, usually while staring at the ceiling during
one of his frequent sleepless nights, Nehemiah was unsettled by what
seemed a fine line between a vision and a bright idea. Ingenious plans
can be created by clever people. He had seen his share of them. Some
survived; most did not; occasionally one made a lasting difference. Visions, on the other hand, inspire, change lives, alter history. But how was
one to tell the difference? Could all his visioning be idle daydreaming, a
plan that would eventually be filed away to gather dust in a drawer along
with other fruitless fantasies? Such thoughts forced beads of nervous perspiration to stand out on his forehead. What if this were merely an unful-
filled longing in his Jewish psyche? Or a savior complex? Even if the idea
were right, the timing could be wrong. What eventually calmed his pounding chest and allowed him to drift off to sleep was the conclusion he always came back to—it was the *call*, not the *plan*, that had to be trusted.
The vision excited him to the core, but it was the uninvited, unshakable
sense of calling that assured him the venture was worth the risk.

Time and time again over the turbulent months and years that followed he would fall back on this bedrock belief—his call. It would embolden him to ask King Artaxerxes for an extended leave of absence and a substantial government grant. It would be his source of courage to face down powerful and cunning adversaries who would stop at nothing to sabotage the vision. It would infuse him with the moral authority to rally a disheartened Jewish populace, mobilize unskilled volunteers to rebuild their city and reinstate the Torah as the law of the land. The calling was his confidence.

If his calling gave him conviction, the vision was his compass. The vision was God-inspired, Nehemiah became convinced. Once it was moving, too many little miracles converged around it for him to come to any other reasonable conclusion. Like the queen's unexpected advocacy and the king's more than generous response to his request for a leave and funding. And the responsiveness of the Jewish people to leave their day jobs to volunteer full time on an audacious wall-building project. There were just too many of these confirmations for him to conclude anything but that this mission was being orchestrated by Yahweh himself.

The end vision Nehemiah could see in living color—a magnificent walled fortress, a thriving center of a Yahweh-worshiping culture, poised high on a mountain for the world to behold. His mission, he knew with growing certainty, was to shepherd this vision to reality. However, the outworking, he would soon discover, would be far from picture perfect. Some things you can just not anticipate from eight hundred miles away, such as the rebuilding of broken walls proving to be less important than rebuilding a fractured Jewish community. Or the major adjustments required in switching strategies from a handpicked, professional Persian construction team to an unskilled volunteer work force—and the resulting compromises in aesthetics. And who could have anticipated that regional strongmen Sanballat and Tobiah would have the audacity to disregard the king's orders and wage a campaign of terror to halt the project? Realities of life have a way of modifying a vision. 🏛

A HISTORIC TRANSFORMATION

On a hill above Atlanta sits a monstrous stone and concrete structure, a vacant hulk that is a reminder of a darker time in the city's history. Known as the Atlanta Stockade, it was a place of brutal inhumanity in the years following the Civil War, a prison that housed both hardened criminals and petty offenders too poor to pay their fines. Men, women and children as young as ten were crowded into large cells where beastly behavior went on unchecked. Some years the venereal disease rate among inmates was as high as 90 percent. There were frequent public complaints that family members who had been sentenced there had disappeared, never to be heard from again. These were, of course, unsubstantiated reports. The official record documented only one death in the prison's entire history—a man who had tuberculosis. It was not until the 1950s, thirty years after the prison had been closed, that highway excavation across the property turned up the skeletal remains of some fifty bodies, with no record of who they were or how they got there.

In 1927 the city leaders decided to rid Atlanta of the stigma of the stockade and voted to demolish it. But there was one problem: the building had been built too well. It had been constructed using what was then a new technology known as steel-reinforced poured concrete. This material, it was claimed, would become harder and harder over time—perfect for prisons since it would become increasingly impregnable as the years passed. The engineering tolerances were not fully tested, however, and the structure was substantially overbuilt. Some of the walls were four feet thick. The roof was sixteen inches of poured concrete. Demolition bids, when they were received by the city, were cost prohibitive and so the building was abandoned. The cavernous building became a magnet for all sorts of debauchery and a major distribution point for an illegal drug trade. Its legacy of inhumanity continued to be a blight on the community. And its barred windows, like hollow eyes, continued to peer down into the heart of the city.

More than half a century after its official closing, and after decades more of decadence, signs of a new kind of life began to stir about the old prison property. Renny Scott, an Episcopal priest who lived a few blocks from the facility, suggested that this might be a good site to convert into a shelter for homeless families. The thought of housing our most vulnerable citizens in a prison seemed to me to be anything but hospitable. But Renny persisted. It was agreed that we should at least invite a group of architects to tour the place and determine if the idea had any feasibility.

Seven architects from several design firms arrived one morning to explore the old monstrosity. All had seen it from the expressway and were intrigued by the gothic architecture, but none had ever been inside. Donning hardhats and armed with flashlights, the group climbed over piles of rubble and trash and inched their way along dark, graffiti-covered halls until they emerged into an opening, a three-story atrium at the center of the structure. Tiers of rusted bars rose toward an open skylight; broken steam pipes protruded from the walls; needles and broken wine bottles were strewn everywhere—the scene was ominous and foreboding. But to the architects it was also breathtaking. They envisioned windows and light, textures and color, space and dimension—a world of beauty invisible to my eyes. When I offered them an ancient set of original blueprints that I had uncovered in my research, it was like handing archeologists the Dead Sea Scrolls.

Over the next hour and a half, I listened to an animated discussion about how this symbol of injustice could be transformed into a symbol of compassion. Then one of the architects asked me about the budget for the project. I told him that money was not an issue, that in fact we had in excess of $3,000 on deposit. Their laughter echoed off the walls of the atrium. It was clear that these men had never built anything by faith before. If they were to offer their God-given talents to the accomplishment of this vision, I gently nudged, we could raise $150,000, maybe $200,000 right here, today. They said they would get back to me on this.

When the seven architects reconvened two weeks later, I discovered that God had planted a vision in the soil of their spirits. They had discussed the matter with their firms and had unanimously agreed that the design community should take on this project pro bono. There was, however, one important condition. The project would require a close working relationship with the general contractor, since nothing in the conversion would be standard. Design decisions would have to be made daily, on site.

"Who is your general contractor?" they queried. "Who do you know?" I replied. When their laughter was once again under control, they set about making a list of the general contractors with whom they had worked over the years. They would invite the city's twelve largest commercial contractors to a breakfast in the warden's office at the Atlanta Stockade. That grabbed everyone's attention—not one of the "generals" wanted to miss this intriguing event. When the morning arrived, the architects had built a makeshift ramp over the debris for easy access, swept a path through the trash, and placed Coleman lanterns along the dark corridors to illuminate the way to the warden's office. A gourmet breakfast on linen and china was spread for the contractors. And standing prominently on an easel in glowing lantern light was a large, full-color rendering of the vision of the transformed stockade.

General contractors are some of a city's fiercest competitors, bidding against each other every day in a dog-eat-dog environment. When the twelve major contractors of a city emerge from a room all pledging to pool their resources to undertake a project pro bono, history has been made. In fact, that is precisely what took place at breakfast in the warden's office. The generals, following the lead of the architects, locked arms, divided the project up twelve ways and set about recruiting their subcontractors and suppliers to join them in the venture. The architects committed the money to pay a full-time on-site architect, and the contractors hired an experienced project manager to supervise the construction process.

It turned out to be a Herculean challenge coordinating donated services and materials from scores of companies. Fourteen electrical contractors volunteered along with six mechanical firms and a generous assortment of demolition, masonry, interior design, carpentry, drywall, painting and landscaping companies. Plans were adapted to accommodate a donated industrial heating and cooling system. Special techniques were required to apply a new exterior sealing product that was provided by the manufacturer. An elevator had to be installed to meet code. Cutting and coring through walls intended to be impenetrable proved to be the largest physical challenge. But there were others. Legal and insurance issues were complex. Each company, no matter if it provided services free or at cost, had to provide liability insurance and worker's compensation coverage for its employees. The premium costs for scores of participants added up to an exorbitant sum. So the "generals" appealed to the insurance brokers who for years had written their construction policies and convinced the insurance industry to do what it had never done before—create a comprehensive package to cover all participants and pick up the cost of the policy!

Project estimates climbed to $3.2 million, a cost far beyond the capacity of our small nonprofit ministry. But momentum was building. First local, then national news media picked up on the historic transformation and began a series of colorful articles. Atlanta mayor Andrew Young presided over a "bar breaking" ceremony as workers with cutting torches opened "a window of freedom." HUD secretary Jack Kemp came and, at a luncheon held in one of the graffiti-covered prison wards, proclaimed the project a model of private-sector initiative. Tom Brokaw even showed up with his filming crew. Churches, foundations and businesses jumped on the bandwagon, and eleven months from the time construction began, the Atlanta Stockade had been converted into sixty-seven beautifully furnished loft apartments without a penny of debt having been incurred. And it had a new name: GlenCastle. With the property free from debt as well as property taxes (a legal firm had taken on the task of having the facility removed from property tax rolls), the rents were set at a rate minimum-wage earners could afford. For $275 per month, an individual or family could move into a furnished efficiency apartment, utilities included. At the time of this writing, fourteen years after GlenCastle opened its doors, the facility remains full, generates adequate cash flow to pay operating expenses, including professional property management and maintenance, and is still the most affordable unsubsidized housing in the city.

It would be misleading to portray the experience as either easy or trouble free, inspiring though it surely was. There were zoning issues and building code barriers that frustrated progress and required no small amount of arm-wrestling by our seasoned professional team. There were disagreements over the size of units, handicap accessibility and amenities. Then, too, construction had its challenges. Immovable staircases were too steep; ventilation had never before been a concern; water pressure was insufficient to supply the required sprinkling system. What proved to be of enormous benefit, however, was having respected, highly experienced development experts involved in every phase of the project. There was no problem they could not solve or negotiate around.

It would also be wrong to create the impression that funding for the project happened miraculously and without effort. Admittedly, the historic significance of the building and the marketing sizzle inherent in a conversion of this nature did make funding the project far easier than raising routine operating dollars for a nonprofit. However, even with the substantial pro bono investments of the architects, contractors, subs and suppliers (which totaled over $1 million), another $2-plus million in cash had to be raised. We hired a development consultant who produced promotional materials, planned fundraising events, developed foundation proposals, designed a direct mail campaign, lined up speaking engagements for staff, issued press releases and managed the entire process. It took nearly three years of preparation before actual construction began, conducting feasibility studies, acquiring the property, organizing committees and task forces, planning the campaign and securing enough commitments to afford reasonable assurances to large donors that the project had a good chance of succeeding.

Certainly miraculous occurrences took place, such as the time the senior executives of Chicago-based Amoco Oil, at their own initiative, appealed to their corporate foundation to give $300,000 as seed capital to launch the project. Neither before nor since has Amoco given this large an amount to a nonprofit, even in their home city. It was our first corporate gift and it served to legitimize the project in the eyes of other corporations and foundations. There were many such surprises (of somewhat lesser magnitude), the convergence of divinely ordered coincidences, reassuring us that this was in fact a vision authored by the Spirit. Nationally recognized gospel singer Larnell Harris, upon hearing of the story, was inspired to write a song about this "castle of hope" and flew in at his own expense to perform it on the prison steps before a group of astonished participants. And then there were the two well-to-do sisters who became benefactors upon discovering the name of their great-grandfather—mayor of Atlanta at the time the prison was built—on the vine-covered prison cornerstone. Such coincidences happened with such frequency that eventually they did not surprise us anymore. They could not be planned or counted on, nor could anyone lay claim to them, but they did not come without the expenditure of enormous amounts of energy on the part of staff and volunteers. Like casting for fish in a lake until they jump into your boat, you don't stop casting, but you can't really take credit for catching the fish either.

One of the leadership functions that Renny and I ended up assuming was that of "guardians of the vision." In addition to drawing in committed volunteers, the project attracted a number of opportunists who saw it as a means for personal gain. While no one was opposed to participants receiving legitimate credit that would have public relations value to their companies, there were self-serving entrepreneurs who attempted to position themselves politically and leverage their association with the project to gain business. Renny and I saw it as our duty to ensure that the mission remained focused on compassionate service and that everyone involved was either volunteering or providing goods or services at cost. Maintaining the purity of the vision became an essential leadership role.

Another opportunity for funds that was dropped in our laps seemed ideally suited for GlenCastle. Congress had just passed the McKinney Act to address the national problem of homelessness. The first installment of funds had arrived in Atlanta, and ours was the only project on the drawing board. The city offered us the entire $3 million allocation to underwrite construction costs as well as ongoing support services for residents. We were ecstatic! It seemed that God was honoring those who had ventured out in faith by providing the sum that was needed to underwrite the project. But as we read through the regulations that accompanied the funding, we became uneasy with certain restrictions. First, the money had to be used to house and treat homeless men only—a significant departure from our vision to provide families a secure and affordable place to get back on their feet. And then there were restrictions on the expression of religious faith that raised concerns. Ours was clearly a Christian ministry, and though we were not heavy-handed in our approach, we valued the freedom to engage in discussions of faith as appropriate. The further we read, the more uncomfortable we became. It became increasingly apparent that the vision would have to be significantly altered if we were to accept these funds. The decision was agonizing, but we knew what had to be done: we declined the funding and went back to square one. (Since then, policy changes introduced by the Bush administration have significantly eased restrictions on faith-based organizations.)

Who would choose to operate by faith if he or she didn't have to? I have concluded that it is far less stressful to take on a project that I have adequate capacity and resources to complete. I have also seen that by limiting my vision to available resources I will not position myself to depend upon divine intervention for its accomplishment. Vision that is divinely authored—the kind that extends me far beyond my own abilities—requires a frightful level of risk taking. It is fundamentally different from strategy planning and goal setting. It requires me to let go of the security of predictable outcomes and venture into uncharted waters with little more than an inaudible internal voice as a guide. Such vision is not a product of human creativity; it is divinely conceived and implanted in the spirits of those who are willing to trust miracle over plan.

WHENCE COMES OUR VISION?

A city without a vision is a city in trouble. A large-scale event (like hosting the Olympics or the Super Bowl) can for a time unify the efforts of a city. But an event is different from a vision. An event is momentary; a vision endures. An event may flow from a vision, but a vision is the source of energy. "Where there is no vision, the people perish," warned the writer of old (Proverbs 29:18 KJV).

Atlanta is rich with creative ideas, but it lacks an orienting vision. It used to be that our clergy were the leaders who spoke of vision for the city. No more. The religious leaders who remain downtown are largely consumed by the task of managing their aging institutions. Preservation, not vision, is their challenge. Public officials have sometimes served as visionaries. These are rare persons of conviction and courage whose vision transcends their personal ambition. But such leaders are scarce today. Public opinion polls determine the "convictions" of our political leaders, and electability decides their causes.

Whence comes the vision for a great city—a city whose heart beats with twenty-four-hour-a-day vitality, whose center is peopled with neighbors rightly related, whose core is as alive with community as it is with commerce? Whence comes the vision for a city whose soul is healthy? Who has the stature to champion such a vision today?

I know of no discipline that is producing visionaries today, save one. There is one unlikely profession that demands the distinctive combination of qualities and skills that is also required for farsighted urban communication skill and intuition. Though controversy often swirls around this group, I am convinced that the new vision that is needed in our city will most likely come through faith-motivated *real estate developers!*

I have witnessed in cities both at home and abroad the powerful impact that a single developer can have on a city. Charlie Shaw is transforming the blighted Lawndale neighborhood in Chicago by converting the old Sears headquarters into a thriving urban community. Leslie Viljoen, one of Cape Town's most successful developers, is creating an ambitious mixed-income, racially blended community that is a model for a new South Africa. And there is our own Tom Cousins, who is redefining public housing by his East Lake project. These are all men whose faith has moved them to employ their considerable talents and resources to attack daunting urban challenges. Their high-risk ventures are reshaping history.

Why is God using real estate developers as his vision bearers today? Think about it. The real estate developer is one who conceives of things that do not exist and causes them to become reality. It is the real estate developer who can capture a vision in a believable package, convince lenders, investors, politicians and communities that the plan is in everyone's best interest, assemble the array of players and structures required for its execution and then orchestrate the creation of a whole new landscape. This breed has a nose for opportunity, instincts for what will and will not work and an irrepressible optimism for a mission they believe in. They understand politics and the value of partnerships and coalitions. They are tenacious, driven, fiercely competitive and at the same time genuinely conciliatory. Risk taking is their life; their forte is forging into uncharted territory.

Successful real estate developers who are motivated by faith are uniquely equipped to be visionaries. They understand the difference between human effort and divine intervention. An internal spiritual compass guides them amid the tensions between the allure of an exciting mission and a commitment to sound business sense. They know, too, that the bottom line cannot always be calculated in monetary gain. And when their passion, imagination and faith are captured by an inspiring vision, developers have the perfect combination of gifts to enable them to rise to the occasion and become visionary leaders.

Atlanta is a city unusually blessed with capable, faith-motivated real estate developers. Imagine for a moment the impact upon our city if our spiritually minded developers came together around the vision of a new heart for Atlanta. Everyone knows the strategic importance for residential development around Centennial Olympic Park. The rebirth of the downtown center into a safe, vibrant community with vested neighbors, charming restaurants and a full range of goods and services is more than a delightful fantasy. There is a broad and sober consensus that the future of our city may depend on this. Based on profitability, it may make little sense, but to a group of faith-motivated developers with a vision, this could be a challenge worthy of their best. It could become the wellspring of new spiritual life for the city.

Christian developers are also men and women who realize the significance of the church in the city. They know that urban churches, which often speak for the poor but offer few solutions for their plight, can be enlisted to champion the cause of reneighboring the downtown community. Under the banner of a just and caring community, and with a mission to establish a wholly new parish, the church could come alive with missionary fire. Chapels in each new development, parish chaplains building community and promoting neighborly relationships—this is exciting new territory for the urban church. And developers, more so than anyone else, have the influence and capacity to bring the church to the table.

Whence comes the vision for a great city whose heart is strong and whose soul is healthy? The leaders with visionary capacity are among us. Will they rise to the occasion?

18

THE DIFFICULTY WITH DOING GOOD

NEHEMIAH HAD NEVER BEEN MORE SURE of anything in his life. He had been called for a special mission. So many coincidences had converged on him—things he could not possibly have influenced—that he was left with no explanation other than God. Little miracles, he called them, not concrete evidence that would stand up in court but mysterious events too curious to dismiss. Like the surprise visit from his brother Hanani with a report from Jerusalem on the very day he had made up his mind to request a royal investigation into the affairs of Judah. And there was more. The persistent obsession he could not shake, the peace he felt only when he released himself mentally and emotionally to the vision, the excitement that surged within him when he allowed himself to play with plans for such a mission—these unavoidable coincidences had all intersected. And so when the king granted his request for a leave of absence to go and rebuild Jerusalem, it was less a miracle than a confirmation of what he already knew to be his divine calling.

It had all gone so smoothly. Securing the funding and materials, the availability of a crack development team, a trouble-free road trip—more confirmations that God was directing this undertaking. Even the transfer of power from Ezra's administration to Nehemiah's had been painless. The people had embraced the challenge of rebuilding the wall with volunteer labor. And in spite of the daunting complexity of the project, the construction had begun without a hitch.

Over these past few months, a new understanding of how God oper-
ates was beginning to take shape in Nehemiah's mind. Years in government had taught him that successful projects require much planning—economic forecasting, political support, feasibility studies and detailed
financial analysis—just to get to the starting line. And then there was always the issue of selecting the right person to put in charge. Everything
had to do with good timing, good planning and good people. But God's
methods appeared to be quite different. Much of the planning seemed
mysteriously to be already done. He was beginning to learn that if he
would concentrate on doing God's work in God's way and in God's timing, the waters would part before him just as they had for Moses. This was
before he hit his first serious roadblock.

The surprise arrival in Jerusalem of regional governors Sanballat, Tobiah
and Geshem was mildly disconcerting to Nehemiah. He had learned from
his intelligence sources that these three had publicly voiced their concern
over his presence in Judah. He had dismissed it as petty jealousy. But when
they accused him to his face of seditious ambitions and threatened to report
him for treason, it was more angering than threatening to Nehemiah.

If that had been the end of it, he would have dismissed the incident as
a minor irritation. But the conflict was far from over. First came the work
slowdown instigated by these cunning opponents. Then the major assault—a massive, well-coordinated military buildup on Judah's borders.
Surely this is not the plan of God, is it? Nehemiah wondered. Why was this
hostility coming against them if they were being faithful to the divine vision? The aggression had certainly provoked a serious prayer meeting,
and the people readily acknowledged their need for, indeed begged for,
divine intervention. There was something to be said for the power of fear
to drive people to their knees, Nehemiah figured. But this was hardly the
smooth sailing that a divine mission was supposed to experience.

And this was not the end of troubles. Loan sharks from among their
own ranks caused another work stoppage. It was then that Nehemiah saw

clearly for the first time that the enemy of Yahweh not only prowled on the periphery of Judah but also stalked the hearts of Yahweh's chosen. A battle of unseen forces was being waged here, a battle he felt unequipped to fight. He would call a public meeting to address the complaints, redress the offenses and secure commitments to abandon all such practices in the future—this a governor could and should do. But Ezra would know far more than he about the war that raged for the soul of the community. Nehemiah was also feeling much less confident about his new understanding of how God works.

Then came yet another round of assaults from Sanballat—a public smear campaign, an attempted ambush and, finally, a more sinister tactic: an effort to lure him onto holy ground where only priest were to go. It was all so exasperating! Doing God's will was not supposed to be so difficult, so treacherous. What happened to the parting of the waters? This was more like trying to paddle against the current of a raging river.

The onslaught of opposition forced serious questions upon Nehemiah. Was Yahweh trying to tell him something? Had he stepped outside the plan of God, taking things into his own hands rather than depending on divine leadership? Had he failed to listen carefully enough to divine directives? Surely he was not expected to consult with the liberal-minded Eliashib, even though he was Yahweh's anointed high priest. That priest was a known collaborator with the enemy. And yet, despite the contempt Nehemiah felt for the man, he had to admit that the old priest's generous orthodoxy did give him pause.

For a moment, Nehemiah toyed with the thought of hearing out Eliashib's perspective. Even Sanballat's. Certainly there are reasons why intelligent people see the world differently. Perhaps behind all the conflict and confusion there were issues he had not given a fair hearing. Dare Nehemiah even listen? 📖

Author Rob Alloway listens with attentive ear to the "other voices" in this drama, searching for the heart of a reluctant high priest and the soul of a political strongman who considered himself part of Yahweh's chosen family. Hear him as he speaks for Eliashib and Sanballat.

ELIASHIB, HIGH PRIEST

I never challenged Nehemiah's right to govern us. He held a Persian writ of office. Tobiah was out; Nehemiah was in. Let it be as King Artaxerxes wishes. Was it Nehemiah's wish to rebuild our city's walls? So be it. My name is first on the list of helpers. It is my sweat that stains the lintel of the Sheep Gate. No one can say I did not render to the crown's appointee his rightful due.

But I was also high priest. That is an office above purchase or persuasion. Once each year it fell to me to enter the Most Holy Place within our temple and seek forgiveness on behalf of everyone. I dreaded that day. It was the only ritual I could not delegate to someone else. Around my ankle would be tied a cord so that my body could be dragged out should Yahweh strike me dead. Into the presence of Yahweh I would timidly proceed. It was the Day of Atonement.

"O Yahweh, we have sinned. I beseech thee, cover the iniquity of thy people. Accept this offering of blood so that we might be cleansed. Remember your promise to Moses that on this day you would put away our iniquities and remember our sin no more."

The people of Yahweh, descendants of Abraham, Isaac and Jacob— forgiven! That was why Nehemiah hated me so much. We did not agree on who was covered by the blood.

"You must speak out against the foreigners who have married among us," the little autocrat ordered me. "Yahweh requires purity from his followers."

"Do not confuse the chastity of your loins with purity of heart," I replied. It was an unfortunate choice of words. Rumor had it that Nehemiah was a eunuch.

"But the law demands it." His spittle assaulted my face.

"The law demanded many things of us in the past," I replied evenly.

"But the prophets have also promised a new order."

"You dare defy Torah?"

"You dare bend it to your cause?"

"Blasphemer!"

That was always the way our conversations went. There was no real talking to Nehemiah. But I could not withdraw.

"Does a Persian cupbearer now presume to teach the law as well? What law do I transgress, Nehemiah? If I am guilty, then name my crime."

"You sanction the taking of foreign wives. The law of Moses is clear: the Hittites, the Girgashites, the Amorites, the Ammonites, the Perizzites, Jebusites, Moabites and Egyptians—all have been excluded from our fellowship."

"And I have admitted none of these to the temple."

"You remain friends with Tobiah. He is an Ammonite."

"His family lived among them. So did our King David once. Would you have excluded him too? Tobiah claims to be a Jew; for me that is sufficient."

"What about Sanballat? He makes no such claim. By his own admission, he is a Samaritan, a foreigner."

"It is you who declared him foreign, not Torah. The Samaritans are not listed. In your bitterness you twist the law of Moses against him. They are our brothers. They seek the face of Yahweh and hold to the prophet Moses. They are what is left of our ten lost tribes to the north whom the Assyrians slaughtered."

Nehemiah raged, "You shall pay dearly if you oppose me."

"Yahweh will judge us all in this matter," I said. But already he had turned away.

Nehemiah, you had it in your power to unite our people as in the days of Solomon, but you would not lift your eyes beyond your ghetto. For all your freedom, you are still a slave in Babylon.

When Nehemiah left us, Tobiah helped fill the leadership vacuum, and I am unashamed to admit that I assisted him. Someone had to govern. My son married Sanballat's daughter with my blessing. Their wedding present was a scroll of the prophet Isaiah. I wanted them never to forget the hope that was our heritage. It reads, in part, "The sovereign LORD—he who gathers the exiles of Israel—declares, 'I will gather still others to them besides those already gathered. These will I bring to my holy mountain and bring them joy in my house of prayer. Their burnt offerings will be accepted on my altar, for my house shall be called a house of prayer for all nations.' "

Why did Nehemiah hate me so? I believed atonement was for everyone.

SANBALLAT

Yes, I had it in for Nehemiah and his grand plans to rebuild the walls of Jerusalem. At least he was truthful in that. But be careful when you read his book—his memoirs of how he restored the city. It is not called vanity publishing in jest. We failed, of course, but our failure only proves that might is not always right.

Nehemiah would have you believe it was all a matter of sour grapes over my losing a share of the Persian taxes I collected in the region. Where is his proof that I exploited my royal writ and feathered my own nest? He would have you believe that Jerusalem was the logical hub for the trade route that connected Egypt with Babylon. Any credible map of the region will expose that hypocrisy. If Jerusalem were so strategic, I could have rebuilt it myself. After all, until Nehemiah's arrival, the rubble he called a city was under my care, managed by Tobiah. But the last thing the people needed was one more tax. There were already enough towns for trade.

Yes, I resented that Nehemiah's satrapy came at my expense. He had bested me in the management of our Persian overlords. I had never met King Artaxerxes, much less cried into his wine goblet. Sanballat? I was just one name on the list of a hundred satraps who did their best to keep peace within Persia's vast empire.

Persia is not amused at satraps who threaten war on their neighboring colleagues, particularly one who was a favorite of the court. Half a loaf is always better than none, and even sour grapes can be made into wine. So what was so important as to risk my life?

Nehemiah sanctioned racism in the name of Yahweh. He dared attach the sacred name of our God to his own deluded quest for ethnic purity. Nehemiah turned politics into a holy cause. It was he who started the contest.

Make no mistake. Samaritans are Jews too, although none of the people who returned from Babylon will ever admit to it. Samaritan means "keepers of the faith," and I am proud of that title, although we prefer the term Israelites, for that is what we are. What faith, you ask? The faith of Moses and of the Torah, whose every word is sacred. What other faith is there?

We differed sharply on a number of points with the Jews who returned from Babylon—we'd been arguing with them for the hundred years before they went into exile. What families don't fight over the details of a shared history?

We weren't happy with a lot of the changes to the way our faith was practiced by our brothers in the south, but we found the grace to tolerate their opinions. Mount Gerizim is still the most holy place, according to Torah, but that didn't mean a temple at Jerusalem was blasphemous. And when the first wave of refugees returned—fifty years before Ezra showed up—we even offered to help them rebuild it.

But no, according to Nehemiah, we Samaritans weren't good enough to work on their temple. We had to choke down the fact that it was a temple built with the coins of our pagan master, who sacrifices for his welfare. And they accuse *us* of compromising our faith!

Why did we first offer to help? Because we were Jews, part of the covenant people. Samaria and Judah, we were both small fish swimming in the unholy sea of pagans that surrounded our communities. It was no time to be splitting theological hairs about who had best preserved the family tree. Viewed against the rest of the world, we were the same. At least that was how we saw it. But not the newcomers from Babylon. In their eyes we were nothing more than half-breeds, the bastard children of the ten lost sons of Jacob.

Nehemiah dares speak of my family. He tells you in indignant tones that I gave my daughter in marriage to Johanan, the grandson of Eliashib, high priest at Jerusalem. The marriage was said to give me a certain influence within the elite of Jerusalem, as if I traded my daughter's life for the sake of political power! Did Nehemiah not read his own book before he published it? Eliashib helped build the wall I tried to destroy. If he was anything to me at all, he should have been my enemy. Why would I seek an alliance with him or trust him in anything?

Eliashib and I dared to dream large—to the point where we risked our children to make the dream a reality. It was a marriage of Jew to Jew, and both fathers longed that it might be the start of a true community built on the things we held in common rather than on the dusty ancestral records of the scribes. It was a moment of great potential.

Our prophets had promised such a day. Look hard enough and you will find that we all came from Adam. We all carry the marks of sin. We all look to a common salvation. Isn't that enough to make us family?

No! Nehemiah would not listen to these corrupting arguments. Ezra had already spoken on these matters. There was no point in rehashing issues that had already been settled. Nehemiah would not torment himself with indecision. He had his mission and he would not allow it to be sidetracked by endless theological negotiation. He was sticking with Ezra.

But why was he being plagued by all these troubles if he were following the designs of Yahweh? Had his ego gotten in the way? His motives were never perfectly pure, he had to admit that to himself. He had always struggled with issues of control, and yes, he did want to look good in the eyes of others. But that was just who he was. God knew that when he called him into this mission.

Nehemiah could not make any direct correlation between his own failures or shortcomings and the troubles that dogged his every step. In retrospect, he could see how good had come out of many of the struggles. Never before had he prayed more intensely or often. Never had he felt such dependency upon God. But for the life of him, he could not imagine how better planning or better listening could have averted any of these troubles.

In most ways, he concluded, managing a divine mission was much the same as managing the king's affairs. Greed, jealousy, power struggles, opportunism, scheming—such is the dark side of humanity. The "little miracles" were inspiring, signals confirming that he was on the right track. But a faith-driven mission was no more exempt from the wiles of human fallenness than was a government project. Neither was a God venture more stress free than a secular endeavor. The difference lay not in the painlessness of the process but in the significance of the mission. 📖

ON TEARING UP TARES

"Are you sick and tired of the lies and games being played by Charis Community Housing . . . ? Martin Street Plaza belongs to you the tenants . . . the money allocated to Martin Street Plaza belongs to *you*. Charis is attempting to take control of the Martin Street Plaza complex . . . has not kept any of the commitments it made to the residents . . . is exploiting residents and using government funds while pretending to help them. They make salaries over $100,000 . . . resident employees make $6.00 per hour. . . . We are sick and tired of people pretending to help poor people and at the same time robbing them. Demand an audit of your fund . . . demand that Charis staff be removed from your project. Join the Coalition to help fight for and demand your rights . . . before it's too late!" This angry statement was signed Geraldine Lowrey.

My righteous indignation would have been burning had these charges of blatant mistreatment of the poor been directed at someone *other than us*. Instead, I was reeling from disbelief. Geraldine Lowrey, a self-proclaimed advocate for the poor who I had never even heard of, mailed several pages of venomous distortions and deceptions to community residents, corporate and foundation partners and political leaders, "exposing" our ministry for ripping off the poor. I was dumbfounded. How could this be happening?

Charis is our housing ministry, which has built modest homes and provided affordable apartments for many low-income neighbors in the community. Martin Street Plaza, a badly neglected public housing project overrun by drug dealers, has clearly been our most monumental undertaking. For more than five years we have worked with the resident leadership to help them wrest the management out of the hands of an incompetent housing authority and raise private donations to rehab the apartments. Of even greater significance, our efforts together had produced a resident-owned cooperative to actually take ownership of the property. It was enormously satisfying when, after long years of effort, we began to see pride gaining an upper hand over depression as families at Martin Street became wage earners, many of them taking jobs in property management, security and maintenance right in their own housing community. They began to refer to their complex as "the gem of the Summerhill crown." Martin Street Plaza became a model of hope that residents, HUD, corporate partners and Charis all felt justifiably proud of. That was before things turned sour and Charis ended up as the oppressor.

"No good deed goes unpunished," says one of Murphy's tongue-in-cheek laws. I am continually amazed at how quickly a positive accomplishment can be undone by the sowing of discord. All it takes is a community leader feeling bypassed or a disgruntled employee claiming discrimination to ignite passions that can spread like wildfire. In no time an angry altercation can rage out of control. For some strange reason, just when things seem to be going well, these unexpected controversies erupt, tempers flare and angry charges spew venom on the ones who have invested the most. I have seen it happen time and time again.

This is obviously not a new phenomenon. A couple thousand years ago, Jesus gave his friends some remarkably contemporary counsel on how to deal with such situations. A farmer plants a field of wheat, his illustration goes. But during the night his enemy scatters the seed of tares, or weeds, in the field. When the wheat springs up, so do the tares. The farmhands offer to weed out the tares, but the farmer says no since too much wheat would be uprooted in the process. He opts for allowing the good grain and noxious tares to grow together until the harvest. Then he can separate wheat from weeds, harvesting the grain into the barns and throwing the tares into piles to be burned (Matthew 13:24-30).

The message is fairly straightforward: it is better to lose face than to lose grain. Wherever good grain is beginning to grow, I can expect that weeds, too, will spring up. Investing time and effort in rooting out these destructive infiltrators of God's work is counterproductive. Too much damage will be done to the tender shoots in the process of ferreting out maligning rumors and false claims. And counterattacking is not an approved kingdom response. Better to suffer the indignity of diminished credibility than to lose the fruit of the harvest to witch hunts. The sorting-out process belongs to the Lord of the harvest. Once again, I am forced back to the basics of faith: can God be trusted with the outcome when our reputation is on the line?

I confess that the farmhands' solution has emotional appeal to me. A little "tearing up" would feel pretty good right now. But then, I'm not the one in charge of the harvest. And for that we should all be grateful!

Fast-forward: It took five years of headlines accusing our ministry of embezzlement, our computers being seized by the U.S. Inspector General's office, lawsuits and independent as well as government audits to finally vindicate us. Fortunately, our books balanced to the dime and the unjustified charges faded away. Martin Street Plaza is now a renovated, affordable, well-managed apartment community. The damage to our reputation and budget was much longer recovering.

ON ACCOMPLISHING GOOD

My day began over an early breakfast at the Good News Café with Chris and Rebecca Gray. They wasted no time diving into a matter that was heavy on their minds. "Why is doing good so hard?" Rebecca teared up as she uttered the words. "We do our best, we are as responsible as we know how to be, we try to stay sensitive to God's leading . . . and something always seems to derail our plans. Our best efforts don't accomplish half what they should for the kingdom!"

The Grays are not complainers. Far from it. They are high-capacity military officers who left active duty four years ago to assume a leadership role in our ministry. But serious fatigue registered on Rebecca's face. An unhealthy weight loss from a stress-aggravated digestive disorder added to her anxiety. Chris, unflappable and rock steady, was wearing a concerned expression.

No couple I have ever met has grasped the essence of urban ministry as well and as quickly as the Grays. The moment they hit the ground in Atlanta, they began to distinguish themselves as capable and sensitive leaders. Called, visionary, unthreatened and unthreatening, they combined all the gifts required to lead FCS into the future. Yet Rebecca implored, "Have we made a huge mistake?"

My day ended at Virginia's, a restaurant in a converted warehouse, over a late dinner with Dana Walker and Kerry Reid. In from D.C. for a conference they had initiated, these leaders of President Bush's faith-based initiative seemed relieved to get away from the hotel congestion to a quiet spot for some agenda-free conversation. "Why is doing good so hard?" they asked as we dipped chunks of sourdough bread into a saucer of garlic and olive oil.

These dynamic, visionary leaders, elevated to positions of responsibility at a high level of government, confessed the weariness of their souls in trying to do their best to accomplish a kingdom mission, only to have their efforts challenged, undermined, ignored and devalued by both the government and the church. The president, committed to the church's reengagement as a service provider, had inspired them both to join him in this mission. But his handlers, they soon discovered, have other priorities, diverting his attention from the faith-based agenda. Then there are the career bureaucrats who are resistant to new ideas that disrupt their familiar routines. And the church is suspicious of government involvement, afraid of "strings," fearful of trading away their message for the seduction of easy money. "We're not sure now that this is where we should be." Consternation and doubt were etched on their faces.

Multitalented, high-capacity people directed by God into positions that severely restrict their ability to execute. How frustrating! All four mentioned the acute temptation to accept job offers that promised more money and less stress. Yet, when I asked them if they knew of any place they could go that would be more in the center of God's will for their lives, they could not. They had been drawn by divine impulse into a place of severe trial of belief, a refining furnace where powerful spiritual, psychological and political forces burn to the essence of their being.

As I wound my way home through dark city streets, I found myself wishing for light—not the kind that repaired streetlights would provide but illumination for the dark night of the soul. On this day, in these exchanges with friends serving at the extreme ends of society, spiritualizing their struggle would have been ill timed. No trite God-has-you-here-for-a-reason advice would be helpful. Their questioning of their own calling, though fearful, was necessary. Questioning God, even raging against God, was honest. Their doubts had integrity.

Surely God does not toy with the emotions of those who desire to follow him. But when we have listened as carefully as we know how and have positioned ourselves as best we can discern in the epicenter of his will, why would we encounter so much resistance, frustration and stress? Spiritual warfare? Lack of faith? Wrong method or timing? All of the above? I can't give an answer. But regardless, there seems but one appropriate response to this holy entrapment: endure.

Could it be that divine calling is not about accomplishment after all? What if success is defined not in measurable productivity but in the quality of our interactions with others? What if the criterion by which we are ultimately evaluated is faithfulness rather than performance? Even more baffling, what if a calling is not primarily about effecting change but rather about being changed ourselves?

One thing had become clear to me as I pulled into my driveway: the testing of one's faith is the same in the urban trenches as in the halls of government. Refining fires burn just as severely whether one is struggling with poverty or power. Who but called ones would choose to continue feeling their way along an uncertain, dimly lit path in the direction of an unseen kingdom when opportunities beckon from all sides? Indeed, who of us would choose to walk by faith if we had any other viable option?

19

WHERE YOUR TREASURE IS

A WARM MORNING SUN WAS CHASING back shadows from the Jerusalem streets. Seven men sat together in a half circle on fallen boulders, sipping mugs of steaming broth. It took considerable imagination to picture this intersection of two prominent streets as a corner park where old men once gathered to talk politics and watch children at play. That was a long time ago. Perhaps someday again in the distant future. But for now it was just another rubble field where a few hearty souls clustered to catch up on neighborhood business.

"Well, what do you think?" Azariah stroked his bushy salt-and-pepper beard and scanned his neighbor's faces. "Is he going to pull it off?" Benjamin and Hasshub smiled and shook their heads with uncertainty. They had heard it all before—confident new leaders blowing into town with convincing talk, getting everyone worked up with their ambitious plans to reclaim the city, only to fizzle before the first gate was set to hinge. Jedaiah and Meshullam, younger men less jaded by disappointment, made no effort to conceal their optimism.

"I think he's the man who can do it," Jedaiah jumped into the conversation. They were all neighbors, each braving an existence on a street that ran along the northwest wall. Benjamin and Hasshub had claimed adjoining properties next to Azariah's house. They were the seasoned homesteaders in that part of the city. The others had rebuilt houses farther down the street but within shouting distance of each other. Even though the wall outside their homes afforded no more protection than a broken-down pasture fence, their neighborhood crime watch was fairly effective in keeping rogues from lingering in their immediate surrounds.

"I guess I ought to volunteer my services," Azariah confessed his intentions without giving away a hopefulness that had been growing in him. He had heard the new governor's rousing inaugural address but had not allowed himself to be drawn in by the emotion of the moment. Yet ever since he had wandered by the temple plaza and had seen the shipments of construction materials being sorted and tagged and stacked for orderly deployment, and then overhearing the new governor barking orders to his lieutenants on the specifics of how the division of labor was to be organized, an optimism had taken root in his spirit.

"I suspect we all should," Benjamin registered his support. "We've already signed up." Jedaiah nodded toward Meshullam. "Don't know what we'll be assigned to do, though." None of them had construction skills sufficient to make a living with. They would have to learn on the job whatever work they would be assigned.

Azariah admitted, a bit sheepishly, his fear of heights as the seven friends walked to the temple plaza the following day. He hoped he would not be assigned to the high wall overlooking the Kidron Valley. There was already a line at the registration booth by the time the group arrived. Name, address, skills, physical limitations if any, family or professional affiliation—the recording clerks were writing as fast as they could ask their questions. "City residents over there." They motioned to the men. In an assembly area roped off from the supply yard, several dozen familiar faces were listening to a smooth-faced man wearing an embroidered tunic, obviously one of the governor's men. He spoke clearly but with an accent—the same deliberate and proper Hebrew enunciations that other Persian-educated returnees used. He paused to acknowledge the seven new arrivals, recapped briefly his earlier instructions, then continued with his orientation. Nehemiah had given orders, he said, for all workers whose personal residences and businesses

were near the wall to work on those sections immediately adjacent to their
own homes. This was good news!

"Clever man, isn't he?" Azariah commented to his friends as they were
marched to another assembly area for a lesson on the basics of wall construction. The governor understood self-interest. These neighbor-recruits
were certainly ready to serve anywhere in the city on any project they were
assigned, but working on the wall section that protected their own homes
was especially motivating. During the days of toil and intrigue that lay
ahead, this would become even more obvious.

Back on their street, Azariah and his companions, joined by several
other neighbors, a Persian-trained supervisor and a small army of farm
boys, set about clearing rubble and stacking stones. The demolition process was mindless, backbreaking work—necessary work in order to get
down to a solid foundation, but boring. It wasn't until three days later,
when they began to select stones to fit back into place, that the conversations became focused and lively. Closeness of fit, thickness of mortar
joints, plumb and level lines—these were engineering issues that would
determine the strength of the wall. But there was more than impenetrability
to consider when building a wall, especially a wall that one would have to
look at out his living room window every day of his life. Aesthetics. By the
time the bottom row of foundation stones had been laid in place just outside Azariah's residence, strong opinions had formed in all the neighbors'
minds of what a residential wall should look like—or should not look like.
Some of the workers, especially the farm boys, had no concept of symmetry or artistic appearance. Keep them on the rock-hauling detail, it was
agreed, or maybe allow them to construct the interior, invisible layers. But
the visible exterior surfaces, like a tapestry of stone, would require artistic
ability. A delegation of neighbors fanned out across the city to inspect the
work of other masons and bring back recommendations for the geometric
style that was most pleasing to the eye.

Four weeks of drenching sweat and blistered hands and aching backs
produced amazing results. In place of a rubble field and vistas of open

Judean countryside beyond, a tightly joined wall became the view from Azariah's front window. It had risen to nearly half its original height, and its shadow was already providing relief from the late afternoon sun. Things are going too well, Azariah thought as he stood admiring the handsome masonry work. And he was right. His thoughts were suddenly interrupted by the shouts of a uniformed cavalryman galloping up the street toward him.

"Enemy troops are amassing on the Judean borders!" the soldier yelled. "Everyone to the assembly area in the temple plaza. Bring all available weapons!"

While Azariah and his neighbors were engrossed in their wall-building efforts, a world of trouble had been stirring just beyond the Jerusalem horizon. And now, Nehemiah was telling them, Jerusalem may come under siege. The little governor, eyes flashing, hair dusty and matted with perspiration, was instructing the crowd to run to their villages and farms and collect every knife, sword, slingshot and shepherd staff—every weapon in Judah—and bring them into the city.

"Yahweh will prevail," he reassured the assembly, "but each of us will have to be ready to fight for our homes and families." Again, the governor's wisdom showed through. Azariah and his neighbors were given orders to post sentries and stand guard on the wall outside their own homes. They were to rotate shifts for round-the-clock surveillance, and if they spied any enemy movement outside their wall, the armed city would rush to their defense.

The threat passed, of course, without anyone's having to shoot an arrow. Yet the crisis produced an effective minuteman defense system for the city and a confidence in the hearts of the people that their own preparedness and Yahweh's power would protect them. And something even more significant emerged from this crisis: ownership. Every male resident of the city from priest to perfumer had strapped on a sword and walked the wall in defense of his city and his home. No longer was Jerusalem a city of tentative squatters—it was a city of owners. The village and farm people sensed it too. Jerusalem was worth fighting for, even dying for if need be. The governor knew something of the power of becoming vested. 🏛

STRATEGIC NEIGHBORS

Something happens inside you when you buy a home in the city. You react differently when you see a prostitute climb into a car or a young dealer at a car window exchanging a plastic baggie for a wad of bills. Once you secretly enjoyed shocking suburban volunteers by casually pointing out these daily occurrences through the van window as you drove them around on ministry tours. That was when you felt a bit proud about your familiarity with conditions on the frontlines. But when you move into the neighborhood—you and your spouse and children—drugs and prostitution become a personal assault on the quality of your life.

The intrigues of the city—the shootings, the break-ins, the police chases—lose their romantic appeal when they occur on the street in front of your house. They outrage you. They push you to take drastic action. You organize a crime watch. You march around the community with your neighbors. You call city hall. You even risk confronting suspicious characters personally. Criminal activity must go—all of it!

There is a world of difference in the attitudes of urban workers who commute into a community and those who have become vested neighbors. Commuting ministers, such as summer college interns, have greater tolerance for, and more patience with, broken people who need treatment for their life-controlling problems. A counselor can be compassionate with an addict during the day when he is able to drive home to a safe refuge at night. Short-term missioners can befriend at-risk children in a high-crime neighborhood for a few days or weeks. But for a neighbor who lives next door to a crack house, exposed to perpetual risk of being caught in the crossfire of a deal gone bad, her compassion will be tempered by the impending threat of harm to her family. When one's home and car are repeatedly being broken into, treatment for the perpetrators becomes a lesser priority than removing predators from the community.

This is why good neighbors are always preferable to good programs. Neighbors who are committed to the health of the community function much like a healthy body. Like white corpuscles in the bloodstream, neighbors rush to the invaded area to surround, neutralize and expel the infection-causing intruder. Their vigilance continues day and night, for they realize better than anyone how quickly disease can spread. They know, too, how difficult it is to root out criminal elements once they have become embedded in the community. Neighbors are concerned for their own families first and their community next. And only when the safety of home and neighborhood is secured can they afford to reach out compassionately to those who pose a threat.

The best thing we can offer an urban neighborhood is good neighbors. We call them "strategic neighbors." These are people who have a deep commitment to loving God and loving their neighbor. They understand this to be a spiritual mandate for their own lives as well as the most effective means for having a redemptive impact on their world. They are frontline troops who go into places where good neighbors are in short supply. They buy homes, join the neighborhood association, help organize crime watches, build relationships with neighbor kids, offer support to single moms, take seniors to the grocery store. In short, they are the embodiment of good news.

Where do these strategic neighbors come from? They are young professionals whose hearts have been sensitized by a mission trip. They are couples who have volunteered as tutors or helped build a house for a low-income family and are ready to take a next step. They are families who have felt a call to serve as urban missionaries. They are normal working adults who have become persuaded through a sermon or a Bible study or a book that faithful Christian living means more than being good church members and pursuing the American dream. Varied in gifts and interests, they all have at least two things in common: they are risk takers and they want to make a difference in their world for God.

After-school programs are needed. Summer camp is great. Treatment facilities are important. But there is nothing so important—so essential to the return of wholeness to an urban community—as a handful of committed neighbors who will make the neighborhood their own. There is nothing so life giving or self-sustaining as sanctified self-interest.

WHERE YOUR HEART IS

"Where will our boys go to school?" Next to our children's physical safety, that was the concern that loomed largest in Peggy's mind. Our decision to move into inner-city Atlanta would have been difficult enough if we hadn't had children. But with two elementary-age boys, the stakes were higher. The tone of Peggy's question told me that she was not willing to sacrifice their futures on the altar of our ministry.

Our house in the city was under construction, and we would be moving in by July. Since we would be living just down the street from Slaton Elementary School, we decided to drop by and check it out, though we were not at all certain that public schools would be the best option for our boys. The principal, we found to our delight, was a Christian for whom public education was as much a ministry as it was a profession. On our first visit to his office we asked to see the most recent standardized tests scores. They were not encouraging—math at the twenty-ninth percentile and reading at the thirty-first. If we were to enroll our boys in the school, we asked, could we assist in their classrooms? And could we bring volunteer tutors into the school? The principal's response was exuberant: "How many and how soon? We need all the help we can get!"

Jeffrey entered the fifth grade at Slaton that fall and Jonathan the first grade. We decided we would keep a close eye on their progress, and if we saw any detrimental effects, we would withdraw them and find an alternative. As the principal had assured us, we were welcomed into the school with open arms. Teachers seemed pleased to have Peggy's support with reading groups and grading. And the volunteers from suburban churches brought new materials and provided one-on-one tutoring for children who were lagging behind. A handful of other middle-income neighborhood residents who had also decided to place their children in the school set to work reenergizing the PTA. The stirring of new life became palpable.

Gwen, a young schoolteacher who had recently completed a summer internship with our ministry, decided to join our staff full time, raise her support and invest her energies in the children at Slaton. She initiated a track and swimming club for troublesome third and fourth graders identified by their teachers as likely dropouts. With consent from parents and principal, she removed twelve of these children from their classrooms and brought them down the street to our church, where she concentrated on academics in the mornings and sports in the afternoon. Within the first year, most of the students had moved up to grade level and beyond and were ready to reenter their normal classrooms in the fall, behavior problems greatly diminished.

Teachers complained that latchkey kids who roamed the streets all summer returned to school in the fall having lost precious academic ground. The first two months of the school year had to be spent in review, bringing them back up to speed. If there were only a way to keep them in a holding pattern, the educational curve in the fall quarter would leap ahead. How about a summer camp, we suggested, with a mixture of academics and fun? The teachers were ecstatic. Since our staff was already geared up for doing camps of various sorts, it would not be much of a stretch for us to adapt to a school setting. Plus, camp sponsorship was a tried-and-true means of raising funds. Several teachers volunteered to help shape and even staff the program. The principal applied for a small grant from the school board and brought in a few donations from supportive friends. The camp for Slaton latchkey kids was off and running. By fall of the following year, the academic performance of the school had lurched forward measurably.

By the time Jonathan, our younger son, took the battery of standardized scholastic achievement tests administered to all fifth graders in the public school system, a remarkable amount of learning had taken place at Slaton Elementary School. The average test score had risen to the seventy-first percentile in four years. This was an achievement of monumental proportions given that the demographics of the school had changed little during that period—still mostly low income and minority. And at least two middle-income parents had learned some important lessons as well. First, a little leaven causes the whole loaf to rise. Second, where your treasure is, there will your heart be also.

20

SERVING OR LEADING?

"IF IT PLEASES THE KING AND if your servant has found favor in his sight, let him send me to the city in Judah where my fathers are buried so that I can rebuild it." It was asking a lot. Nehemiah knew that. So did King Artaxerxes. This request was for more than a leave of absence. It involved money—a great deal of money. And the authorization to lead.

Rebuilding a city is a large-scale public works project requiring massive amounts of human effort, materials and expertise. The king was hardly naive about such costs. He understood, too, that an undertaking of this magnitude would require more than funding. Nehemiah would need authority to reestablish Jerusalem on a solid footing. The city would need strong leadership. This was not meant to cast any negative reflection on Ezra, who had been governing Judah for the past twelve years. As a religious leader, Ezra had strengthened the role of the temple and had inspired sporadic spiritual renewals, but he was a scribe and clearly not cut out to rule. Nehemiah, on the other hand, was qualified to be far more than a project manager of a construction job—he was exceptional leadership material. And so the king drafted and sealed a royal proclamation naming Nehemiah the governor of Judah.

This *could* prove to be an unpopular appointment, Nehemiah worried. Ezra had been such a national hero among the Jews and was held in great esteem across the empire as well as in the homeland. No doubt some in Jerusalem would recognize Nehemiah's name since he had risen to such a high government position. But an Ezra he was not. And if replacing Ezra caused a rift within the Jewish community, he would have a difficult time reestablishing Jerusalem. Rebuilding a city was at least as much about unifying the spirit of the people as it was about constructing new walls and gates.

The issue seemed not to concern the king in the least. Many years of political chess playing with the countries of an often-turbulent empire had made him wise in the ways of governance. A capable leader learns how to navigate political crosscurrents without alienating people. An effective leader learns how to forge alliances, organize coalitions, build consensus and use muscle when needed. Of one thing this king was sure: authority without popularity may have its limitations, but popularity without the authority to execute is untenable. When Nehemiah departed Susa for his new assignment, he had everything he would need to reestablish Jerusalem, including what he had not asked for but would soon be grateful he had—the full authority of governorship.

In his first act as governor, his appreciation for the king's wisdom increased substantially. On the temple steps, staring into the faces of fellow citizens he had never met, Nehemiah knew there could be no doubt in anyone's mind about his right to initiate this project. The nobles of Judah might question the feasibility of the undertaking. And they might have concerns over the advisability of launching the mission in the midst of a drought. But certainly no one would ask the question "By whose authority?"

This authority issue was no small matter. Earlier attempts at temple reconstruction by some inspiring and capable men had been derailed for decades for this very reason. Religious wrangling had interrupted the first construction schedule. The second attempt was blocked by disgruntled locals who bribed Persian government agents to interrogate Zerubbabel and Jeshua—able Jewish leaders but without gubernatorial powers. Bogus charges were filed against them for initiating an unauthorized building project. The resulting stop-work order halted construction while the case inched its way up through channels to Persian courts in distant cities. Petty squabbling—that's how King Cyrus viewed it, and he had little time for it. He had an empire to worry about. So the matter dragged on and on, through two subsequent dynasties, until King Darius ascended to the throne. It took another two years for the case to work its way up to Darius's high court. At long last an order was issued to search all government archives to see if any decree existed authorizing the reconstruction of a Jerusalem temple. An investigation finally turned up the dusty document in an archive room in Ecbatana, three hundred miles north in the land of Media. Cyrus's original authorization, signed in the first year of his dynasty, settled the matter once and for all and the temple project was finally back on track. More than fifteen years had been lost in the delay.

All politics are local. King Artaxerxes understood this well. From the time he was a child growing up in the royal courts, he had watched his father, King Xerxes, strategize endlessly to quell political strife that seemed always to be erupting like geysers from subterranean hot spots throughout the empire. And he was not unfamiliar with the turbulence in Palestine. His father had once put a halt to the rebuilding of Jerusalem because of accusations of sedition that arose from Samaritan informants. As a matter of fact, he himself, in his first year on the throne, had issued a stop-work order on Jerusalem reconstruction because of concerns fueled by jealous regional governors that Jewish ambitions would surely lead to the secession of the whole territory west of the Euphrates. It was essential, Artaxerxes knew from personal experience, that a relationship of trust and a clear line of authority be cemented up front.

Local politics can be ugly indeed, Nehemiah would discover for himself. No sooner had he begun to organize the wall-rebuilding effort than did the provincial governors alliance attempt the same strategy that had worked in the past to stall the rebuilding of Jerusalem. *Ah, the wisdom of Artaxerxes*, thought Nehemiah, mildly amused. A relationship of trust and a clear line of authority established up front—how vital to the success of a mission!

In the ways of politics and governance, Judah had never seen finer than Nehemiah. With a natural ease, he organized systems, appointed leadership, issued orders and imposed regulations. But there was one arena he took great care not to enter—the domain of the ceremonial law reserved for the priests. Even though the line of demarcation between church and state was blurred in many places in this temple-centric culture, there was nonetheless a realm clearly outside his sphere of governance. Priests alone were ordained as the intermediaries between Yahweh and the people. They alone could sprinkle the sacrificial blood on the altar. They alone were permitted to enter into the inner holy places, and then only the chief priest—highest of their order—could venture behind the temple veil into the presence of Yahweh. This was a world that a layperson dare not enter.

Authority has limits. Authority to govern is not the same as spiritual authority—a distinction Nehemiah honored and respected. This is not to say, however, that religious authorities are above the law. A priest, even a high priest, cannot reinterpret or disregard divine ordinances to suit his own ends. Pagan marriage is off-limits, no matter how politically expedient it might be. Leasing out temple space for irreligious uses, though perhaps not specifically prohibited by law, is clearly outside intended purposes. "This is not right!" Nehemiah was not timid to declare when he saw such abuse of religious power.

Authority rightly used is a great blessing; authority misused is a curse. 🏠

CROSSING THE LINE

Some would call David VanCronkhite a prophet or at least a visionary. He had always been a high-energy, go-for-broke business type, but midway up his climb to the top of his career, the divine interrupter invaded his life. Nothing was ever the same again for David. A passionate concern for the poor replaced his business obsessions. He was mysteriously drawn to the streets of the inner city, where he spent disproportionate amounts of his time and money assisting addicted and homeless men. Eventually, he left his career path altogether and was commissioned by his church as a full-time urban minister.

David dove into his urban calling with the same intensity that had propelled him upward in the world of business. He cut deals with grocery stores to supply surplus food for a feeding program. He harnessed Christian rock groups to do open-air concerts for street people. He set up barbeque grills in vacant city lots and hosted "love feasts" for the hungry in body and soul. He secured a vacant warehouse to provide shelter for the homeless. Soon hundreds of broken people were crowding in to partake of the hospitality and hope that David and his growing cadre of volunteers freely offered.

People of all sorts were attracted to David's frontline mission. Broken people, for sure. But the affluent as well. College students, successful professionals, middle-class couples and social elites—those with tender hearts and adventuresome spirits showed up at the warehouse ready to serve. From around the country they came, some ready to trade their security for a cause worth sacrificing for, all offering themselves in selfless service. They came to change lives, and in the process they themselves were changed. Some stayed; others took away with them a burning in their souls that would ignite fires of compassion in their home cities. Some went abroad to carry the flame to the poor of the world. A movement had begun. They called it Blood and Fire.

David was clearly the spiritual leader. Some called him Reverend, but he hardly fit the description. His hair grew long, an evocative T-shirt stretched tight over his muscular chest, and a radical Harley chopper was his transportation. His fiery sermons stirred the souls of street people and suburbanites alike. His charisma was as alluring as it was terrifying. The vision that grew large in him was to plant churches of the poor in the cities of the world. His message and methods were radical and prophetic.

But a prophet, though powerful and persuasive, does not possess all the gifts of the body of Christ. David could rally and inspire and challenge, but he could not manage. He could induce architects to redesign the warehouse into an efficient, multipurpose ministry center, but the press of human need often diverted his energy away from the plan. He could motivate real estate developers to contribute expertise and materials to the renovation, but the money raised to pay subcontractors sometimes went to buy food for street people instead. He could stir business leaders to use their connections to generate funds but would be off on a trip to start new churches rather than being available for appointments.

David understood his limitations. He knew that he needed to surround himself with capable people who could bring accountability and management expertise to the movement. That's why he recruited from the business community a group of well-connected Christian leaders to serve as his board of directors. These were men and women who believed in the mission of Blood and Fire and also understood the importance of budgets and planning and audits and systems. They knew that, in addition to a capital campaign for building renovations, a day-to-day operating budget had to be raised to keep the ministry functioning. For the first time since the movement began, an audit was conducted. Organizational structures were clarified and accounting systems were put in place. And for the first time, the movement had a business plan with time lines and financial goals.

But there was a problem. David had always been free to move with the promptings of the Spirit. If God told him to give next month's insurance payment to a person in dire need, he would do it and trust God to supply for the insurance. If God told him to board a plane for South Africa, he would charge the ticket and count on money to appear in time to pay the Visa bill. Responsiveness to the Spirit was to David the essence of faith. The board, of course, had a different view of doing God's will. In their judgment, spiritual freedom was not without bounds. That's what budgets are for. To spend funds reserved for one purpose on some unplanned, unbudgeted need and then trust God to come through with a miracle was simply not good stewardship; it was irresponsibility. With each spontaneous expenditure, the tension between David and the board grew more stressful.

Chris Franklin seemed to be the solution. Chris had been working at David's side for several years. He had a heart for hands-on ministry, an obvious understanding of the inner workings of the organization and the gift of administration. David trusted him and so did the board. It was a great relief to everyone when Chris accepted the position of executive director. He immediately brought order to the chaotic environment. However, when it came to cutting checks, Chris felt caught in the middle between David's spur-of-the-moment directives and the board's expectations of responsible financial management. The dilemma was temporarily resolved by the board's decision to give David a much-needed six-month sabbatical. It had been fifteen years of nonstop trench warfare, and battle fatigue was taking its toll on him.

While David spent long, leisurely days reading, reflecting and rebuilding his relationship with his family, the ministry at Blood and Fire ran smoothly. The board raised significant dollars to finish the reconstruction of the warehouse and assumed the task of funding a daunting operations budget. The staff and congregation of misfits missed David's fervor, but the programs and worship remained steady under Chris's guidance.

The day David returned from his leave, batteries fully charged, the prevailing calm was shattered by an avalanche of new visions for the movement. His enthusiasm was contagious and his new revelations stirring, but Chris and the board immediately applied the brakes. Things were going well in the ministry, and these new ideas, if approved, would have to be phased in over time. David was impatient. There was a dying world out there—homeless men freezing under bridges, kids ensnared by drugs, abused women and their children sleeping in abandoned cars. This was no time for caution. This was a time to risk everything for the kingdom.

A train wreck was about to happen. David, flamboyant mouthpiece of a movement built on a trust in God to do the impossible, found himself under the governance of pragmatic, responsible directors to whom such impulsive behavior was foolhardy if not unscrupulous. David could not capitulate to their caution; neither could the board fly by blind faith. Exercising their prerogative and responsibility, the board fired him.

A line had been crossed. A cadre of fine Christian laypersons with every good intention had lopped off the head of a spiritual movement. In the name of fiduciary conscientiousness, they had inserted themselves between a visionary and his vision. These well-meaning outsiders had seized the reins of control away from a priest and his parish—a parish they supported but one in which they had no membership. It was in the best interests of the poor, they had reassured themselves, and to preserve the credibility of the ministry in which they had invested substantially. In good businesslike fashion, they changed the locks, secured the bank accounts and mailing lists and appointed Chris to take David's place.

But the spiritual leadership of a movement is fundamentally different from corporate decision making behind closed boardroom doors. The board was soon to discover just how different. Blood and Fire leaders from other cities, some as far away as Cape Town, flew in to confront their decision. Ministers who had served as board members in the early days of the movement began to appear at board meetings, asserting that they had never formally left the board and challenging the legitimacy of David's termination. Incensed congregation members—former addicts whose lives had been transformed—pushed their way into meetings to voice their protest. The board listened politely to one appeal after another imploring it to reconsider its position. The directors appeared to be genuinely conciliatory, but in private they stiffened their resolve, consulting with counsel in case legal action might be required.

It was the desire of everyone involved to resolve the matter in a just and godly manner. During weeks of earnest discussion, the expanded board, which now included former members, wrestled with various scenarios for holding on to both David and fiscal accountability. But again and again the debate returned to an underlying theological impasse: with whom does the final authority for a God-given vision lie? Some argued that the board had both legal and ethical responsibility. Others held that the visionary had primary authority, confirmed by and accountable only to the movement leadership.

It would take a miracle to resolve this stalemate. But no miracle came. Fractures only widened along philosophical fault lines. It degenerated into power plays between current and former board members, legal saber rattling and the squeezing off of the cash flow from the board and its deep-pocketed allies. It was not a pretty process. In the end David was reinstated by a margin of a single vote. All of the board members were then asked to become advisers rather than directors so that the authority for governance could be shifted back to Blood and Fire elders. It was the end of a costly experiment in the exercise of spiritual authority.

Blood and Fire continues to grow under David's leadership, though it took a serious financial hit when its well-heeled board members withdrew. Chris left immediately upon David's reinstatement, along with some of his loyal followers. The ministry is back to trusting God for its daily bread and light bills, not knowing when or whence its next sustaining donation will appear.

For better or for worse, divine visions seem to be entrusted to individuals, not committees. Boards, bean counters and benefactors, though essential to the life of a movement, are not the source of its spiritual fire. Visionary leaders, while certainly needing a level of accountability, must be free to roll out their visions as the Spirit reveals it to them. It is, however, a risky business. No one hears the voice of God with absolute accuracy. But clip the wings of the visionary and the vision will never get off the ground, let alone soar.

ON SUBORDINATING AUTHORITY

If Summerhill taught me anything, it taught me not to subordinate control to the local community. Sound insensitive? Politically incorrect? Maybe so. But when you have sustained critical wounds in the crossfire of neighborhood politics, when you have lost your capacity to repay loans or deliver on promises made in good faith, when you see twenty-five years of credibility disappearing down the drain, you should learn *something* from the experience.

Servanthood. That's what I called it when I first got involved in the neighborhood of Summerhill. I was there to serve the community. And God knows it needed help. Its twenty thousand residents had dwindled to twenty-three hundred, half of its homes had burned or rotted to the ground, its churches and business were boarded up, its leadership had long ago fled to the suburbs. Crime stalked the streets like a plague, destroying the vulnerable and stealing the futures of the young. But who in their right mind would oppose after-school programs and summer camp for the kids? Not even rogues and predators would be that cold. So that's where our ministry began—with the youth. And with their families. And then their housing conditions. In time, new homes began to appear on vacant lots—the work of eager hands and caring hearts willing to give up their Saturdays to provide needy families with a decent place to live. A vision began to emerge out of the brokenness, a hopefulness that had long been absent from the community. And as visions do, it began to draw new life around it.

A neighborhood meeting, organized by a group of former and existing residents and several of our ministry staff, culminated in a first-ever Summerhill reunion. It was a grand success. Hundreds of former neighbors, some of whom had not been back in the community for two or more decades, returned for a festival of listening to music, feasting and remembering the days when Summerhill was a wholesome place to raise one's family. It was an event that fueled momentum to restore health to the neighborhood. Not long after, we formed a community development corporation (CDC) and a dreaming-planning process began. Other professionals, excited by the potential for rebirth, donated their services to create a master plan for a revitalization of the area. A blue-ribbon board of leaders joined in to lend their support to community residents. Real estate developers offered to build out at cost entire blocks of mixed-income housing. Foundations pledged substantial philanthropic dollars. It was one of the most energizing and inspiring visions I have ever been involved in.

Those outside leaders—partners, we called them—who were drawn into this vision (many of whom I recruited) came out of a sincere desire to serve the poor. The array of marketplace talents and skills they represented could not have been purchased for any amount of money. Their more than adequate capacity to implement what soon escalated into a multimillion dollar plan gave a measure of security to lenders and investors. But as the vision rolled rapidly forward into staffing, structuring, land acquisition and construction, the sound business sense of these capable leaders yielded to the sometimes unsound wishes of the community board members. In the name of servanthood, unsecured loans were negotiated based on the credibility of board members, contracts were entered into with inadequate backing, promises were made with good intentions but without due diligence.

It might have all worked out had we possessed the foresight to ensure that those higher-powered board members making the commitments would remain in legal control until all obligations were fulfilled. But early on, hard-nosed reason had taken a back seat to a soft-hearted charity. We were supporting partners, here to serve, we avowed—not to negotiate, not to take control. And so, seasoned businesspeople checked their marketplace savvy at the door. Wishing desperately to avoid old stereotypes of "controlling white boys" and prove that we were beyond the racist and patronizing past, we supported deals and decisions that we would have never condoned in our own organizations. The house of cards finally came crashing down when community board members, disgruntled by outsiders having too much sway, held an unannounced meeting and fired the board chair—a highly respected developer whose reputation was unsurpassed in the Atlanta business community. Other board members, alarmed by the sudden ouster and sensing that their presence was becoming less welcome, began to submit letters of resignation. In the end, the community alienated its support, lost its capacity to fulfill its obligations and set race relations back decades. The exciting vision, of course, was dead in the water.

After a three-month depression, I began to regain enough energy to reflect on what went wrong. We had called it a "partnership," which had such a fine, nonpatronizing sound. But in retrospect we had never taken the time to figure out the difference between servanthood and partnership. Unlike servanthood, which offers unilateral assistance, partnership is an interdependent relationship. It has a mutually agreed-upon mission, negotiated roles and contingencies for each party, limits of responsibility and specific outcomes. Summerhill was clearly not this. Sterling leaders offered their advice but not their decision-making ability; they offered their deal-making expertise but not their best business sense; they offered their social capital but not their professional responsibility. This they (we) did in the name of serving the community. I am beginning to suspect that servanthood may not be in the best interests of a community.

What could we have done differently? Real partnership, if it has integrity, offers some promise. Like the way we are attempting to do it in the South Atlanta neighborhood, for example. Here we engaged in a dreaming process, much the same way as we did in Summerhill, and came up with a comprehensive plan that both fulfilled the community's wishes and made good development sense. But when we came to the point of implementing the South Atlanta revitalization plan, we took a decidedly different tack.

We sought partners to commit to the various tasks and roles required to accomplish the master plan—community organizing, acquisition and development of land, recruitment and selection of new homeowners, provision of agreed-upon social services. In each case a clear line of authority was established, each partner assuming full responsibility for funding and completing assigned tasks. When zoning issues have come up, the building partner leads the charge. If it requires a public hearing, the neighborhood association rallies its members to provide support. When it comes to clearing truckloads of trash from vacant lots, the association takes the lead, with some of the other partners lending a hand. Youth programs are coordinated by our community chaplain with a host of church groups and volunteers participating. In the delicate matter of screening prospective buyers for the affordable homes, community representatives serve on the selection committee. The final decision is the responsibility of the builder.

Joint ventures, I am seeing, are more effective than servanthood in the rebuilding of a community. There are doubtless problems with both approaches, but at least the starting point of partnership is healthier than servanthood. And the objectives are more honest. Joint ventures lay self-interest right out on the table. Each partner has something tangible to gain or lose. Each partner needs the other. Servanthood, on the other hand, is based on the perceived deficits of another, though this is not usually admitted openly. It usually diminishes the dignity of the ones being served.

Such a negative treatment of servanthood may seem to fly in the face of the long-held belief among many Christians that to serve others is central to our mandate. I do not disagree. It is the unhealthy way we have practiced servanthood with which I take issue. Even Jesus seemed to imply that there was a better way for the family of faith to relate: "I no longer call you servants. . . . Instead, I have called you friends" (John 15:15).

21

CONFLICT OF INTEREST

NO SOONER HAD JERUSALEM BEEN SECURED by a strong
wall and grand new gates than did the land speculation begin. It didn't
take a genius to figure out that this location would soon attract business
from all over the region. If trading had persisted for years under threatening conditions when Jerusalem was without walls, it was certain to bur-
geon now that a credible government and an armed security force were
in place.

There was money to be made in Jerusalem, especially in real estate.
Prior to Nehemiah's arrival, property values had never recovered from the
siege of 586 B.C., when the walls had been systematically destroyed and
the gates burned away by Nebuchadnezzar's troops. Though a new temple had been erected and a few homes and government buildings rebuilt,
whole sections of the city still lay in ruins. Clean-up crews had removed
tons of rubble in preparation for the wall dedication, and the streets were
now passable. Amazingly, the basic infrastructure of the city was still intact. Hezekiah's tunnel, which had been carved through a quarter mile of
solid rock, still channeled water from Gihon Spring, and the cavernous un-
derground cisterns on temple hill were structurally sound. But what reignited the real estate market was not only the wall or infrastructure but also
the construction of Nehemiah's new residence.

The first hint that new economic life might be stirring was the renovation of a few old homes and storefronts. But when the sounds of new construction were heard throughout the city—the governor's home, no less—it was a tip worth betting on. Speculators who had never had any interest in Jerusalem property started circling like buzzards over carrion. The competition immediately drove prices up. Land that only a few months ago you couldn't give away was all of a sudden bringing prices not seen since the glory days of Solomon. So intense was the bidding that Nehemiah feared property values might become too expensive to permit a healthy and balanced repopulation of the city.

The title work was expensive. It sometimes took months to trace the chain of title to its original owners prior to the fall of the city. Tracking down heirs was another challenge. The siege had scattered most of the original property owners to the four corners of the earth. Most of those families had never returned. Other than the temple complex and some government land, property ownership had gone to anyone courageous enough to homestead it. It had become a city of squatters, you might say, and for more than a century no one cared. The wall had changed all this. The city was now attracting professionals who hadn't done business here since the days of independence—genealogists, lawyers, skip-trace investigators and investment bankers, to name a few.

For any economy to flourish, at least three factors have to exist: a strategic location, a stable government and favorable trade policies. Jerusalem had all three. And two of the three were under Nehemiah's direct control. His first acts as governor were to secure the city, establish military and civil defense protection and appoint a capable administration. Convoys of merchandise could now travel Judean roads in safety, free from the threat of ambush and highway robbery. A regional governor possessed by personal greed could levy burdensome tolls and tariffs on trade routes that crossed his borders—a practice not uncommon for the shortsighted. But Judah was different. It had Jerusalem! And any governor who had a modicum of economic savvy would realize immediately that overtaxing the trade stream would choke the goose that could lay golden eggs for the region. And given its strategic location, right in the crossroads of the Middle East, Jerusalem would soon become a prosperous city.

It was no naive decision to build his personal residence in the city. Nehemiah knew the signals this would send. New construction, especially residential construction, is a sure sign that someone believes the city is coming back. Someone is willing to risk personal resources on that belief. What's more, if people are willing to establish a personal residence there, they put their own bodies on the line. Nehemiah moved in. Those who watched from the sidelines—suburbanites intrigued by urban life, speculators sniffing a new market, foreign visitors investigating new trading opportunities—all concluded the same thing: this smart little governor was going to be here for a while.

Nehemiah was investing in Jerusalem, and everyone with business sense knew that he was poised to do very well. He could control how the city developed, what areas would be zoned for commercial revitalization, where residential development would move. This knowledge positioned him and the insiders in his administration to stay a jump ahead of the real estate market and make tidy profits, even if they did nothing but buy and flip properties. He could even allocate tax dollars for infrastructure improvements to facilitate the process. A governorship was a windfall.

But this assignment was more than a governorship to Nehemiah. It was a divine calling. This mission was not about amassing more personal wealth, though no one could have faulted him for making legitimate returns. It was about restoring Israel to a place of respect among the nations and exalting Yahweh as the one true God. That is why Nehemiah determined up front that he and his administration would refrain totally from land speculation. And further, he would not accept even a modest salary or living allowance from the people. He wanted to avoid the appearance of conflict of interest.

During the early months of his administration, before the harvest failure inflicted such a hardship on the people, Nehemiah did engage in some lending for a reasonable return. It was a healthy way, he reasoned, to infuse much-needed capital into the economy. But after hearing the outcry of the poor whose homes and farms were being confiscated because they could not repay their debts, he appealed to everyone engaged in lending to forgive these debts and in the future to refrain from charging the poor interest. This was the end of Nehemiah's personal lending practices.

Some would have counseled that it was perfectly legitimate for Nehemiah to invest his own money in valid business deals and real estate projects in Jerusalem. But Nehemiah understood human nature, and he knew the seductiveness of the deal. He knew how one self-serving decision would make the next a little bit easier. He knew himself too. If he were going to keep a single-minded focus on his mission, he must put a check on the intoxicating allure of wealth building. So he drew a line in the sand— no mixing of personal business with ministry.

ON METHODS AND MOTIVES

When I asked real estate developer Billy Mitchell if he would consider serving as chairman of the newly formed Summerhill Neighborhood Development Corporation (SNDC), he agreed to give it some prayerful thought. Billy would be the ideal head of our new CDC—impeccable credentials, a highly respected CEO in the Atlanta business community and a master deal maker. I figured a week was enough time for prayer, so I approached him a second time. He would do it, he said, on one condition: if Herman Russell, a black developer friend of his who had been born and raised in Summerhill, would agree to be his cochair.

Billy and Herman were highly successful businessmen whose lives were already overloaded with responsibility. But the vision of the rebirth of Summerhill was compelling. Though the neighborhood now lay in desolation, it had once given birth to many noteworthy Atlanta leaders. And now, once again, it was poised to become a significant player on the Atlanta landscape. The 1996 Olympic Games were coming to Atlanta, and Summerhill was the prime location to be the host community. Its location—right in the heart of the city—made it the ideal setting for the new Olympic stadium. And if the neighborhood could be restored to the beauty and health it had at one time boasted, it could be a model to the world of how a devastated urban ghetto can be resurrected.

Billy and Herman agreed to provide leadership to the redevelopment effort. And they committed themselves to something that no one had asked of them but that would become vitally important: they agreed that they would take no profits from the community. Opportunities abounded for lucrative real estate deals. An 840-bed Ramada hotel sat vacant on a prominent corner, a perfect site for Olympic housing. Blocks of vacant residentially zoned land lay waiting for new housing. A boarded-up commercial strip could be reignited into a vigorous business district. All of this could be developed at unprecedented speed with the Olympic time clock ticking down toward opening ceremonies. Yet Billy and Herman decided to draw a clean line in the sand between their business interests and their public service.

The challenge that loomed largest before the fledgling SNDC was to maximize every opportunity for the benefit of the community. A once-in-a-lifetime window of opportunity lay before us with an immovable deadline. The press corps of 180 nations would converge on this one spot, making it for one glorious moment the hottest advertising and public relations location on the globe. Corporations would want to display their logos on visible buildings, the networks would want to secure the best camera placements from the top of the hotel, the city would want to be sure that its host community would have its best face on. It was indeed a golden opportunity.

The pace was fast and furious. Billy took his responsibility seriously. He recruited several other capable board members to bring additional horsepower to SNDC. He brought in a trusted young real estate friend to run the corporation. He enlisted business partners to acquire, refurbish and run the vacant hotel and to build a mix of attractive and affordable housing. Deals were cut to buy land, restore vacant homes and rehab dilapidated apartment complexes. Money flowed into the neighborhood in unprecedented sums. Foundations pledged millions, the city issued bonds, banks took risks and corporations invested in speculative ventures. For a developer, the environment was intoxicating.

No one could have imagined that anyone would want to sabotage a vision so noble and well conceived, one that elicited so much goodwill for Summerhill. In retrospect, it was surprising just how quickly and easily the progress could be derailed. All it took was one volunteer lawyer who became offended by Billy's rejection of his request to join the board. Hurt by the decision, the lawyer began to raise questions about the motives of some of the white board members. In behind-the-scenes conversations with neighborhood leaders, he planted suspicions that some of the board members pretending to be friends were actually positioning themselves to make millions at the expense of the community. In no time at all, what began as well-intentioned partnership turned into a battlefield with volleys of hurtful charges and countercharges being launched from each defensive position.

Community members charged that the white businesspeople were taking over their vision. Business leaders said they were merely expediting the plan they had been asked to deliver. The community claimed that there was no attempt to empower neighborhood people. The businesspeople said there wasn't time to teach residents the skills needed to make complex real estate deals and run large-scale development projects. The community charged that they were being encumbered with a huge debt that would take them many years to dig out from under. The businesspeople tried to explain that debt was the standard way of doing deals. With every accusation the distrust deepened. The breaking point came when, in an unannounced board meeting to which the chair was not invited, the community board members elected new resident members and with their new majority dismissed Billy as their chair.

The firing of Billy Mitchell sent shock waves all over the city. Companies that had committed to invest millions began to pull out. Foundations canceled grants and took action to recover unspent money. Promises that were made on the basis of the reputation of the board were not delivered on. SNDC, devoid of its business strength, had no way to complete its development projects and thus no way to make good on its loans. The house of cards came crashing down.

There was a call for accountability. Who was to blame for this fiasco? The press had a heyday. There was ugliness enough to report on, but one thing they could not find—an ulterior motive in Billy Mitchell. For all his months of tireless labor, often at considerable expense to his company and his family, he had taken not a penny of compensation. His company, which could have leveraged substantial benefits from Olympic contracts in Summerhill, was discovered by investigative reporters to be uninvolved.

In the months and years that followed, Summerhill was analyzed by students and researchers and writers from all over the nation. It became a case study in what can go wrong with well-intentioned community development projects, a prime example of efficiency colliding with empowerment. Many postulated on what could have been done differently—better communication, more racial sensitivity, less ambitious plans. And had Billy Mitchell or any of the other board members been discovered making a profit from the effort, greed would surely have topped the list as a leading cause of the collapse. But when all the probing and digging was done, only naiveté and faulty judgment could be blamed. Motives remained unscathed on the high road. Even in the rubble of broken dreams, character counts for something.

22

CHURCH AND COMMUNITY

THE GREAT OX UTTERED AN UNEASY MOAN, throwing its massive head from side to side. Beside it stood its owner and the owner's eldest son, both holding ropes that pulled taut against its powerful neck. Behind them stretched a river of shifting, tugging, bellowing animals, each tethered to a human, each jumpy from the noise and confusion. Goats and lambs and cows and bulls, even some small birds, called out their displeasure in a cacophony of bawls and bleats and cheeps. All the way back to the Sheep Gate they waited impatiently in the morning sun for they knew not what.

Responding to a jerk from its master's rope, the bull moved forward until it stood directly before the high stone altar, where four priests in bloodsplattered robes waited. One of the priests handed the owner a large knife and motioned him to use it. With symbolic meaning, the giver of this peace offering placed his hand on the creature's head, and before the great animal knew what was happening, the blade was plunging deep into its neck. Down to its knees the ox dropped, blood gushing in a stream from the wound. A priest moved in quickly to catch the flow in a silver bowl. It was over in less than a minute.

While with practiced efficiency the priests assisted the worshipers in gutting, skinning and quartering the animal, the cleric with the silver bowl climbed the steps to the altar and, walking ceremoniously along each side, paused at each of the four corners to sprinkle the blood. This accomplished, he rejoined the others, spilling the remaining blood on the ground before the altar. Together they began carrying the butchered parts up the steps to the fire. The valuable leather hide the priests kept. Certain of the organs were thrown into the fire and consumed as the law required. The meat was arranged on hot grates, breast and right thigh going to the priests, with the remainder for the worshiper and his family to feast on.

A prize yearling lamb was next in line. Then came a fat male goat. The sacrificial procedure was the same—a gentle hand on the head by the owner, a sudden knife to the throat, blood collecting and sprinkling, dismembering and braising, and then the feasting began. There was, however, a noticeable variation of the process when a poorly dressed man approached the altar with a hand-fashioned cage containing two small turtledoves. The birds were obviously undomesticated and flapped wildly as the worshiper attempted to grab one of them. In the confusion the other dove saw an opening and broke free, leaving a handful of feathers swirling behind. With the remaining fowl firm in his grasp, the embarrassed man held it out toward the waiting priest. A flash of the ceremonial knife and the little bird's head was severed, a few drops of blood squeezed into the silver bowl, a hasty ascent to the altar, a toss of the feathered carcass into the fire. It lasted but a few seconds. The man disappeared empty-handed into the crowd, bird cage swinging at his side.

Worship was such a wonderful experience. For most folks at least. What was not to love about it? The smoke that billowed heavenward from the altar was like visible prayer ascending to Yahweh. The offerings of flawless animals were expressions of gratitude from the hearts of the people. And the sheer joy of a whole week to relax with family and friends, free from the cares of daily life, feasting on prime livestock and the best produce of the land—this was celebration at its best.

Even in this lean year, there was somehow more than enough food for everyone to feast on. Perhaps it was the promise of better days ahead inspired by the new city wall and gates that caused folks to dig deeper into their assets. There was certainly ample reason to be optimistic and thankful. And so by the thousands, families from all over Judah packed into the city with their choicest animals, sweetest fruit, plumpest vegetables and finest wine—all to present ceremonially before the Lord and then to consume in vigorous feasting. The only distraction from the merriment was the day-labor crowd that always showed up on feast days. Like hungry buzzards, they peered from the periphery at the parties, waiting to pounce on leftover scraps. Most of the respectable families tried to ignore them, though there was occasional snickering at their pitiful attempts to dress up in festive attire. An unsightly lot they were—migrants, squatters, dirty-faced kids forever scavenging for a handout—but usually not much more than a minor aggravation. Usually. But *this* feast was taking a turn that was far from usual.

Early that morning the silver-tongued Ezra had done a public Scripture reading that turned into a mass meltdown. No one had ever seen anything like it. The whole congregation broke out in spontaneous sobbing, so touched were they by the power of the reading. Governor Nehemiah had to take the podium and quiet everyone down. He reminded the crowd that this was a feast day, not a fast day, and encouraged them to return to their parties. It was his concluding instructions that disturbed some folk even more than Ezra's reading. "Go and celebrate with a feast of choice foods and sweet drinks," he told them, "and share gifts of food with people who have nothing prepared." *Share*, he said, not just leave scraps. Sharing with the priests was fine, but sharing their finest meats and produce and wine with vermin was a tough order to swallow. This was not the first time this pushy little governor had pulled something like this. Nor would it be the last.

In the months to come, temple worship in the reborn Jerusalem would take on a whole new life for the Jewish community. All feasts, indeed, would be shared with the needy, but there was more. Much more. In addition to enforcing a per-capita tax to underwrite basic temple operations, a 10 percent tithe of all grain, oil and wine would be delivered to the temple storehouses to supply a year-round welfare program for the needy. And this was only the beginning. The firstborn of all flocks and herds would also be donated to the temple—this in addition to the livestock offered at feasts. All firstborn sons would be required to volunteer one year of community service to help run temple programs. Usury laws were reinstated that forbid charging the poor interest. All debts were to be forgiven every seven years. Yes, these were Yahweh's commands, Ezra attested, to be viewed as acts of worship. And Nehemiah purposed that under his administration the law of God would be the law of the land.

Self-interest, like gravity, has a powerful and persistent pull. It was Nehemiah's greatest disappointment. The children of Jacob, chosen to be a light to the nations, secure once again in their Promised Land, seemed to be infected by the same self-centeredness as the pagans back in Persia. Repentant in the morning and by afternoon hiding their best foods from the poor. Good theology does not good people make. Reinstituting the prescribed feasts and celebrations was the easy part—these had a self-reinforcing capacity—but sharing food with the poor was difficult to measure. The temple tax could be cleanly recorded, but tithing was a slipperier matter. If everyone did as the Scriptures instructed, the temple storehouses would be full to overflowing in good years and at least steadily supplied during leaner times. But it was a constant battle with attrition. The system almost collapsed while Nehemiah was away from Jerusalem on a visit back home in Susa. Amazingly—or perhaps not so amazing—the celebrations and feasting had continued uninterrupted.

Were the old prophet Amos still alive, he would have shouted out again: "I hate all your show and pretense—the hypocrisy of your religious festivals and solemn assemblies. I will not accept your burnt offerings and grain offerings . . . all your choice peace offerings. . . . Instead, I want to see a mighty flood of justice, a river of righteous living that will never run dry." Piety without justice is a mockery. 🏛

CHURCH BY THE BOOK

They knew how to do church—that was undeniable. Not only had they grown into one of the largest megachurches in their denomination, but they had planted sister churches all over the metropolitan area. Church planters and denominational leaders came from around the country to study their model and learn from their experience. Their method was not complicated: biblical teaching, relevant worship and quality leadership. It would take three years, they had learned from experience, for the right organizing pastor to develop a committed core group from a home gathering to a self-supporting congregation. They had written the manual on how to do it.

Their experience, however, had been exclusively among people like themselves—educated, mostly professional and almost exclusively white. But the principles they had learned would work in any setting, they were confident. These were not just pragmatic organizational methods; these were biblical foundations. And in this confidence they launched into what church growth experts had told them was the greatest of all challenges: the inner city.

Their target area was a rough one. The neighborhood was filled with fatherless children who roamed the streets day and night. Drug dealers and prostitutes hung out on the corners. A felony conviction here was a badge of honor—the harder the prison time, the greater the prestige. Establishing a church in this environment would be an enormous challenge. But the church was confident that truth, rightly presented, would have a transforming impact on the lives of the residents. They also believed deeply that where the darkness is the most intense, there the light of the gospel will shine the brightest.

Leadership is key; this they knew from earlier hard-learned lessons. The organizing pastor had to have the right combination of leadership skills, personal warmth, communication ability, cultural sensitivity and several other characteristics, all of which could be accurately profiled through a battery of psychological tests. Finding the right candidate for this urban plant proved to be more of a challenge than they had originally imagined. Capable black ministers who wanted to join a conservative white denomination were in short supply. Fewer still were those who would consider moving into a crime-ridden community to start a church from scratch. The candidate they eventually settled on was a compromise. He was an attractive enough young man who had once lived in that very neighborhood. He had been long enough away, however, and well enough assimilated into the larger society, that he felt estranged from the environment he grew up in. And though he never told a soul, there were moments when the culture of poverty was a source of embarrassment to him—an unflattering reflection on a past he had tried hard to overcome. But he did pass the church's theological litmus test and met criteria to satisfy minimal church-planter requirements. And so he was hired.

The young minister and his wife were determined to give the mission their best effort. In no time their home was filled with affection-starved children, soaking up attention and devouring countless bowls of popcorn and cases of soft drink. Curious mothers soon appeared, checking out these new neighbors and warming quickly to the hospitality that was extended to them. It was surprisingly easy to initiate an after-school program for the children to help them with homework and teach them stories from the Bible. But summer camp was when things really mushroomed. More kids than could be managed streamed into the minister's back yard, jostling for places at craft tables, bouncing on the trampoline, vying to be chosen for games. Fortunately, volunteers from the mother church were there to maintain a semblance of order. Several neighborhood moms showed up and pitched in with refreshments and clean-up. By the end of the first week, it was clear that a limit had to be imposed on the number of children allowed to attend—a difficult but necessary decision. It was a good problem, in a way. It created the perception that the new church was growing faster than its capacity to accommodate all those who wanted to join. By summer's end, many of the children and two mothers had responded to the message of Christ's love and were eager to participate in a new Sunday school program that the pastor initiated. The church was off to a good start.

The numbers were encouraging. The number of children at least. But it soon became obvious that attracting adult members to this house church would be a tougher challenge. The handful of women who began attending regularly were eager enough to accept small responsibilities—nursery duty, preparing and serving food for church dinners, that sort of thing. But they were not of a spiritual maturity level to assume leadership roles. Three of the four regulars had children out of wedlock, and the other was living with a man to whom she was not married. But it wouldn't have mattered anyway. The mother church was quite clear on its conviction that women could not serve as church officers. On occasion, men did show up for a service or a meal. Usually, however, they seemed more interested in filling their stomachs than in nourishing their souls.

By the end of the second year, it was obvious that this church was not going to meet the expectation of being financially self-sustaining in three years. The women who had joined the church lived at or below the poverty line, and their offerings were not sufficient to fund even a modest church budget. The church had yet to elect its first elder or deacon and there was not a man in sight who could begin to meet the biblical criteria. The mother church had toyed with the idea of commissioning some of their suburban members to join the new congregation for a period, but the scheme was abandoned as being too artificial. If this were going to be a true urban church plant, it had to grow out of the culture of the neighborhood.

Year three only confirmed what everybody by this time already knew: this was turning out to be a money pit. Some were now questioning the young minister's competency. The young pastor complained that black people would not come to a home to worship; church had to be in a church building to be culturally appropriate. But how could any ministry be self-supporting in this neighborhood? And how could it find leadership that would meet the prescribed qualifications of officers? Perhaps if the church invested its energies in community youth, disciples might be raised up over time as leaders. But that would require a long-term commitment and a great deal of money over an extended period of time. This was definitely not the model the mother church had bargained for.

Years five through eight were marked by sporadic attempts to bolster the ministry through workdays, mission projects and summer volunteer programs. By this time the expectation of the ministry ever becoming self-sustaining had been abandoned. The missions committee charged with the oversight of the project agonized over just how long this experiment should be allowed to go on. It did provide a base for their suburban churches to serve the poor of the inner city. That was worth something. But that hardly justified a full-time pastor's salary and benefit package. Such volunteer out-reach could be done through partnerships with other urban ministries at a fraction of the cost. Yet to cut funding would be to admit defeat, and that was not something they were accustomed to.

Year ten—an in-depth analysis by the mother church. Their model, they assessed, needed tweaking, a few cultural adaptations, but in principle it was still sound. For unexplained reasons, their doctrines relating to church lead-ership and gender—doctrines that obviously did not work well in this envi-ronment—went unexamined. The established theology of the church was not on the table for discussion. The problem with this urban church plant attempt, they concluded, was due to compromises they had made in leader-ship selection. Then they quietly declared victory and pulled the plug.

Church of the Culture

It had never been Wayne Gordon's idea to become a minister, let alone start a church. Not that he was opposed to ministry. In fact he had started a Fel-lowship of Christian Athletes program in the inner-city Chicago high school where he coached and found that to be fulfilling. But pastoring a church was the furthest thing from his mind. He was much more comfort-able having guys hanging out at his storefront apartment, lifting weights, snacking on junk food, joking around and frequently talking about serious issues in their lives.

When his new bride, Anne, moved into the 'hood with him, the gather-ings at their apartment took on a coed flavor. The girls were fascinated by the Gordons' marriage—how long they had dated, why they decided to get married instead of just living together, how Wayne treated her now that they were married. The boys listened a lot. As trust deepened between Anne and Wayne and the youth, so did the questions. And the candor. Before long the young people were delving into matters of morality and spirituality, raising hard questions about whether the values the Gordons held had any relevance to their street-oriented world. In time several of the youth took the bold step to become followers of Christ. This was the beginning of a journey no one could have anticipated.

These new believers needed to be involved in a good church, Anne and Wayne believed. But the young people weren't buying it. After an in-depth Bible study together on the subject that lasted several weeks, the youth determined that their fellowship *was* a church—a deduction Anne and Wayne had not expected. And further, the youth concluded, Wayne was their pastor!

Over Wayne's protests (and eventual concession), the small group of disciples set about the task of defining just what kind of church they ought to be—when and how often they should meet, how they should worship, how they would make decisions. The process was as exciting as it was chaotic. The word soon spread among their friends, and before long the Gordons' storefront living room was packed to capacity. Word spread, too, among Anne and Wayne's white college friends, and soon guitar-strumming, mission-minded young professionals were showing up to lend their support.

Early in their first year as a church, a concern arose that demanded attention. The white guitar-playing folk, with their musical ability, leadership skill and knowledge of proper church practice, had been asserting influence over the young church and were shaping it toward their own cultural preferences. The duly elected teenage "elders" called a closed meeting to discuss the matter. In their naiveté they passed a unanimous ruling that would set the course of the church for its entire future. Only residents of the neighborhood would be allowed to belong to their church, they voted. It would be the most momentous decision that church would ever make.

The motivation of these fledgling elders could be questioned, but their intent was clear: their church would be, by definition, a church *of* the neighborhood. Lawndale Community Church, they named it. Others could attend, but only those who lived in Lawndale could be members and leaders. In time a handful of curious parents showed up and eventually were invited to join, adding a modicum of maturity to the congregation. As young people graduated from high school and found jobs in the Chicago economy, they wanted to stay involved in the church, which of course meant staying in the neighborhood. Some went off to college but agreed to come back in the summer to help run a summer camp the church had decided to initiate. A few professional outsiders, inspired by the vitality of the church and drawn by the opportunities to serve, decided to relocate in the Lawndale community and become members of both the neighborhood and the church.

A larger place was needed for gatherings, since the Gordons' apartment could no longer contain the crowd. A dilapidated warehouse down the street could be picked up for a song but would require thousands of dollars to make it usable. To the kids, it was perfect. So they made what some might call a foolhardy decision and, with the help of a few adult friends, bought the building. Without much of a plan, hundreds of willing hands began clearing debris, patching leaks, erecting makeshift partitions, painting walls and creating usable space for weightlifting, worship and all sorts of other activities. They started a tutoring program to help kids with their homework. Then a basketball team. Simple painting and carpentry skills learned working on the warehouse enabled several young men to start a program for fixing up neighbors' homes. A physician friend moved in and started a part-time health clinic in one corner of the warehouse.

Managed chaos—that's what it looked like. And some days the "managed" part seemed nonexistent. Some would say it was generous to even call it a church. Leaders who were immature inner-city kids with every problem imaginable, worship that often sounded more like a rock concert than a church service, theology that had to be worked out on the fly, programs heavy on enthusiasm and light on substance—no denomination worth its salt would endorse such a strategy. Yet few could deny the impact this church was having on the lives of a growing number of youth. Talk about ownership. These kids were vested—in their church, in their faith, in their community—a thousand times more than any well-run youth group in a suburban church.

Lawndale Community Church, a church of street kids, developed over the following two and a half decades into a powerful agent of community transformation. Today six hundred families, almost all community residents, attend Sunday services. It has created a development corporation that has reclaimed entire city blocks and rebuilt hundreds of new and deteriorated homes. It has started small businesses run by neighborhood entrepreneurs that employ scores of workers. Its health clinic handles nearly a hundred thousand patient visits each year. Its residential drug rehab program houses a hundred men and deploys them into productive employment in the local economy. Its educational and recreational programs involve more than a thousand community youth. More than any other church in Chicago, this church has had a redemptive impact on every facet of neighborhood life.

One has to wonder what impact would have resulted had Wayne held to his original strategy of integrating youth into other established churches. And wonder, too, how different would be this church's influence on its community had the young elders allowed the church to follow the normal pattern of commuter church growth.

23

BIBLICAL TITHING

NEHEMIAH WAS FEVERISHLY WORKING on what might be one of his most important addresses. He had just led a procession of leaders—all the senior priests, nobles and patriarchs of Judah—to the temple portico for the signing of documents that would officially reinstate the Mosaic code. The day had been an emotional catharsis unlike anything people could remember. This day, public confession and repentance had gushed forth like water from artesian wells. The crowds that now pressed in to witness the signing ceremony had earlier in the day voiced their enthusiastic support of all the "new" ordinances. Nehemiah's timing was superb, though he was prepared for resistance. This would probably not be a perfunctory scratching of signatures on a symbolic scroll. The elders would likely want to examine every word of the document. And the imposition of a temple tax could spark an unwanted debate.

It was not at all a new idea, this temple tax. Moses had first instituted it when the temple was a mere mobile tabernacle. One-fifth of an ounce of silver was the amount he had levied. But the practice, along with the various other tithes and offerings, had come and gone with centuries of turbulent history. Now, with the dawning of a new day in Jewish history, it was time to reinstitute the law Yahweh had given to Moses. It was time to reestablish the temple as a stable institution and the center of Yahweh worship for all Jews everywhere.

Nehemiah had done the numbers. According to the latest calculations, the basic temple operating budget—building maintenance, a full calendar of religious events, ceremonial supplies, salaries of clergy, musicians and choir, ministry program staff and administrative personnel—could all be underwritten if every adult male would make an annual pledge of one-eighth of an ounce of silver. This was less than the one-fifth of an ounce that Moses had required. Perhaps the leadership would view one-eighth as a bargain rather than a burden.

As it turned out, Nehemiah's anxiety was wasted. Not a word of dissent was raised about the temple "assessment," as he finally called it. The leaders agreed to this amount as a reasonable obligation to maintain temple functions. Nor was there any argument with the tithe of their produce and livestock. Neither was there resistance to the additional offerings of first-fruits of the harvest or the firstborn of every flock and herd. The financial commitment was substantial, but the spirit of the people was remarkably generous. They agreed to cease all commercial activity on the sabbath and even supported the reinstatement of the sabbatical year during which no crops would be planted and all debts to fellow Hebrews would be canceled. It was an inspiring day indeed.

The documents had been prepared in advance. In Nehemiah's mind it had never been a question of *if,* only *when.* And that time had arrived. The contract contained regulations on how the tithes and offerings were to be collected and disbursed—all in accordance with the Mosaic code. Silver for temple operations; sheep, goats, cattle and oxen for ceremonial sacrifice and sustenance for the priests and Levites; firewood lottery to keep the altar burning year-round; grain, wine and oil stockpiled in temple storehouses for staff use and for distribution to those in need. Of course, sacrifices presented to the Lord at feast weeks and scheduled celebrations—the best of the flocks and herds and vines and fruit trees—were to be consumed on site by the families who brought them, with a portion going to the priests. The poor who had nothing but snared doves to offer were to receive a share of the bounty so that everyone could celebrate before the Lord with grateful hearts and full stomachs.

First to take quill in hand was Nehemiah, who scrawled his signature in large script at the top of the document. Senior clergy and Levites eagerly followed suit, which was no surprise to anyone. Next in line were elders representing each branch of their family's tree. Though it was a sobering commitment, the whole affair felt more like a celebration than a legal transaction. Unlike the taxation imposed by the Persian government that paid for distant royal palaces and monuments to kings in faraway lands, this "tax" produced immediate benefits for every local citizen. It was an act of worship, surely, but it was more than that. It was an investment in the social order, in education and music, in the preservation of history. It established moral boundaries. It was obedience to Yahweh's statutes, and to live by those statutes assured a healthy and just society. Even the most pragmatic of the elders could see this. Wholeheartedly they affirmed, "So we promise together not to neglect the Temple of our God."

The emotional crescendo of the fall festivals disappeared with the first hard freeze. As the season for storing and pruning and sheltering against the winter winds set in, treks to Jerusalem became infrequent. By the time planting and lambing season arrived again, every Judean family was obsessed with the perennial gamble against the unpredictable forces of nature. Too little rain would shrivel the crops and grazing pastures; too much would wash the seed away. This year, thanks to the Jerusalem militia, no one worried much about Bedouin marauders. But there were the other pestilences to be concerned about: wheat fungus, beetles, foot-and-mouth disease—enemies every bit as dreaded as foreign invaders. But this was the life Judah understood. It had been this way for centuries. All the high-profile drama in Jerusalem had little to do with the anxieties of daily living.

It was understandable that people would want to hedge their bets against the capricious whims of nature—hold back a bit on firstfruit offerings until one had a better feel for the bushel-per-acre yield, postpone the livestock tithe until mortality rates could be assessed. After all, what good would a thriving temple program be if everyone were too poor to enjoy it?

Perhaps it was true that the land would somehow yield greater abundance if folks would risk giving to Yahweh first. The priests preached this all the time. But their theology was hardly without self-interest.

Were it not for the visits of itinerant priest-Levite teams, who came with blessings from the temple and a watchful eye over the Lord's share of the increase, payments might well have been delayed much longer. As it was, it was almost impossible to monitor with any accuracy which lamb or calf had actually been born first and which vines were producing the sweetest grapes this season. If the tithes and offerings didn't come from the heart, there was a lot of room for slippage. Especially was this true of the allocations for the poor. It was hard to sympathize with those who didn't have enough drive or ingenuity to start their own flocks and who had no trouble manipulating the pity of others to feed their families. Widows and orphans were a different matter, but able-bodied men who had enough energy to father children but not enough to put in adequate crops to feed them were hardly deserving of compassion. Fortunately the temple staff who managed the community welfare program handled most of the dealings with this type. Where it became touchy was at the feasts and festivals where families had to share their grade-A meats and fine wine with this lot.

The Nehemiah contract, with its if-then contingencies of blessings and curses, produced a vigorous religious life in Judah. Perhaps not every solution is in the system, but the order and accountability and consistency of Nehemiah's administration produced a stability in the land that had not been known since the days of the great kings. Judah was blooming once again like a flower in the desert. Twelve years of diligent development had been both demanding and rewarding for Nehemiah. It was time at last for him to return to his home in Susa, give King Artaxerxes a personal account of all that had been accomplished and take a much-needed leave from his gubernatorial responsibilities.

He failed to note in his memoirs the length of his stay in Susa, but he did record in detail what he found upon his return to Judah. All of the Levites—the worship leaders, musicians, gatekeepers, program staff, administrators—had been laid off and sent back to find work on the farms. Temple storehouses were bare, with not a kernel of wheat, drop of oil or sip of wine to be found. The altar grate was black and cold. A skeleton crew of priests kept the temple open, but all of the programs, with the exception of the feasts, had been canceled.

What was missing from Jerusalem's religious life was more than made up for in her economic life. Perhaps that was part of the problem. The demand for temple activities declined as the price of cattle, wool and wine increased. The boom market was seducing otherwise devout people into working not just long hours but sabbath hours—hours once devoted to worship. And with near full employment in the land, what sense was there in topping up welfare reserves for the needy who should be working for a living? Levites could be called back to work as needed to staff the feasts and festivals. It was all depressing to Nehemiah.

He would pull out the contract and call the people back to accountability. That he could do legally. But the spirit in which it was originally signed could never be mandated by the law. 🏠

BIBLICAL TITHING

I told a group of ministers recently that Peggy and I had spent some of our tithe money to fund a Fourth of July barbecue for the neighbors on our street. As you might imagine, it set off a lively debate that sent the group scurrying for their Bibles.

The tithes and offerings are to go to the church, one pastor insisted. It's called storehouse tithing—and Scripture commands God's people to bring 10 percent of all their earnings to the temple (or church, as we call it in the New Testament era). Another said that it was an Old Testament law not required under the dispensation of grace, but it serves as a guideline for giving, a minimum standard for the Christian. The tithe is to support the work of the church, they all agreed.

As they thumbed through their Bibles, a rather complex picture emerged as to the purpose and proportion of the various tithes and offerings. Some of it was to be offered up as burnt offerings before the Lord. Some went to support the priests and Levites who led worship and ran the temple. Some was to be brought into the temple storehouse for distribution to those in need—a welfare system of sorts. Some was to be spent for meat and strong drink and consumed during weeklong religious festivities. The one thing that did become clear, however, was that the uses of the tithes and offerings that Jehovah prescribed for the children of Israel had little resemblance to the church budgets of any of these ministers.

It was apparent that while my pastor friends had little inclination toward adapting their budgets to square with the Old Testament allocation, they seemed quite comfortable telling their congregations that tithing to the church was a biblical doctrine. It's God's money and it is to be used for God's work, they affirmed.

And is God's work done exclusively in and through the structure of the local church? I probed. Well, one pastor retorted, if everybody gave their tithes and offerings to whatever ministries or activities they chose, the church would suffer. Elders, he said, are to have oversight of the resources of the church. How God's money is spent is not an individual decision; it's the responsibility of the corporate body under the guidance of ordained leaders.

And what of God's mandate to care for the poor? How am I to support struggling single-parent families—the widows and orphans of our day—who live in my neighborhood but who may never become members of my church? Aren't the people of God to be agents of compassion and peace in their own communities? To invite my neighbors to join together in a thankful celebration with games for fatherless kids and free barbeque for those whose earnings are meager—is not such a feast an acceptable offering before our God?

But you shouldn't use tithe for it, came the response. *Hmm.* Now, if this were about being biblical, then joyful celebrations and sharing food with the poor must surely be as legitimate as paying priests their salaries and keeping the temple candles burning, right? I sensed little interest in going there. Church picnics, maybe. Benevolence budgets, perhaps. But for an individual to divert God's money to support acts of compassion among his neighbors—well, that would undercut the church.

Then I saw it. Their argument made perfect sense. At least it would have fifty years ago when churches were an integral part of the neighborhoods around them. If the church were still the primary promoter of love of neighbor, the initiator of programs for community children, the orchestrator of charity for families in need, then tithing to the church would have a beneficial impact on the whole community. But such is no longer the case. These pastor friends, like most ministers these days, were leaders of commuter churches largely detached from the neighborhoods where they were located. Few had the time or budgets for much community outreach—a reality that became commonplace years ago when ministers and members moved out of the neighborhood. (This is undoubtedly the reason why urban churches often thrive while the communities around them disintegrate.) For these pastors, keeping their sermons relevant, their programs engaging and their churches growing was an all-consuming effort. Little wonder why they lacked interest in such a disruptive endeavor as restoring the doctrine of tithing to its intended purposes.

Our pastor recently preached a series of sermons on tithing. The messages were thoughtful and winsomely delivered, intended to stimulate the congregation to consider seriously the stewardship of the resources God has entrusted to us. We were encouraged to reach for a goal of 10 percent—an Old Testament law that serves as a good New Testament standard. And to those who were already tithing 10 percent, he appealed to consider an even greater spirit of generosity. The content, though not new to us, was convincingly presented and triggered some lively dinner-table discussion between Peggy and me.

The tithe, our pastor said, was to be given primarily to the church. But what about the frontline urban ministries who are doing heroic work but are not on the church's radar screen? Perhaps our church would add them to the budget if we designated some of our tithe for their support. A meeting with our associate pastor to discuss this proposal was cordial but not encouraging. The elders were entrusted with the responsibility to prayerfully allocate the church's resources, he explained. If members took it upon themselves to channel money toward their individual preferences, the system would break down. It would be best if we directed some of our above-tithe offerings to such ministries, he counseled us.

For the first time since joining the church, I became interested in its finances. As best I could tell, the church budget reflected responsible planning: the largest portion for staff, programs and building maintenance; nearly one-fourth for missions; a small percentage for benevolence and homeless ministry. I suppose I could have split hairs over a few line items, but that would miss the point. My concern was not over budget allocation; my concern was that my church does not encourage me to give where my God-given passions lie. Nor does it encourage me to give sacrificially to care for my neighbors.

But I am not surprised, really. Not even disappointed. I appreciate deeply the role the church plays in my life. And I will concede that the church as an institution must be vested in its own self-preservation; otherwise it would not survive. The church universal, on the other hand, survives *only* by giving itself away. *If you would save your life,* the Jesus principle goes, *you will lose it. But if you lose it for my sake, then will you find it.* I suspect that an institution can't do that. Only people.

And so I will continue to appreciate my pastor's challenges to increase my tithing level. But my gifts will not be exclusively, even primarily, to preserve an institution, as much as I value my church. You might like to read the resolution that Peggy and I came to in the letter we sent to our pastor.

Dear Pastor:

As a result of your excellent series of messages on stewardship, Peggy and I have engaged in lengthy and lively discussions over the past several weeks about our personal giving. We have finally come to a decision and want you to be first to know about it.

We value highly the role our church plays in our lives. It is a pri-

mary place of our spiritual nurture. The worship, preaching, music
and fellowship nourish our spirits and encourage us in our faith walk.
We certainly want to continue to support the church with our financial giving as well as our service.

You were gracious to encourage the congregation to give to good
ministries beyond the church budget. We certainly understand and
appreciate why you feel that the majority of our tithe should go to the
church. However, because we have been called to minister among the
poor, you can doubtless understand why we would feel drawn to invest the majority of our energies and resources in urban ministry. We
are in relationship with so many wonderful, called and capable urban
workers who live sacrificially in order to pursue their ministries. Many
of them, especially minorities, struggle financially because they get little support from their churches and, of course, those whom they serve
are unable to provide financial support.

We have decided to meet and exceed your challenge to tithe our
gross income at the 10 percent level. This year we have decided to give
15 percent. And we will give a tithe of this tithe to the church. The
balance we will invest in the frontline troops who are engaged in kingdom work in the urban trenches. Enclosed is our pledge card that
comes with our deep appreciation for you personally and for the important ministry of our church.

With prayerful consideration and much joy,
Bob and Peggy Lupton

24

HOME IN THE CITY

"**HAVE YOU EVER STAYED IN THE CITY OVERNIGHT,** Grandfather?" The innocent question revealed fears that had been troubling the six year old's mind. Athaiah, towering patriarch of the proud tribe of Perez, lifted young Zechariah to his lap and wrapped an arm around him. In all the excitement and confusion of moving preparations, he had given no thought to the childlike concerns that might be stirring in the little ones.

"Yes, I have, child," the old man reassured him. "Many times. The city will be a wonderful place for us to live. It's safe now and there are lots of things for a boy to do. They are even starting a school for children at the temple, which you can attend."

A small child picks up on the anxieties of his parents, and there was no shortage of anxiety around the Perez household on this day. Ever since the great wall dedication, the men had been talking about relocating to Jerusalem. Even Athaiah, who had the greatest stake in the hill country of northern Judah, seemed energized by the thought of rebuilding a city home on the historic site of the Perez family in Jerusalem.

"Why leave our homes and vineyards and neighbors?" the women argued. It made no sense to trade a comfortable rural lifestyle for a city where strangers lived virtually on top of one another. Yet it was not merely the disruption that troubled the women; it was concern for their children that weighed most heavily on their hearts.

Jerusalem had always been a scary place for children. Family trips to the temple to offer sacrifices, even feast days, were always marred by fear. There were muggers who would snatch your valuables and disappear into the back alleys of the city. There were con men who were always scanning for opportunities to swindle the unsuspecting with their fast talk and sleight of hand. There was the fear of staying too long and having to return home in the dark—or worse, having to spend the night in the city. It was a dangerous place, ugly and gloomy, indefensible against predators who lurked in the shadows and preyed upon the vulnerable. And even after the wall had been rebuilt and new gates hung, the fearful memories remained.

The men were somehow able to overcome these negative recollections. For them, scary childhood episodes became the grist of folklore, repeated and embellished for entertainment at family reunions. Many of the men had worked on the wall and had shared in the excitement of reclaiming the city. To them it was no longer a frightful place but a field of dreams ripe with new opportunities. But the women, for whom security was a prime concern, passed along to their children a nearly innate anxiety about anything urban.

The boy nestled close to Athaiah's chest. "It will be fine, little Zech," assured the patriarch. "You are a Perez; you have David's royal blood flowing in you. Your father and your brave uncles and cousins are going with us to Jerusalem to reclaim our rightful place. God has given us back our city. It is your inheritance." In his mind the old man knew that the child would not grasp the significance of this decision. But in his heart there was an assurance that this day would make an indelible mark on the little one's life.

Second only to Nehemiah's decision to build a new governor's residence in Jerusalem, Athaiah's decision to relocate in the city was of seismic proportions. The Perez family—well chronicled in the sacred writings—traced their lineage back through King David to Judah (Jacob's fourth son). Now, as then, they held a position of respect throughout the Jewish community. The whole of the land of Israel now bore their ancestral name: Judah.

There were leadership genes in the Perez lineage. Perez men distinguished themselves as powerful military leaders under King David's rule. They remained strong long after Israel split up into separate kingdoms, and even when they were defeated and enslaved by Nebuchadnezzar, they somehow held the family together. They would be among the first to return to the homeland when King Cyrus issued his repatriation orders. And now they were leading again. This time they were rallying their strength to rebuild and repopulate Jerusalem. Their decision would send unmistakable signals all over Judah that the city was surely on the rebound.

Not everyone in the Perez tribe would make the move. But Athaiah the patriarch, by his mere presence, would reestablish the Perez identity in Jerusalem, and with him would be 468 distinguished men of the tribe, along with their families. Their fine new homes, now ready for occupancy, had risen out of the rubble of the section of the city their ancestors had called home during the glory days of David and Solomon.

On his unforgettable first day in the city, little Zechariah had the best view of anyone. He was riding high on his grandfather's shoulders, wearing the brightly colored coat he had received on his sixth birthday. Through the massive city gates they passed, surrounded by wide-eyed cousins and aunts and uncles as well as burros and camels laden with furniture and pots, bedding and clothing. The gatekeepers must have known his grandfather, for they waved the family through without asking to inspect a thing. The city seemed friendly enough. People watched and waved from the street and out of windows and shop doors. Even the uniformed soldiers who carried gleaming swords were more reassuring than scary. But what comforted the boy the most was that he sensed in his mother an excitement that had not been there before. Her fear of the city was less apparent now. He had heard his mother talking with his aunts about their new homes and about such things as new ovens and shops with fresh fruit and Persian carpets for their floors. The dread of staying overnight in the city, he realized, had mostly disappeared from his mind. This was turning out to be a real adventure!

At first Zechariah's mother would not let him out of her sight. But since he was too small to be of much help unpacking and moving their belongings into their handsome new residence, he was soon chasing up and down the street with his cousins from one house to the other. By late afternoon, most of the furnishings had found places in their new homes and the women were giving thought to preparing the evening meal. It wasn't until then that the boy's mother realized that she hadn't seen him for quite a while.

Nor had the other women in their company, she learned as she raced from house to house, inquiring frantically and calling out his name at the top of her lungs. Wild thoughts attacked her from every direction. Could Zech have been kidnapped and smuggled out of the city? Could he have fallen from an abandoned building and be lying unconscious on a pile of rubble? The men tried to quiet her, reassuring her that he was probably playing with some new friends he had made in the neighborhood. But she would not be quieted. By this time the other women had called their own children together, partly to inquire if they had seen the missing child but mostly to reassure themselves that all their own were accounted for. A couple of children had seen him chasing a goat, they remembered. Heading in the direction of the temple.

The commotion attracted no little attention as a screaming mother followed by a score of Perez men entered the temple plaza. A little boy with a brightly colored coat was missing, the woman shouted, and Athaiah and the men inquired among the priests and worshipers who were gathered for evening sacrifices. Yes, one of the clerics confirmed, a child in colorful garb, along with several priests' children, had been chasing after a goat that had bolted from the altar to escape the knife. The children couldn't be far away.

The sight of the small child emerging from a narrow street, leading a goat by a frayed rope and followed by an entourage of laughing children, unleashed a rush of emotions over his mother—an explosion of joy followed by enormous relief and then anger. Zechariah knew in an instant that he was in serious trouble; the look on his mother's face told him that. But in his grandfather's eyes he detected something other than disapproval. It was something like pride. His grandfather could see that on his first day in the city this youngest Perez had already distinguished himself as a leader.

Life in the city proved to be different from the placid, predictable world Zechariah and his family had left behind. Instead of the crowing of roosters to wake them up at daybreak, there was the rumble of wagon wheels in the street and shouts of traders getting an early start on the day. And the scents were so different. No sweet smell of fresh-cut hay from the fields or the heavy odors of lanolin and damp fleece at shearing time. In the city, smells were more immediate, more complex. They changed a dozen times in one short walk to the corner store. Pungent balms from the perfume shop, tantalizing aromas from the bakery, the stench of spoiled vegetables behind a produce stand, incense wafting from an apothecary, fresh horse manure in the street, and the ever-present cloud of burning wood and wool and animal carcasses that rose from the temple altar to permeate the city air.

And their neighbors were so unusual. There were more kinds of fascinating people in the city than one might encounter in a lifetime in rural Judah. Like the fish merchant from Tyre whose shop was less than two blocks from the Perez homes. He was Phoenician, he said, and spoke several languages. Not only was he literate in Hebrew and Aramaic, but he could write in a script called "alphabet" that he said was widely used among the Greeks. There were always strangely dressed people in his shop who told stories about ships that sailed to distant lands in search of exotic treasures. Sometimes these visitors brought with them carvings of strange-looking gods and gold coins that bore the pictures of foreign kings.

For anyone with an ear for music, Jerusalem was like heaven. The temple orchestra and choir practiced daily, performing traditional anthems as well as new pieces that were constantly being written. The best musicians in the land, some trained in Persian schools of music, had been drawn to the city along with their array of instruments—brass, woodwinds, timpani and all manner of stringed instruments. The public was frequently invited to these rehearsals, and each sabbath there were performances for all those who gathered to worship. But there was more than Hebrew music to be enjoyed. Traveling musicians who arrived with caravans from other lands often performed in the plazas for coins that an appreciative audience dropped into their cases.

There were certainly negatives, the boy's mother was quick to remind his father. She and the other women had an unending litany of gripes— the noise, the congestion, the homesickness, the claustrophobia. One thing, however, could be said about the city: it was never boring! The speed at which life rushed by was dizzying but stimulating. It was the right place to raise a child who would be a leader. This his mother, after several years, conceded.

By then she could never imagine living anywhere else. 🏠

A THEOLOGY OF OCCUPATION

Approach the intersection of Second Avenue and Boulevard Drive any time, day or night, and you will see the raw and unchecked version of street life when crime takes over a community. Clusters of men congregate on the corner in front of a row of storefronts, openly selling drugs to the passing traffic. Across the street, cars pull in and out of the parking lot of a boarded-up fast-food chicken place, stopping long enough to exchange stolen goods for cash with the entrepreneurs who have moved in on this abandoned turf. In the wooded lot behind the chicken place, prostitutes conduct their business under the watchful eyes of their pimps. The gas station on the other corner swarms with "mechanics" stripping automobiles of parts they can sell. Beside the station, a large Victorian house, partitioned into cheap rental rooms, houses addicts who burglarize the neighborhood by day and descend into their own private hell by night.

Welcome to East Lake! The pride and charm that once characterized this Atlanta neighborhood disappeared years ago as its children grew up and de-

parted for greener pastures. Weeds and trash eventually took over mani-
cured yards and graffiti replaced attractive streetscapes. Absentee landlords
who bought up the properties cared less about the quality of community life
than about doubling their rental revenues. The elderly who stayed were condemned to a life of isolation behind drawn shades and deadbolt locks. As
fear crept in, the police, dependent upon community vigilance and support,
lost their ability to keep the peace. With leadership depleted, the community degenerated into a wild, unsecured territory, wide open to thieves and
thugs and other predators who thrive in lawless environs.

Is there a way to turn around a neighborhood that has been overrun by
crime? Can East Lake ever again become a healthy community in which to
raise children? Yes, most assuredly. But it will not happen simply by passing
tougher anticrime legislation or putting more police on the streets. Nor does
street evangelism or church-sponsored midnight basketball offer an adequate solution, as important as they may be. Life on the corner of Second
Avenue and Boulevard Drive is determined by two critical factors: occupation and leadership.

Those who occupy the land at this community crossroads, and the type
of leadership they exert, will determine its quality of life. Currently, roguish
renters and predatory leaders occupy this turf. The weak and vulnerable are
withdrawn into the surrounding shadows. But introduce a couple of committed neighbor-leaders into the territory and the dynamic begins to shift.
Victims begin to show themselves and courage starts to resurface. Police
sense that they have some new allies and are energized to renew their peace-
keeping patrols. Illicit activity on the corner, which does not do well under
scrutiny, becomes more cautious and gradually drifts away. Neighborhood
energy, long consumed in personal protection, begins to refocus on community well-being. The playground is reclaimed. A legitimate grocery store is
sought. Zoning enforcement is solicited to close down overcrowded apartments. In time the land is reclaimed for redemptive purposes and health returns. The defining factor is who occupies it and who will assert leadership.

Sound like wishful thinking? Just take a few snapshots of this corner.

(You might want to use a little caution if you drive by with your camera right now!) Six months from now this intersection will seem noticeably different. Two years from now you won't recognize it as the same place. A few faith-motivated visionaries have decided to put their talents and resources to work reclaiming this community. In low-key manner they have been getting to know the goodhearted neighbors in the area. Jeffrey, our twenty-six-year-old son, has been caught by the vision. He has just purchased a home near the corner and is gathering intelligence on the activity around him. Others have been quietly buying up vacant lots and derelict houses. They've torn down a couple of crack houses that were beyond repair. They have leased one duplex to a Christian couple who will be good resident managers. The Victorian rooming house is currently under contract. This month Charis (our housing ministry) will break ground on the land that prostitutes now use; seven new homes will be built here for key families who are making serious commitments to reclaim their community.

In religious terms, we might describe this as the practical theology of occupation. It raises the question, does it matter where the people of God locate themselves? At a time of unprecedented global urbanization, the issue of *where* we live out our witness has enormous consequences. Grand strategies to evangelize the world via megagatherings and satellite and other state-of-the-art communication methods may have their place. But the task of redeeming our cities will be accomplished on the ground, one block at a time, by courageous people who take the daily risks that bring life to their corner of the world.

"Occupy till I come" (Luke 19:13 KJV) was the Lord's parting instruction as he illustrated how his kingdom is to function in this world. Never have marching orders been more strategic.

RELOCATION IS NOT ENOUGH

It was a large downtown church with a tall steeple. The skyline of the city rose to its north; a blighted neighborhood lay to its immediate south. The music and preaching were superior—that's why it had grown to several thousand members.

Ten years ago I was invited here to speak at an urban missions week. The church seemed serious about reaching out to their community, so I decided to take a calculated risk. I told them that if they really wanted to change the neighborhood, they needed to move in, become neighbors and begin to take seriously the command to love God and love their neighbors as themselves. A couple of members had already taken this courageous step. I encouraged the pastoral staff to lead the way for others in the congregation. That was ten years ago.

Last month I was invited back. The pastor's son, now an associate minister, led me to his office and showed me a large map of the city. Blue dots pinpointed where every church member lived. To my amazement, the neighborhood around the church was nearly solid blue.

"How many members do you have living here now?" I asked.

"Nearly two hundred fifty!" He smiled. He and his wife had bought a home here, he said. So had his dad and a number of the staff. I was speechless.

"And so what has happened in the community?" I was eager to learn. They had started a number of programs, he told me—an after-school tutoring program, summer camp, ESL classes, a counseling ministry to single moms. They had formed a community development corporation and had hired a full-time director to coordinate these programs and mobilize volunteers to run them.

"And what is happening in the community?" I asked again. The pastor's son seemed confused by my question but courteously repeated the list of programs he had just described.

"Yes, but what is happening in the community?" I persisted. "Has crime gone down? Has drug trafficking dried up? Has prostitution left? Has the education level improved in the neighborhood schools?"

"No, not really," the young pastor admitted. The streets were still unsafe. There were still a lot of break-ins, a lot of crack houses. The schools were still bad. "Sometimes I wonder if our living here really makes any difference," he confessed quietly.

I picked up a note of discouragement in his voice. Property values *were* edging up; he was pleased about that. But the neighborhood association was ineffective, run by a few loudmouth activists who were always bickering over city grants and never getting anything done. No, the neighborhood hadn't really changed much.

I was stunned. I had obviously made a wrong assumption. I had assumed that if resourced Christians relocated into an area of need, they would have a transforming impact on their neighborhood if for no other reason than self-interest. I was wrong.

How could 250 committed Christians, all desiring to care for the poor and sufficiently motivated to relocate in the inner city, have so little influence in changing their community? In the meetings that followed with the pastoral staff and other church members who had moved in, I probed deeper. The programs were definitely helping some of the kids and families, they told me, but their converts were not coming to church—the class and cultural divide was too great. Their vision for a multiracial church was not working as they had hoped. They were now exploring other options. Should the church change its style of worship to accommodate more ethnic diversity? Or perhaps they should start new churches where the poor and immigrant populations would feel more comfortable. Each time I asked about life in the neighborhood, the responses seemed to end up on the issue of church. Was there a vision for the community? I pressed. The question drew puzzled looks and more talk of evangelism and getting people into the church.

And then it dawned on me. These were suburban Christians, born and bred in individualism, who had brought with them into the city a church-centric theology of personal salvation and corporate worship. Ministry to the poor—ministry to anyone—was evangelism driven. A vision for the re-birth of a community could only be understood through the lens of saving souls and adding to the church rolls. The reclaiming of dangerous streets, the regeneration of fallen systems, the transformation of corrupted political power—these were aspects of God's redeeming work in the world that had somehow been omitted from their biblical teaching. Of course they had no vision for their community; they had no theological framework on which to fashion one.

It would be a serious error to diminish in any way the wonder of God's transforming work in the heart of a woman or man. It would be equally wrong to devalue the importance of worship. Yet if this church was to ever grasp a vision for the transformation of their community, they had to consider that there is more to salvation than the saving of an individual soul. Redemption has societal implications, not merely personal. Closing down a crack house that is destroying the lives of youth is as least as redemptive as rescuing a child from its clutches. Organizing a crime watch to eliminate break-ins is an important part of establishing the shalom that God desires for all his creation. The love of neighbor—not a small concern to God—is best seen and certainly more effectual on the streets where they live than behind the walls where they worship.

A theology of occupation is a huge step in the right direction, but it is not enough. I had to be honest with them about it. It must be coupled with a theology of engagement—an understanding of how the people of faith are to engage in activities that transform places as well as people. If the fullness of the gospel is to have redemptive impact on the city, it must penetrate into every strata of urban life.

Strange, isn't it, how we feel called to a mission of saving others, only to discover that the calling ends up being at least as much about our own salvation?

FOREVER CHANGED

The question most often asked of Peggy and me about our decision to live in the city is "What about your children?" Certainly the influence of an urban environment upon our boys has been our number-one concern, ranking well above our own safety. Our quiet, ever-present fear has been that we might end up sacrificing our children on the altar of our ministry.

When Jonathan, our younger boy, came home this Christmas from his first semester at Eastern College and showed us a paper he had written for one of his courses, we were moved to tears. The childhood incident that he describes was one of those traumatic events that tore at our hearts and caused us to question the wisdom of our choice to raise our family in the city. Even now, with our boys both out of the nest, we wonder about the long-term effects of early exposure to harsh urban realities. Jonathan's paper is much-needed reassurance.

FOREVER CHANGED

A Personal Story by Jonathan Lupton

A day of celebration was in order to congratulate the Atlanta Braves on their "worst to first" baseball season of 1991. My mom even agreed to let me out of school early on this joyous occasion. Downtown Atlanta was alive with activity. The sidewalks were so filled with people that the overflow had to scale telephone poles, signs, cars and even billboards. Every window along the parade route was filled with faces anxiously anticipating the coming of the heroes who had kept them up past their bedtimes during the World Series. I joined the multitudes by climbing onto a mailbox to watch the players go by. The crowd cheered as their favorite team members passed by. Kids on their parents' shoulders screamed at the passing parade cars. The amount of energy along the winding streets of Atlanta was tremendous.

I had gone downtown to witness this celebration with two of my friends, Susan and Ashok. Susan was an innocent-looking, pale-skinned young woman who rarely came downtown. Her parents gave their permission this time because of my male protection. Ashok was a dark-complexioned Indian who stood about six foot three and had the build of a football player. We had joined in the screaming as our favorite players rode past. After the parade passed by, the barricades that held back the crowds came down and people flooded into the streets.

On the way back to the car, as we rounded a corner, we found ourselves in the midst of a street full of what appeared to be high school
students like ourselves. I soon became aware that I was the only white
male within sight. I'd be lying if I denied being tempted to turn
around and take an alternative route. But another side of me asked,
who am I to assume that I am in danger simply based on the fact that
the crowd around me is African American? I made a decision that day
not to judge based on the color of people's skin but to respect people
as individuals. So the three of us began to make our way through this
sea of faces. Our pale faces were like stormy whitecaps of tension on
the large but smooth waves of activity in the street. It felt like every
eye in this surging audience was focused on me. I watched my feet
carefully to avoid kicking anyone or stepping on anyone's toes. I still
felt guilty for feeling frightened.

Suddenly an elbow jammed into the back of my neck and knocked
me to the pavement. I found myself the target of kicks from I don't
know how many pairs of legs. Instinctively, I cradled my body into a
fetal position to protect my face and vital organs. I don't know how
long I lay there absorbing this abuse. The shock of the incident gave
me a feeling like I was in a dream. I felt no pain and was no longer
afraid. I felt distanced from the situation, like a bystander might feel.
This couldn't be happening to me.

Then the kicking stopped. I felt a pair of strong arms grasp me. A
man feigning possession of a gun was helping me to my feet while
fending off my attackers. I scanned the faces of the crowd that pushed
for a view of the beating. Susan was in tears, her face filled with terror.
Ashok looked at me sympathetically and apologetically, for he had not
attempted to rescue me. And the crowd seemed like an excited circus
audience, with me playing the part of the clown. I could not understand the excitement, even pleasure, that I saw in their faces. I looked
down at the bloodstains on the knees of my jeans. I felt my face and
discovered that it was also bleeding. Was this some sort of an outra-

geous joke? I didn't get it. With the help of our unknown rescuer, we were hurriedly escorted to the safety of a police car.

I was comforted by the repeated questions from my friends. "Are you okay?" "Do you want to go to the hospital?" But the only questioned that remained in my mind that day was "How will I feel when I get back home and my black friends and neighbors greet me?" Despite the fact that the man who rescued me was black, I wondered if this experience had forever turned me into a racist. I was scared again.

When I got home, I was still in shock. I recounted the episode to my mom like I was telling the story about someone else. Her worst nightmare about living in the city had come true. I told her that I just needed a nap and went into my bedroom to sleep. I was awakened first by my dad, who attempted to console me by explaining what I was going through psychologically. This didn't answer my greatest concern of whether I had become a racist. My big brother was the next to call. I had to hold the phone away from my ear as he expressed his anger at the event. He told me that he had a Louisville Slugger in his trunk and that if I ever saw these guys again, I should just give him a call. This wasn't the answer either. Later, my black friends from two doors down, having heard the news, came into my bedroom and embraced me. At this moment I knew that I no longer saw the color of these guys I grew up with.

The next morning, on the way to school, I sat in the back of the bus as usual. On this bus of friends and acquaintances, I was liked and respected, and again mine was the only white face present. As I listened to the conversations of the morning, one story had a familiar sound. A couple of seats ahead of me someone was telling the humorous story to a couple of giggling friends of some white guy who got the crap beat out of him downtown yesterday. I leaned forward to inquire of the location and time of this beating. Their report confirmed my suspicion. I calmly said to them amid their laughter, "That was me." They laughed louder at what they thought was another one of my jokes.

Their expressions slowly sobered as they realized how serious I was. Suddenly they put a real person, even a friend, in the place of a punch line, and the joke was no longer funny. A few made attempts to apologize, but most, including me, just sat there silent, forever changed.

A New Christmas Tradition

One of the special joys of serving in the city happens at Thanksgiving and continues on through Christmas. During this festive season, the hearts of many caring people turn toward the less fortunate. Families blessed with abundance become especially mindful of those who have little. I have the enviable position of bringing urban and suburban families together so that joyful sharing can fill the holiday season with special meaning.

I have organized such giving since long before we moved into the inner city. I gathered lists of needy families with the names, ages, sizes and special needs of their children and matched them with families who would deliver on Christmas Eve a bounty of delicious food and wonderful presents. It was a holiday tradition that gave me great satisfaction. But all that changed the year we moved to the city.

We had been feeling pleased at how quickly our family was embraced by our new neighbors when we moved into our inner-city home earlier that year. We were soon frequenting each other's homes and getting to know more about each other's personal lives than we had in the ten previous years of running an urban ministry. When the holiday season arrived, we found it much easier to list special needs and wants for the "adopting" families to supply. But this year, as we sat in the living rooms of the poor when the gift-bearing families arrived, we saw something that had escaped our attention before.

The children, of course, danced with excitement at the stacks of presents arriving at their door. And the mothers were generally gracious to their well-dressed benefactors, though they seemed self-conscious and subdued. But the fathers, upon hearing the knock at the door, would disappear from the room and not return until the gift givers had departed. For the first time a darker side of our giving tradition became evident. I saw parents in their own homes, in front of their children, being exposed for their inability to provide for their families. Our system of kindness was destroying their pride.

A new way of doing charity was clearly needed. The following Christmas season, I asked our giving friends to consider an additional gift. "Give the gift of dignity to the dads," I requested of them. "Give the gift of pride to the parents of our community." And here's how we decided to do it. Instead of delivering gifts to homes, we encouraged donors to bring them unwrapped to our Family Store, where we set up a special "toy shop." Each gift would be ticketed with an affordable price tag. Parents from the community would then be invited to come shopping and purchase those items that would delight the hearts of their children. Parents who had no money would be offered jobs so that everyone could share in the dignity of earning and purchasing and giving.

Our second Christmas in the city had a different spirit about it. The idea made sense to donors, and a wonderful array of toys and clothes flowed into the "toy shop." Parents in our neighborhood were overjoyed to find such bargains. Not a single one complained about not receiving free toys. That year our new neighbors taught us some important lessons about human dignity. We learned that low-income parents would much rather work and earn and shop for their families than stand in free toy lines with their proof of poverty. We learned that everyone, rich and poor, loves to find a bargain but no one wants to be someone's charity case. But clearly the most important lesson we learned was that the deepest poverty of all is having nothing of value to exchange. Our one-way charity had been subtly communicating, "You have nothing of worth that we desire in return."

Why had it taken us more than ten years to see these things? Doubtless for the same reason that churches continue to feel good year after year about their soup kitchens and the Marines keep promoting their giveaway Toys for Tots program. A gift seems compassionate until it is seen from the recipient's side. And that doesn't often happen unless you are sitting together as neighbors on each other's couches.

AN ANNIVERSARY DINNER

We had been planning it for weeks. The two-year anniversary of Peggy's
breast cancer surgery was a sweet event to savor. She is a survivor! And with
each passing year, the chances that the cancer will not return continue to improve. The best setting for this occasion was dinner at home in front of our
fireplace in the house Peggy built. Aged Parrano cheese on crisp bread wa-
fers for appetizers, a good cabernet, thick filet mignons on the grill, fresh
corn on the cob, a salad, lights turned low for some intimate conversation—
we eagerly anticipated this special evening.

The grill was heating when a car pulled into our driveway. Louise Adam-
son, an aged urban missionary who welcomed us when we first moved into
the city, hobbled up to our front door. A distressed look on her face, she
handed me an envelope that contained a letter from our housing ministry
addressed to a low-income homeowner who had fallen behind in her house
payments. As I unfolded the letter, a returned check fell out—insufficient
funds. Louise began pleading the case of this single mother who is raising
her own child as well as the four children of her drug-addicted sister. We
would work with her, I assured Louise. Back to the grill.

We were savoring our medium-well steaks when the phone rang. We decided to let the answering machine take it until we heard the voice of our
executive director, Chris Gray, recording the news that the mother of our administrative assistant had died suddenly. Peggy simply had to pick up and
get the details firsthand.

Our corn on the cob was well past ideal eating temperature when the
phone rang again. It was Eddie, a neighbor down the street whose wife is
seriously ill with an ailment doctors have yet to correctly diagnose. He
wanted Peggy. He left his number and asked her to call as soon as she could.
This might be something serious. We downed the rest of our meal and Peggy
returned his call. Eddie's mechanic job required him to wear a uniform to
work and a button had popped off his pants. Did Peggy have any buttons?
And would she . . . uh . . . mind . . . uh . . . maybe sewing it on for him? In

a few minutes Eddie showed up at our door carrying a bundle of greasy-smelling work pants—seven pairs, to be exact—all missing at least one button. We spent what was left of the evening watching TV while Peggy sewed buttons.

The final call of the evening was from Carolyn, a mother who leans on Peggy for support, especially when she is struggling to resist the powerful urges to return to her alcohol and crack habits. Peggy picked up. It had been a pretty good day, Carolyn said, though she hadn't been able to eat anything—cirrhosis of the liver acting up again. Just needed to talk.

Peggy and I smiled at each other as we climbed the stairs to our bedroom. It was hardly the romantic evening we had fantasized about, but it was special in its own way. It was a rich mixture of joy and pain, of deep gratitude and mild irritation, of tantalizing aromas and heavy automotive oil. It was a tolerable measure of life in the city—a life that we have come to embrace as our own. We drifted off to sleep, hearts full.

EPILOGUE

"Remember me, O my God, for good."
NEHEMIAH 13:31 ASV

ONLY ONE WHO HAS FACED THE DARKER SIDE of his own soul, one who has come to grips with the mix of motives that contaminate his best work, one who knows that his highest accomplishments have been achieved at high costs to others—only such a person would end his memoirs with a plea to be remembered by God for the good he has attempted to do. No epilogue, no closing summary, no recap of his notable achievements. Nehemiah ends his journal with a humble, heartfelt prayer. A prayer for absolution, you might say, with a Lord-be-merciful-to-me-a-sinner tone. It would stand throughout history as the final word in the chronology of Old Testament Scripture.

Any community builder who has enough time on the streets to encounter the ugly underbelly of effecting change will relate to this layperson's prayer. Younger visionaries who charge naively into troubled territory will not understand it, at least not at first. With confidence and compassion, they move in next to crack houses, take vulnerable children into their homes, reach out to struggling moms. They nurture kids, help parents find jobs and patch widows' leaking roofs. But in time they, too, will run into the systems that are destroying their neighbors' lives—a drug economy, racism, slumlords who squeeze profits from deteriorating property. As surely as darkness follows daytime, they will encounter the enemies of good. Suddenly, ministry becomes much more complicated.

Compassion, the community builder soon learns, is essential but not sufficient. Evil must be confronted. It is not enough to know the drug dealer on a first-name basis, not enough to have his children in your summer camp. He must be put out of business one way or another. If he is not open to heart change, then other approaches must be used—straight talk, a neighborhood watch, a protest march, a call to the police, legal action. Compassion must step aside while war is waged.

Confronting evil is a messy business. Righteous indignation can push one to behaviors he or she would never consider under normal circumstances. Adrenalin surges. In the heat of conflict, anger at injustice easily becomes anger toward the perpetrator of injustice. And when the battle becomes personal, all sorts of ugliness boil to the surface. Nehemiah even found himself resorting to violence—snatching lawbreakers up by their beards and throwing their personal belongings into the street. Not so different, perhaps, from bringing the full weight of the law, the courts and the media down on the head of a neighborhood drug kingpin. Such conflict may indeed be necessary, but it certainly does not bring out the best in a person. The end too easily can become the justification for whatever means are necessary.

But even in the doing of good (rather than opposing evil) there are unintended consequences. Setting high moral and religious standards, so essential to the ultimate peace and prosperity of Nehemiah's Judah, inflicted untold suffering on the mixed families who were torn apart. The caring advocate who intervenes to stop the abuse of a child may cause even worse pain when that child is wrenched from family and friends. Urban pioneers build new homes for themselves and for their needy neighbors and in the process drive up property taxes. Involved neighbors pressure code violators to fix up rental properties, only to see rents raised and the families they intended to help forced out. The Hippocratic Oath—"Above all, do no harm"—is no simple matter for a physician or a city builder to keep.

"Remember me, O my God, for good." It is a prayer well suited for those of us whose hearts are right, whose intentions are good and who, with all our best efforts to renew the city, end up with less than perfect outcomes. It is an admission of our flawed character, a recognition that lasting results are in the hands of the God who shapes history and a hopeful affirmation that in the divine economy no act of obedience is ever wasted.

NOTES

ABOUT THE AUTHOR

BOB LUPTON HAS INVESTED MORE than three decades of his life in inner-city Atlanta. In response to a call that he first felt while serving in the military in Vietnam, he left a budding business career to work with delinquent urban youth. Bob and his wife, Peggy, sold their suburban home and, along with their two sons, moved into the inner city where they have lived and served as neighbors among those in need. Their life's work has been the rebuilding of urban neighborhoods where families can flourish and children can grow into healthy adults.

Bob is a Christian community developer, an entrepreneur who brings together communities of resource with communities of need. Through FCS Urban Ministries—a nonprofit organization that he founded—he has developed three mixed-income subdivisions, organized two multiethnic congregations, started a number of businesses, created housing for hundreds of families and initiated a wide range of human services in his community.

He is the author of the books *Theirs Is the Kingdom* and *Return Flight* and the widely circulated newsletter *Urban Perspectives: Reflections on Faith, Grace and the City*. Bob has a Ph.D. in psychology from the University of Georgia. He serves as a speaker, strategist and encourager to those who seek to establish God's shalom in the city.

For further information about FCS Urban Ministries, to order books or to sign up to receive the monthly newsletter *Urban Perspectives*, please visit the website <www.fcsministries.org>. If you would like to contact the ministry personally, it can be reached at the following address:

FCS Urban Ministires
750 Glenwood Avenue SE
Atlanta, GA 30316
Phone: 404-627-4304
Fax: 404-624-5299
Web: fcsministries.org